Delavan L. (Delavan Levant) Leonard

A hundred years of missions

or, The story of progress since Carey's beginning

Delavan L. (Delavan Levant) Leonard

A hundred years of missions
or, The story of progress since Carey's beginning

ISBN/EAN: 9783744740548

Printed in Europe, USA, Canada, Australia, Japan

Cover: Foto ©ninafisch / pixelio.de

More available books at **www.hansebooks.com**

A HUNDRED YEARS OF MISSIONS

OR

THE STORY OF PROGRESS SINCE CAREY'S BEGINNING

BY

REV. DELAVAN L. LEONARD

Associate Editor of the "Missionary Review of the World."

Introduction by Rev. ARTHUR T. PIERSON, D.D.

[Printed in the United States.]

NEW YORK
FUNK & WAGNALLS COMPANY
LAFAYETTE PLACE

CONTENTS.

CHAPTER.		PAGE.
	PREFACE	1
	INTRODUCTION	3
I.	THE CHRISTIAN IDEA OF MISSIONS . . .	5
II.	MISSIONS IN THE EARLY CENTURIES . . .	12
III.	CONVERSION OF NORTHERN AND WESTERN EUROPE	19
IV.	THE NON-MISSIONARY CENTURIES . . .	27
V.	REFORMATION AND DISCOVERY OF AMERICA	32
VI.	ROMAN CATHOLIC MISSIONS	36
VII.	PREPARATION FOR FOREIGN MISSIONS . .	40
VIII.	PROTESTANT MISSIONS BEFORE CAREY . .	53
IX.	THE CAREY EPOCH	69
X.	THE GREAT MISSIONARY REVIVAL . . .	81
XI.	GENESIS OF MISSIONS IN AMERICA . . .	97
XII.	THE PHENOMENON OF MISSIONARY EXPANSION	126
XIII.	MISSIONS IN INDIA	142
XIV.	MISSIONS IN AFRICA; MADAGASCAR . . .	187
XV.	THE ISLANDS OF THE SEA	247
XVI.	TURKISH EMPIRE; PERSIA	281
XVII.	CHINESE EMPIRE; KOREA	307
XVIII.	MISSIONS IN JAPAN	339
XIX.	MISSIONS IN SPANISH AMERICA	365
XX.	MISSIONS AMONG THE AMERICAN INDIANS .	389
XXI.	THE LAND WHICH REMAINS TO BE POSSESSED	403

PREFACE.

This volume is the outcome of a need experimentally ascertained, and of an evidently increasing demand. That is, having urgent occasion to investigate matters relating to the beginning and development of modern missions, it was found impossible to gather the facts required without a long and laborious search, and so little by little the determination arose to fashion what could not be found. The works of Brown and Choules belong to the infancy of efforts for the world's evangelization, and handbooks like Christlieb's, Warneck's and George Smith's, though of great value, are yet unsatisfactory at various points. And then, besides, the remarkable growth in recent years of interest in missions has increased tenfold the number of such as are in eager quest of information concerning the spread of the Kingdom of God among the nations. This notable phenomenon led finally to the conviction that a book like this, comprehensive but of moderate size, might prove of valuable service to not a few.

All along the design has been to tell, not a little about everything, but rather enough about certain important and characteristic things pertaining to missionary history, fields, etc., to make the narrative interesting, and supply also as much as the average reader would desire. This limitation will explain why some of the newer work, or regions where large results have not as yet been achieved, are left without mention.

How vast the area to be covered! The entire heathen world, with a multitude of nations, and religions by the score. Hundreds of societies engaged, and toilers by the ten thousand. And the instrumentalities employed are numerous and exceedingly varied. In endeavoring to compass a task so well-nigh limitless it is enough to hope for moderate measures of success.

From first to last the Christian youth of the land have been kept in mind, especially such of these as are connected with the Student Volunteers, Christian Endeavor, Epworth Leagues, and kindred organizations. The desire is fervent that many a one whose ears have been opened to hear with solicitude the Macedonian cry will find in the following chapters somewhat to quicken to prayer unceasing, to giving systematic and liberal, and to lifelong toil for the diffusion of the blessed Glad Tidings to the ends of the earth.

OBERLIN, OHIO, May 20th, 1895.

INTRODUCTION.

It is sometimes a question how far an introduction helps the book it introduces. If the author is well known he needs no such formal entrance into the literary world; if he is as yet unfamiliar to a wide circle of readers, his book itself is his best recommendation.

Dickens used to say that it was an easy thing to "come out into society, but a difficult thing to prevent going in again." And so a book or an author that proves unworthy of the introduction to the public, can not long float, notwithstanding the outside supports intended to give it buoyancy.

In the case of the author of this volume, introductory words seem doubly needless, inasmuch as he has for years earned his right to the public ear. Aside from his well-known service to Home missions in the superintendence of this work in Utah and surrounding territory for six years, he has for several years been one of the editorial staff of *The Missionary Review of the World;* and has won his way to the readers, the world over, by his facile pen, his scholarly research, his high ideals of service, his accurate historical knowledge, and his vigorous style.

The outline of thought covered in this "Hundred Years of Missions," is unique, and has been followed in no other book of which we know. There will be found here a review of the century's work in this and other lands, which will both instruct and invigorate the reader.

It is perhaps to be regretted that the modesty of the author forbade his embracing in this volume a resumé of his experiences among the Mormons of Salt Lake Valley, and of the methods which he employed to establish schools and churches in those western districts over which he patiently plodded in prosecution of his great work.

A good book is a seed of the kingdom. May God use this, as the means of a new harvest of consecrated lives, and of gifts sanctified by the altar on which they are laid.

Arthur T. Pierson.

A HUNDRED YEARS OF MISSIONS.

CHAPTER I.

THE CHRISTIAN IDEA OF MISSIONS.

It cannot but be well worth while, by way of introduction, to dwell for a moment upon the basis and scope of the obligation to undertake, and with all faith and ardor, and in spite of all obstacles, to continue resolute attempts to spread gospel truth and righteousness even to the ends of the earth. There are two words in common use, the one derived from the Latin and the other from the Greek, which have the same meaning, to send. The first is mission (*mitto*) with its various derivatives. Thus a missile is something sent, as from the hand, or from a gun, and a missive is a communication sent—commit, commissioner. The other term is apostle (*apostello*) with its derivatives. Hence an apostle, or missionary, in the original sense is one sent, sent as an ambassador, sent to bear some message, to perform some especial service. "Call" also has the same idea in effect. In the particular case before us the mission, the apostleship, the sending, relates of course to publishing everywhere abroad the need and the fact of redemption through the sacrifice of the Son of God, or to the founding and building throughout every continent and island that blessed and glorious kingdom which is **righteousness, and peace, and joy in the Holy Ghost.**

And the all-important question is, Who are called to be apostles, missionaries? Or, Who are sent upon this supreme business, are commissioned and commanded to go? According to the New Testament conception of things, that is. Is it the few, or the many? Certain ones peculiarly gifted by nature and carefully trained besides, or the small and the great together, the whole multitude of disciples, in a word, everybody? We are accustomed to distinguish men by classes and occupations, and division of labor in our day more than in any former time is the law of civilized life. And we say properly, To every man his work. Let the shoemaker stick to his last. Is there anything corresponding to this in the great matter of announcing to all men the glad tidings?

Certainly, with the Gospels and the Epistles as our guide, but one reply is possible. All are missionaries, every one of every age, class, and condition; all without exception, and all equally. The obligation (or better, call it privilege) is universal, being inherent in our calling as Christians, the followers of the Lord Jesus. To be missionaries, apostles, witnesses, heralds, ambassadors, is our chief business on earth: for this were we made, and for this were we saved, renewed. Every soul is sent on a mission which is life-long, and to the whole world. Or, all are drafted into the Lord's army —rather are expected to volunteer—for the tremendous campaign to vanquish sin and to rescue the race. There is no commutation for money, nor are substitutes allowed. Thus enlisted, under orders and drill, it is for each one to be able, and always ready and eager, to endure hardness and make the largest achievements. Of course not all go to foreign lands any more than all enter the pulpit. As somebody well expresses the fact: "It is only some who are called to the heathen, but all are called for the heathen." The divine Captain assigns to service as he will; it is ours only with alacrity to obey. Some do duty as home guards, some in the field and at the front. Scouts are required and skirmishers. There is the indispensable infantry arm, and the cavalry, and the artillery, the engineer corps, and the hospital detail. Three sisters dwelt in Edinburgh who said: "All of us should not stay at home. One of us can go to the foreign field, and the two remaining will support her." A teacher in one of the public schools of Scotland receives a salary of $1,000, lives upon half, and with the other half maintains a missionary in China. It matters not what, or where, so long as the same evangelistic spirit bears sway. All are equally in the service, are true missionaries of the cross, and will share equally in the blessed day of reward.

The Moravian Church, as no other since the days of the apostles, has caught this New Testament conception of things and from first to last has held it steadfastly. The entire membership constitutes an organized missionary body. It lives only to establish and maintain evangelistic undertakings in the lands of darkness. It has no other errand so important upon earth. As Bishop Levering admirably explains: "Whenever men or women unite with us in church fellowship we endeavor to make them feel that they are entering a great missionary society." A wonderfully large proportion of the members are actually toiling upon pagan soil. But what is even more to the purpose, those who remain at home by no means count themselves free from responsibility, and at liberty to look on without concern and be at ease; but hold themselves subject to call, and by warm sympathy, by prayer constant and fervent, as well as by gifts of money which cost no slight self-denial, lend inspiration and courage to the sorely burdened toilers at the front, and hence effectually help forward the work. And, unaccountably, the Mormons, whose name not unjustly has become a synonym for divers moral abominations, from the beginning have possessed something of the same idea of the general duty and privilege, and it is in this marked feature of their church polity that much of the secret of the phenomenal growth and endurance of the Latter-day organization is to be found. Every young man is trained to fitness for missionary service, and when appointed by the authorities is expected to go no matter where, to lands near or remote, and wholly at his own charges, in reaching the field designated, in supporting himself while engaged in seeking candidates for baptism, nor less in returning when permission has been granted.

In Carey's phrase: "Over yonder in India is a gold mine; I will descend and dig, but you at home must hold the ropes." And something such of deep solicitude and hungering desire for the world's redemption as Carey had, belongs to every disciple. Carey of whom his sister says, that from the date of his conversion she never heard him pray without putting up a petition for the "poor slaves and the perishing heathen." And further, that more than once she had seen him standing in his garden with face long upturned and gazing into vacancy, wholly lost to his surroundings as he contemplated the woful condition of the millions without knowledge of a Saviour. And if the principle thus laid down as the only one able to pass muster as truly

Christian, applies to the multitude, to the rank and file of the children of God, how much more to the elect ones who stand as leaders, teachers, and exemplars to the body of believers! The minister of the gospel who is not a true missionary in spirit, in aim and in daily endeavor, has certainly mistaken his calling and is where he does not belong. At a most vital point such an one is unfit for the sacred office and a hinderer of the work.

This then is the conclusion: Every minister, and every member, in every church, is an apostle, a missionary, and as such is in duty bound to go into all the world, and preach the gospel to every creature. And that solemn command signifies for substance at least as much as this: Learn to pray continually and meaning what we say, Thy kingdom come, Thy will be done on earth, since, as Carey so pertinently suggested to his brethren—who for years had been assembling at stated times to supplicate for the universal spread of Christianity, though with folded hands—"to pray while attempting nothing is but mockery and hypocrisy." And that tremendous petition includes not merely "my church," "my beloved denomination," the United States, Great Britain, the regions where the richly-endowed Anglo-Saxons dwell, or within the bounds of Christendom, or where civilization bears sway. We are to be well-informed, deeply interested, full of solicitude and longing, all aglow with zeal for the entire work of the gospel, whether in America, Europe, Asia, Africa, Australia, India, China, Thibet, Patagonia, or the islands of the sea. Even so extensively are we to seek to save lost men, and to stir up others to do the same. Each saint has an undivided interest in the whole stupendous task, an interest which is equal to the sum total of all that lies within the limit of his ability. As Paul affirmed, "I am debtor to all."

Exactly so it was that the first disciples of Christ understood the import of their calling, and accordingly we find them almost at once, and one and all, with glowing love and a faith which knew not how to flinch, engaging in labors most abundant for the diffusion of the new faith in every direction. This characteristic is all the more significant because with respect to proselyting, wielding an aggressive force against antagonistic religions, Judaism was at the antipodes to this, for its spirit was strangely indifferent and even exclusive. Nevertheless, some of the loftiest souls which Palestine produced, and especially the later prophets, plainly foresaw and foretold in language remarkably definite and most inspiring, a happy time when all barriers between Jew and Gentile should be thrown down, when idolatry and superstition should everywhere be destroyed, and Jehovah receive universal homage. A stone cut out the mountain without hands was to become a great mountain and fill the whole earth. His dominion shall be from sea to sea, and from the river to the ends of the earth. All shall know me from the least to the greatest.

It is true that when Jesus commenced his ministry, for a season he appeared to confine his attention exclusively to the chosen people. Thus to the Syro-Phenician woman he declared, I am not sent but unto the lost sheep of the house of Israel. And sending out the Twelve on a tour of evangelization he commanded, "Go not into the way of the Gentiles, and into any city of the Samaritans enter ye not." But all this was exceptional, and provisional. And over against it, as the substance of his teaching, the marrow of the gospel is this: "God so loved the world. And I, if I be lifted up, will draw all men unto me." The look of the Lord Jesus is world-wide, the horizon is at the ends of the earth. His parting command to his disciples is most explicit. He had already affirmed, "This gospel must first be preached in all the world, for a witness unto all nations." And now the bidding is, "Go ye into all the world, and preach the gospel to every creature. Ye shall be witnesses unto me, both in Jerusalem and in all Judea, and unto the uttermost parts of the earth."

CHAPTER II.

MISSIONS IN THE EARLY CENTURIES.

It was with such commands and promises sounding in their ears, that the Master left the little company of faithful ones which he had gathered, and ascended to the skies. These were the marching orders, this was the mission on which they were sent. And though for months, and even years, they little apprehended the prodigious length, and breadth, and height, and depth of its import—for the vast Roman Empire constituted but an insignificant fraction of "the world," and fifteen centuries were destined to pass before the western half would be made known—they set out in dead earnest to obey. At least when at Pentecost the Spirit of power had been shed upon them from on high, and the transcendent results to follow were foreshadowed in the marvelous gift of tongues, and the various nations (not less than fifteen, and coming from three continents), through their representatives then gathered providentially in Jerusalem, and in order first to share, and afterwards to diffuse, north, south, east and west the heavenly enduement. Apparently months elapsed without any disposition arising to journey far from the vicinity of the temple to tell of the crucified and risen One, and divine compulsion was required to thrust these evangelists out into a broader sphere of activity. By the sharp persecution which followed the death of Stephen "they were all scattered abroad throughout the regions of Judea and Samaria, except the apostles," and they who were thus expelled " went everywhere preaching the word." Among the rest, to the Samaritans, and a notable ingathering ensued. Then Philip under a special commission went southward on the road to Egypt, met the Ethiopian eunuch and revealed to him the way of life, and thus perhaps the gospel was carried to the distant region of the upper Nile or beyond. Next, constrained by a heavenly vision, Peter took a daring step, and made an innovation which to many was startling and shocking. For salvation was offered to Cornelius, an out-and-out Gentile, resident in Cæsarea, a city almost wholly Roman, and standing upon the coast of the Mediterranean, the sea destined to play such an important part in the future history of Christianity. And a little later still we hear of the advent of the new faith into Antioch, some three hundred miles to the north of its birthplace, that stirring and magnificent, but most vile metropolis of Syria, and wholly under the sway of heathen ideas and practises. Here also many were found ready to embrace the truth as it is in Jesus. The city soon became an illustrious center for evangelistic movements, and for centuries was a rival to Alexandria, Constantinople, and to Rome herself for Christian learning and ecclesiastical influence.

But now missionary operations are to enter upon another and most momentous phase of development. The conversion of Paul had occurred some years before, his high calling as apostle to the Gentiles had been announced and accepted, and he was ready and waiting to begin his stirring and memorable career. And how impressive is the language which tells how he was inducted into his life work. As " certain prophets and teachers" in Antioch "ministered to the Lord, and fasted, the Holy Ghost said, "Separate me Barnabas and Saul for the work whereunto I have called them." An ordination service followed, and then they sailed for Cyprus on a tour of evangelization, passed through the entire length of the island, and then crossed northward to Asia Minor visiting various important centers of population. After returning to Antioch to report to the church the incidents and results of this venture for Christ, by far the most extended and systematic which had yet been made, a second missionary journey of much greater length was taken the year following, at first through the same portions of eastern Asia Minor to revisit the churches they had formed, and then mysteriously led, almost driven, westward towards the Ægean.

About twenty years had passed since Pentecost, and down to this date to only a little corner of a single continent had the heavenly message been imparted. But now was to be witnessed a significant enlargement, and Europe also was to share the unspeakable gift of God. Here again it was not mere human desire and planning which directed, but direct divine impulse and guidance were vouchsafed. The words are among the weightiest to be found in the Scriptures. "Now when they had gone throughout the region of Phrygia and Galatia, and were forbidden to preach the word in Asia, after they were come to Mysia, they assayed to go into Bithynia; but the Spirit suffered them not. And they, passing by Mysia, came down to Troas." Like the Hebrews at the Red Sea, they were hedged in upon the right hand and the left, and were also impelled from behind, and next they were to be beckoned forward. So how completely was the path marked out by the finger of Him who had promised, "Lo, I am with you alway." "And a vision appeared to Paul in the night; There stood a man of Macedonia and prayed him, saying, Come over and help us." What a universe of meaning that cry contained. In it, coupled with Paul's prompt response, was involved the redemption of Europe; through Europe the redemption also of America, and through Europe and America together the redemption of all the continents and islands upon the face of the globe! "And after that he had seen the vision, immediately we endeavored to go into Macedonia, assuredly gathering that the Lord had called us to preach the gospel unto them." Taking ship they cross "in a straight course" to Neapolis, and journey thence, preaching as they go, to Philippi, to Thessalonica, to Athens, to Corinth. Finally the master-missionary appears in Rome, the metropolis of the world, though going thither as a prisoner in chains. As some hold, Spain also from the lips of Paul heard first of Christ and Him crucified. So far from the place of beginning did the knowledge of salvation penetrate in a single generation.

The attempt will not be made to follow in detail the spread of Christianity during the early centuries. Suffice it to say that before two hundred years had passed the name of Jesus was known and revered in regions as distant as Arabia and Abyssinia, in Armenia, Persia, Media, Parthia and Bactria. Also along the whole southern coast of the Mediterranean, past Carthage to the Pillars of Hercules. By this time, too, missionaries had gathered harvests for the gospel in Spain, Gaul and Britain. Britain and Bactria then constituted the western and the eastern boundary of the Church. It is not surprising therefore that we find Origen, who died in 258 A. D., expressing the confident belief that Christianity "by its inherent power, and without help of miracle, would supplant the religion of the heathen." It is estimated that the number of Christians was not far from 500,000 at the end of the first century, had increased to 2,000,000 by the close of the second century, and to 5,000,000 after another hundred years. Some authorities give 10,000,000 as the not improbable figure for 325 A. D., which would amount to nearly one-tenth of the population of the Roman Empire. For the most part these striking gains had been made in the cities, of which those containing churches are reckoned at 1,800 at this date, 1,000 being located in the eastern portion of the realm of the Cæsars. So few were the converts gathered from the rural districts that presently the terms villager, countryman, agriculturist, had become equivalents for heathen, pagan.

And how came it to pass that such wonders of advance and conquest were accomplished in so brief a period? The explanation lies in part in such suggestions as these: (1) The disciples were as yet in the fervor of their first love, or the Christian faith was still in the enthusiasm and vigor of youth. (2) The number of missionaries engaged was relatively very great. It was the general business of believers to publish the glad tidings. Professional missionaries were not numerous, but the delightful task was taken up voluntarily, spontaneously, and by those who in the midst of their daily toil were evangelists. The gospel was preached extensively and most effectively by merchants, craftsmen, travelers, sailors, soldiers, even captives and slaves. (3) We must recall the fact that hitherto the victories of the cross had been won within the limits of the Roman dominion, and hence among civilized peoples; in lands unified by subjection to a common law, as well as by the use of a common language, the Greek. (4) Besides, the Mediterranean was an all-important aid to evangelization, situated as it was in the very heart of the empire, with its innumerable bays, and its extensive commerce. In connection with this feature of the case is also to be named the matchless system of military roads stretching forth from the capital city to all the principal provinces, and in that day, for facilitating the missionary movements of Christ's ambassadors, the counterpart of the railroads and steamships of our time. (5) And, a most impressive providence, over the entire extent of territory under view, multitudes of Jews were scattered, made peculiarly accessible to the truth by their language and training in the Old Testament, and at least in the first century constituting "the foundation and framework of the churches, and the bulk of their membership." There were perhaps some 7,000,000 in all, especially numerous in northern Africa, Spain, south-eastern Gaul along the Rhone, and on the Tiber, and numerous also in Armenia, Parthia, southern Arabia and Abyssinia.

Here, then, was found a population of at least 100,000,000, covering an area of at least 2,000,000 square miles, lying in the temperate zone and about the shores of a great internal sea. Surely for situation nothing could be more favorable. It was largely because of these same facts that Rome conquered so easily, and retained her dominion so long. "With the Roman government to police the world, with highways and harbors to facilitate journeys by land and sea, with a universal language at their command, and with Jewish people and prayer-houses distributed all over the empire, the apostles went forth to conquer." No wonder then that by Constantine's day the Christian faith had become so prevalent in the provinces, from the Euphrates to the Atlantic, from the German forest to the cataracts of the Nile, that it was no more than wise statecraft on his part to grant it full toleration, and for his successors to adopt it as the religion of state. And thus it had come to pass in a little more than three hundred years, and with no weapons but truth and righteousness, loved and lived, and taught, that the crucified Nazarene had vanquished Cæsar! By the close of the fourth century paganism in the empire was practically extinct.

CHAPTER III.

CONVERSION OF WESTERN AND NORTHERN EUROPE.

BEFORE Christianity had supplanted idolatry within the limits of Roman rule, these capacious bounds had been crossed at various points by fervid souls in eager search of trophies for their Master. Armenia was the first country remote from Palestine to be completely evangelized. This achievement was accomplished early in the fourth century, with Gregory the Illuminator as chief instrument, and a translation of the Scriptures into the vernacular was supplied to the people. As early as 320 A. D., by Frumentius and others, many flourishing churches had been planted in Abyssinia. And it was probably not much later than 350 A. D. that Jesus and the resurrection were proclaimed in exceedingly distant southern India. The St. Thomas Christians of the Malabar coast, who were "discovered" a century since, trace their descent from that ancient beginning. The power of the gospel had also been felt by the Goths dwelling to the north of the Danube, having been introduced by captives taken during a foray in Cappadocia, and so many were presently baptized, that in 348 A. D. Ulphilas was sent as bishop to these barbarians, who constructed for them a written language and translated into it the Word of God. Then it was that, esteeming the Gothic saints already sufficiently bloodthirsty and fond of war, this distinguished apostle felt called upon for prudence's sake to omit from his version the books of Kings and Chronicles! The significance of their conversion appeared later when under Alaric overrunning Italy and capturing Rome, (402-10), and later still when pouring over the Alps a resistless tide into Gaul and Spain, (466-88), the Bible was carried with them, and among various other savage tribes were diffused such moderate measures of Christian doctrine and virtue as they themselves possessed.

By the period which we have now reached, a radical and most vicious innovation had been introduced into the means and methods employed for the propagation of the faith. Heralding for Christ, evangelizing, making proselytes, had come to be a task altogether too lofty and sacred for the common herd to perform, and therefore it was committed entirely to the hands of a class, the clergy to wit, with the monks as prominent coadjutors, and later was given over mainly to the various religious orders, like the Franciscans, Benedictines, Jesuits, etc. It was in 398 that lay preaching was finally forbidden. Not far from the same time, and as a part of the general serious departure from the spirituality of the early centuries, church and state went into permanent partnership, and thus politics began to defile and degrade religion, while kings and armies began to compel an outward acceptance of established doctrinal beliefs and ecclesiastical rites. This lamentable apostasy, though in part the cause, was also the effect, of the heathenizing and barbarizing process now everywhere going on through the irruption into all quarters of the empire of horde after horde of ferocious Goths, Vandals and Huns. And we find here also the reason why from henceforth the progress of the kingdom of heaven was so slow as compared with first centuries. The rank and file of the Lord's army was kept not in constant campaigning and at the battle front, but on dress parade, or busy seeking each his own safety, while only the officers were found playing the soldier's part, engaged in the thick of the fight, inflicting blows and wounds upon the foe.

As yet only a portion of Europe had been redeemed from the worship of false gods. For centuries to come, and by the hundred, and the thousand, missionaries will be required to push forward into the central regions of the continent, and to make their way to the furthest limits upon the west and north and east. The general course of advance was as follows. Already the Greek and Roman peoples had accepted the yoke of the gospel, the next to be subdued were the Celtic tribes, after these followed the Teutonic races, then the Scandinavians, and finally the Slavs.

Britain had been Christianized in some degree while under the sway of Rome, but in the fall of the empire the legions were withdrawn, the Anglo-Saxons made conquest of the bulk of the island, and a lapse into paganism followed. It was nearly a century and a half after the famous landing of Hengist and Horsa that Augustine was sent (596) from Italy to rebuild the walls of the church. He wrought resolutely and with skill, worthy helpers and successors carried on the work, but it was not until King Alfred's day (871-901), or after four hundred years, that little England could be considered wholly Christian. Why then should it be thought a strange and discouraging fact that in giant India, after a single century of toil, and in giant China whose gates have been unbarred less than fifty years, there yet remaineth very much land to be possessed ? It is to St.

Patrick that the honor belongs of being pioneer and founder in Ireland. Born in Scotland and taken thence as a slave, it was in 440 that he began his evangelizing career, and such were the fervor and energy with which he labored, that ere long Erin had become the "Isle of Saints." That is, it was abundantly stocked with monasteries, and from these for generations and centuries poured forth a succession of monks in swarms, burning with ardent desire to make proselytes to the faith in all the dark places of heathen Europe. In 563 Columba with twelve like-minded companions crossed over from Ireland to Scotland, and founded upon Iona a monastery destined long to remain "a beacon light for Christianity for all of north-western Europe." For four hundred years after him his spiritual children were known far and wide "as representing at once pure gospel teaching and discipline, sound learning and Christ-like zeal." Little by little, by influences flowing forth from Iona, Scotland was brought from darkness to light, and England besides as far south as the Humber. Moreover from that same island-sanctuary was despatched a host of monks, "an army of Scots," to invade the Continent, spreading themselves over Gaul and Germany in particular, bent on errands of salvation. It happened also that at the same time missionaries were entering the same regions from the south, and under an impulse from Rome. The conversion of Clovis and his Franks (496) was eminently characteristic of the times. Before a great battle with another horde of barbarians, and looking anxiously in all directions for powerful auxiliaries, he made a vow, that if victorious, he would accept Christian baptism. His enemies were duly vanquished, his part of the bargain was faithfully kept, and with three thousand warriors he received the sacred rite. It was this same royal neophyte who, hearing a glowing sermon upon the crucifixion, and being much wrought upon thereby, exclaimed with warmth, generous, if not exactly evangelical, "Had I been there with my loyal Franks, that most wicked deed would have been avenged upon the Jews!"

This was the general mode of procedure in those days. A monastery was founded in some convenient location, and was made a center from which the monks issued in all directions to preach the truth to their pagan neighbors. Thus Columba, the apostle of Gaul, built a celebrated one in the fastnesses of the Vosges mountains which became the parent of several, and his friend Gallus another in Switzerland, later known as St. Gall. From these, as from scores and hundreds of similar institutions, light was shed on thousands and millions of benighted souls. In southern and central Germany Boniface was the most eminent teacher and organizer, though by 720 when he entered upon his labors, extensive beginnings had already been made by the Irish evangelists. This gifted and perfervid ecclesiastic is said to have baptized 100,000 pagans; he rose to the rank of archbishop and apostolic vicar, and finally in the midst of a most remarkable career died a martyr to his zeal, perishing by heathen hands. As yet the Saxons were wholly untouched. And the measures employed for the subjugation of these determined worshipers of false gods, though in frequent use for centuries before and after, can scarcely be catalogued as according to New Testament precedent. Charlemagne was the zealous leader in the long crusade, and the sword was the exceedingly efficacious instrument of salvation. After many campaigns (772-804) and incredible slaughter, such of the sturdy tribesmen as survived gave up the struggle, and by the wholesale were baptized. What is it but surprising to find that in the Reformation days it was from these same Saxons, brought into the church by the dire compulsion of threatened death, that the purer faith should find many of its stanchest friends!

The Scandinavian nations were next taken in hand, and one after another, Denmark, Sweden, and Norway were persuaded to forsake Odin and Thor, and swear allegiance to Jesus Christ. Alas, too often by the mandate of the civil power, and the stress of brute force, though Ansgar (826–45), a monk of spirit most apostolic, also played a prominent part. From Norway the gospel was carried to Iceland (1000), and to Greenland (1126).

And finally redemption came to the Slavs in eastern Europe. But not from Rome, from Constantinople rather, and the Greek Church. The famed instruments were two brothers, Cyril and Methodius, and 860 is the date of their advent to the scene of their evangelizing activity. Methodius was a painter of power, and finding the pagan heart most obdurate, and not easily reached through the ear alone, he produced on canvas a picture of the Last Judgment, so realistic, and terrible withal, that the mighty monarch beholding, was struck through with terror, and in his trepidation was glad to submit to baptism, and his subjects followed his example. A version of the Scriptures helped to deepen the converting work and render it more lasting. Russia was among the last countries of Europe to turn away from the worship of heathen divinities, and the momentous revolution was wrought on this wise. Olga, the grandmother of King Vladimir, had embraced the truth some years before. But as for the monarch himself, he was emphatically a man of blood, a thorough-going savage and brute, and among the rest possessed of a superabundance of wives. However, for some reason, he concluded to change his "religion," and sent out ambassadors to investigate the theological tenets and ecclesiastical forms, in particular, of Judaism, Mohammedanism, the Roman and the Greek churches. The magnificence of the worship prevalent in Constantinople pleased him most; and so, combining politics and piety in an elegant manner, he promised the Eastern emperor to turn Christian on condition that he would bestow his sister in marriage; and strengthened the offer with a threat of war in case she was refused him. The wedding came off, Vladimir with his twelve sons were baptized in the Dnieper at Kieff, the chief idol was flung into the same stream, and then the entire population immersed themselves while Greek priests read the baptismal service from the banks! This spectacular event occurred in 983. And who is able to estimate the results of this "conversion" so earthy in all its phases? For so it was that Russia was changed, at least in name and form, from pagan to Christian, and Siberia also when it was conquered by Russian arms; so that in this strange way something like 100,000,000 were brought within the pale of Christianity, and not far from one-fifth of the area of the globe!

Mention should here be made of two other noteworthy historic incidents which belong to this period. The Nestorians from Persia were active for centuries in spreading the gospel (498-1100), and from the very midst of the deadly Mohammedan foe continued to evangelize far to the south and east. Little can be told of the scope or results of their efforts to make Christ known, though one monument still survives to demonstrate that missionaries crossed the tremendous deserts and mountains of interior Asia, and halted not until the Chinese Empire had been entered. At Si-ngan-fu an inscription cut in stone fixes their presence there in 781.

But in the meantime, while the Church had been making these most substantial gains in various directions, in other quarters losses almost commensurate had been suffered. For the Prophet of Mecca had finished his career (642), and his fanatical followers had carried the crescent triumphant from the Euphrates to the Straits of Gibraltar. Palestine was now Mohammedan, and much of western Asia. Egypt also, and the whole of northern Africa. In Spain, too, the Moslem had vanquished the Christian. We can scarcely appreciate the appalling calamities which befell the Church during three or four centuries, marked by the repeated and overwhelming irruptions of the barbarians, and followed so soon by other centuries of resistless onsets from the Arabs, Saracens, Mongols, and Turks. The marvel is that from such boundless confusion and catastrophe Christianity emerged possessed of any aggressive force, with life even.

CHAPTER IV.

THE NON-MISSIONARY CENTURIES.

During the thousand years which had elapsed since the Great Commission was given, the glad tidings had been carried from Ireland to China, or across two continents, that is, over one hundred and twenty degrees of longitude, more than a third of the distance around the globe; and from the Arctic regions in Iceland and Greenland, to the equator in India and Abyssinia. Europe was now quite thoroughly evangelized. But during the next five centuries, a period just about half as long, no further advances were to be made, and instead most serious losses of territory were to be suffered. The Christian Church had become semi-barbarized and semi-paganized as a result of the overthrow of the ancient civilization by the irruptions of the Teutonic, Slavic and Tatar hordes, wave upon wave, and by the baptism on such easy terms of so many millions. A long term ensued of anarchy and chaos, civil, social and religious, and of spiritual vigor there was next to none. And besides, in the east and south Islam had made terrible encroachments, with others yet in store. Spain had been invaded by the Moors in 711, and was destined to remain Mohammedan for nearly eight hundred years. In 1453 Constantinople was captured; the Ottoman arms swept all before them to the Adriatic and the Balkans, while as late as 1529, and again in 1683 Vienna was besieged. In Russia for centuries

(1238-1462) the "Golden Horde" was in possession. And further east by Tamerlane and his successors, the Nestorians, long famous for missionary zeal, were so savagely dealt with and so nearly annihilated, that they never in any degree recovered their proselyting ardor. Such were some of the unspeakable calamities which in long succession befell the kingdom during the Dark Ages.

During a large portion of the period between the completion of the conversion of Europe and the outburst of the Protestant Reformation, whatever of religious enthusiasm and zeal and aggressive force Christendom contained were expended, either within its own bounds upon heretics and such like, or else upon the Crusades (1095-1291). These astounding undertakings, so sublime in some of their aspects, and in others so absurd, may not improperly be counted as missionary in a sense. The Christian world was now shut in by the Atlantic on the west, and by Arctic ice on the north, while Mohammedanism formed an impassable barrier on the south and east. Therefore if the boundaries were to be enlarged in any direction, it must be by re-conquering lands now under the sway of the prophet. For almost two hundred years popes and princes by the score devoted themselves to the accomplishment of this result. And their design, pursued with incredible ardor and persistence, and looking to the deliverance of the Holy Sepulcher and Holy Land from alien and accursed hands, though attended with such appalling expenditure of treasure and life, and ending in complete failure, in its results, direct and indirect, was notwithstanding of immense value to Christianity and civilization.

In the meantime "home missions," of a sort characteristic of the times, were not forgotten. In other words, the civil and ecclesiastical powers that be, were closely leagued together to annihilate heresy root and branch. The course of events of this kind was this in brief outline. The Albigenses were taken in hand for rigid discipline in 1180-1229. The "Holy Office," which at a later date blossomed out into the Spanish Inquisition, was instituted in 1229. In 1415 John Huss was burned at the stake for his offenses against Rome. The woes of the Waldenses began in 1475 and were not over until 1561. From 1482 to 1498 Torquemada was hot against Moors, Jews and heretical saints, with dungeon, rack and flame. In 1498 Savonarola sealed his testimony to gospel truth and righteousness with his blood. From 1535 even down to the French Revolution the Huguenots suffered all manner of sorrows and pains for conscience's sake, the climax of woe following the revocation of the Edict of Nantes in 1685. In 1555, under Bloody Mary, Latimer and Ridley perished at the stake, and Cranmer the next year. In 1567-98 Philip II. of Spain undertook to punish the heretics of Holland with the Duke of Alva as his precious instrument. And in 1572 occurred the dreadful massacre of St. Bartholomew.

In the midst of these days of darkness only one name appears at all worthy to rank among the fore-runners of Eliot, and Ziegenbalg, and Carey, and Judson. It is Raymond Lully, the portion of whose career that is pertinent to these pages is included between 1271 and 1315. In every particular his story is characteristic of the lamentable times in which he lived. After a term of shameless excesses we find him suddenly turning about, and in a monastery seeking the salvation of his soul. Here he became the susceptible subject of divers visions, by which he was led to dedicate himself to measureless and lifelong toil for the conversion of Mohammedans and heathen. During four and forty years he pursued this one object, without once turning back, or turning aside. For assistance in carrying out his schemes, application was made to one pope after another, and to this sovereign and that, but for the most part without the least success. In casting about for measures and methods with which to further his plans, he hit upon his famous *Ars Magna*, a wonderful logical contrivance, which "by mechanically presenting all the predicates which could attach to any subject, was adapted to answer any question on any topic, and would by the cogency of its inferences necessarily convert the unbeliever, be he Moslem, or be he pagan." This invention perfected, Lully traveled far and wide to spread the knowledge of his "great art," and endeavored to secure the founding in England, France, Spain, and Italy, of universities for teaching oriental languages and training missionaries. In 1292 he sailed from Genoa for Tunis to apply in person his irresistible convincing process to the reason and conscience of the obdurate followers of the man of Mecca. A challenge was sent out to the scholars to meet him in high debate, and some impression seems to have been produced, for presently he was ordered to leave the country. Some years later making a second attempt to evangelize in Algiers and Tunis, it was only to be set upon by a furious mob, from whose hands he escaped only by the aid of a friendly Arab philosopher. In 1214, bent on the same sacred errand, he entered the same region a third time, lived in seclusion for a season, but then venturing to preach openly against the Koran and its author, was driven out of the city with stones, and was so cruelly pelted as to die in a few hours. Lully's glory lies in this, that he alone of his generation, and indeed of the centuries just preceding and to follow, appears to have cherished any deep concern for the spiritual well-being of the great non-Christian world. And we cannot but love and admire him for his boundless devotion and self-sacrifice, though marveling much that he should have expected to be able to lead sin-cursed humanity captive to the truth as it is in Jesus with logic only as a trusted weapon. But such was the wisdom of the wisest in the days of the hair-splitting schoolmen. Perhaps the chief value of this pathetic incident in the history of missions is to be found in the glimpse it affords of the kind of Christianity current through all the middle ages. The church itself has sore need of redemption. Therefore, though perishing in sin, better let the world wait until error, superstition, and ungodliness are driven forth from the kingdom, until revival, and restoration to primeval purity and simplicity have been vouchsafed from above.

CHAPTER V.

THE REFORMATION AND THE DISCOVERY OF AMERICA.

WE have now reached the vicinity of two events for importance seldom surpassed in the history of the race, which sprung in no small degree from common causes though so unlike in character at many points, which also occurred so closely together (1492 and 1517), and in results were in most intimate and effectual co-operation. Of course the reference is to the Discovery of America, and the Protestant Reformation. For centuries the tremendous import of these achievements as touching the spread of the gospel did not in the least appear, nor even yet by many is their value fully appreciated. But the recent Columbus celebrations have greatly helped us to understand what his immortal deed was worth to humanity. And the meaning will be disclosed, if we endeavor to frame a reply to the question, What if his unquenchable faith and heroic endeavor had been omitted altogether from this world's occurrences? Among other things, the voyage of four hundred years ago was destined to uncover half the globe to the knowledge of civilized men, and so to double the possible area of the kingdom of heaven on earth, and furnish a field for the advance of the Lord's hosts beyond conception vaster and more varied than any ever dreamed of by prophets and apostles. When Vasco da Gama, and Magellan, and Cook, and a score of others had completed what Columbus began, "the world" no longer meant merely the Mediterranean Basin, or the Roman Empire, the paltry spaces peopled by civilized men. Instead of only one continent entire, and a portion of two others, six continents were included, besides such land-masses as New Guinea, New Zealand, Java, Sumatra and Madagascar, and lesser islands by the thousand. Yes, and the immense bulk of Africa was in due time to be made accessible from the coast on every side to the very center. From henceforth to the end of time, the circumference of the globe, the distance from the equator to the poles, were to be the limit of "all the world," and of "every creature."

Then as to the part to be performed by the Reformation. Religion pure and undefiled was to be restored, its original evangelizing and conquering energy was to return, together with material auxiliaries to help, increased an hundred-fold. And hence to these new lands, and to the old ones also, a faith and practise worth possessing, and worth imparting, might be transported, a type of Christianity which wore, at least in some fair measure, the celestial image of its Lord. This same reformed church was to hold within itself the seeds of a higher general intelligence than had ever yet been seen, of freedom also both civil and religious, democracy included, and so a splendid sphere for the immeasurable gifts and graces of the masses. Especial mention must be made of Bible translation among the regenerating forces of the revolt and revival set on foot by Wyclif, and Huss, and Luther, and Calvin. Hitherto for the most part the word of God had been kept hidden in the dead languages, Hebrew, and Greek, and Latin, and so was inaccessible to the mass of Christians, who in addition were unable to read. But to make a bad matter worse, the Scriptures had long since been relegated to the rear as a source of authority and of spiritual life, while the church, the sacraments, the priesthood, had become the all in all for supplying truth and motives to right action. But from that day forward, at least in every Protestant country, the Bible was to be found in the vernacular, and with the timely aid of societies formed for the express purpose, was to be scattered broadcast, and to find a place in every home. "The vernacular Bible became a missionary book, first to Christendom itself, and after two hundred years to all mankind." Nowadays a herald of the cross who should fail to teach his converts to read at the soonest, and to supply them with the New Testament and the Old, would universally be held to misread most grievously his duty and privilege, and to omit an essential element of permanent gospel work. Zeal which is according to knowledge is to be sought.

In their larger aspects the Discovery and the Reformation together included the astonishing spread, and colonization, and dominion, of the virile Anglo-Saxon race and speech—one of the most impressive phenomena in the entire range of historic events. The ruling religious influences of the future were to be not Latin and Catholic, but Teutonic and Protestant. Great Britain was providentially chosen to be directly and indirectly by far the mightiest world-force for civilization and Christianity. In the New World were first to be tried, under auspices remarkably favorable, certain novel, radical and most momentous experiments in civil government and ecclesiastical order, which all the world was to watch with amazement mingled with incredulity, and then sooner or later to begin to imitate. Among these were popular government combined with popular education; an intelligent people everywhere in authority, and the absolute separation of church and state. In the midst of the Western Hemisphere an immense area had been held in reserve from the beginning, almost empty of inhabitants, and waiting to be possessed. Here the institutions of religion, Christian belief and practise, should be able to cast off the trammels of a defective past, the errors and abuses inherited from the ages of darkness, and enter upon an unprecedented course of development toward perfection. A Republic should arise, a nation blessed with numbers, wealth, and aggressive evangelistic zeal, in readiness when the fulness of times should arrive to become one of the foremost factors of Christendom in bearing to every continent and island the teaching which centers in Calvary. And to aid not only in the redemption of the New World, but of the Old World also. Already for more than half a century the striking spectacle has been looked upon, of missionaries by the score and hundred toiling with heroic faith and fervor for the restoration of the gospel to Bible lands, Palestine, Persia, Egypt and the rest, and sent forth to their mission from a country on the opposite side of the globe, a country of whose existence Bible saints had never dreamed! How altogether wondrous are the ways of God with his people and kingdom! And finally, the triumphs of the printing press, and the railroad, and the steamship, and the telegraph, and countless other mechanical inventions were to follow, and all were to unite as messengers from heaven to bear the name of Jesus to the earth's remotest bounds.

CHAPTER VI.

ROMAN CATHOLIC MISSIONS.

From this date forward evangelizing effort divides into two streams as to dominant ideas, methods, and results. For the Christian Church itself by a terrible convulsion had been rent in twain. At first and for several generations, for reasons most cogent which will be given in detail further on, missionary activity and gains were almost wholly upon the side of the Papacy. It is enough at present to recall the fact that during a long period after the discovery of America and the doubling of the Cape of Good Hope and Cape Horn, with the consequent frequent voyages to the East Indies for trade, the entire naval power and commercial activity of the world were in the hands of Catholic Spain and Portugal, and therefore they alone came into personal contact with pagan peoples. But besides, the outburst of zeal for propagandizing now to be briefly mentioned came to pass as a result of a sharp reaction within the Roman Catholic church against the rising Reformation. So much territory had been lost to the Papacy by the stunning spread of Protestant ideas in central, northern, and western Europe, that something extraordinary must be done at once to secure elsewhere gains to match. It was the enthusiasm excited in this counter-reformation which helped to start a host of daring and venturesome souls over sea and land to bear into new regions the glorious cross of Christ. The instruments employed to seek subjects for baptism were the members of the various religious orders, with the Benedictine, Dominican, and Franciscan among the chief, composed of monks without family ties and entanglements, and under solemn vows of obedience and readiness to endure. All these were pliant tools in the hands of the church leaders, and to them was now added (1540), for the express purpose of exterminating heretics, and toiling for the "greater glory of God" (*ad majorem gloriam Dei*), the redoubtable Society of Jesus, a body military and merciless in its discipline, its members bound to be absolutely passive under commands, and to hold themselves ever ready to set forth at an hour's warning for any clime under the sun.

And though we can not but deem these missionaries at many points seriously misguided, and feel compelled to condemn not a few of their doings, nevertheless certain of them we must also admire, and reverence, and regard as brethren in the Lord, because of their evident sincerity, their limitless courage, devotion and self-denial, their almost over-willingness to suffer and die. Francis Parkman's noble volumes on France and England in the New World contain just panegyric in abundance in giving the thrilling story of men like Le Jeune, and Brebeuf, and Jogues, and Lalemant, who intrepidly assayed to subdue to the meekness of the spirit of Jesus the Hurons and the terrible Iroquois, in the effort taking their lives in their hands and suffering untold tortures, with exultation even. To some, as Hennepin, Marquette and Joliet, we also owe much for what they achieved as explorers in the Great West. Or take Xavier the most eminent of them all, indeed ranking among the great evangelizers of Christian history. His zeal consumed him, and his labors were truly apostolic. His career in heathen lands was but brief, and yet in those ten years (1542-52) spent in India and Japan he is said to have baptized not less than 1,000,000 converts. And in those countries, as well as in China, the East Indies and Africa, his successors planted numerous missions. In the New World South America was well subjected to the Christian faith, that is, according to the peculiar Roman pattern. Among the docile natives of Paraguay was planted a veritable Jesuit's paradise, an ideal state of society, in which the church was the alpha and omega, and to an extent truly fearful and wonderful supplied to the faithful reason, judgment, conscience, everything. In Mexico and California some substantial results were achieved, while at Quebec and Montreal, with the exceedingly paternal civil rule of Louis XIV. to co-operate, in the way of rigid discipline and blind obedience there was not much left to be desired.

However, for some reason, nor is the cause far to seek, as a rule the work of these Roman Catholic evangelizers, though so extensive, and for the time in deceitful appearance so successful, was as to results but unsubstantial and fleeting. Great stress was always laid upon the mere ecclesiastical externals of religion, and unchristian and disastrous compromises with heathenism were not uncommon. Probably the most scandalous case occurred in connection with Robert de Nobili in southern India (1606-30), who gave himself out for a Brahmin from the West, suffered none but men of high caste to approach him, forged what he declared to be a fifth Veda, etc., etc.; so that even Rome, never squeamish over such trifling matters, could not tolerate his departures from the gospel. Then further, the spirit of the missionaries was too lordly, they meddled too much with political affairs, and thus stirred up against themselves fear and deadly hatred. It was on account of such blunders and sins that they were driven out of Japan (1614) and China (1618), and in great numbers their poor followers were tortured and put to death. After a steady decline it had come to pass a hundred years ago that Catholic missions, in foreign lands where they had once been prosperous, were in many cases almost extinct.

CHAPTER VII.

PREPARATION FOR MODERN MISSIONS.

WHAT in the meantime were the Protestant churches doing to enlarge the boundaries of the kingdom of heaven? The Luthers, and the Melanchthons, the Calvins, Zwingles, Knoxes, and their successors? The humiliating and perplexing answer is, Practically nothing for a hundred years. And for two hundred years next to nothing. All the names worth mentioning of men possessed of the missionary spirit, praying and toiling to publish the gospel proclamation, can be counted on the fingers of one hand. Yes, for three centuries the attempts were but shockingly few, and the fruits but meager. At best there was only here and there an individual soul oppressed with profound sorrow and sympathy for the pagan world lying in wickedness. As for the Reformed churches as a whole, they did nothing, and they cared nothing. Luther had no look to spare for lands lying beyond the pale of Christendom, could only lament over the condition of the benighted Papists, the stiff-necked and stony-hearted Jews, and occasionally of the dreadful Turks, who made their presence felt in those days by resolutely endeavoring to push their dominion northward and westward in Europe. As for Calvin, he could comment upon Matthew and discover no trace of duty or privilege for the disciples of Christ as touching the world's conversion. Too many of the theologians had no faith in efforts to win the heathen to the gospel, especially if these were in a barbarous state, were bitterly opposed to such attempts, even regarding them fanatical and sinful. And why was this? How shall we explain the phenomenon? We might sum up and set forth the reason in few words, with the suggestion that the world was not ready, the fulness of times for the universal spread of Christianity had not come, and centuries of preparation must first intervene. It can not but be exceedingly profitable to review the history of the last four hundred years with this thought in mind, and take note of the manifold and marvelous overturnings in all realms, high and low, religious and secular, all of which have worked together to usher in this glorious century of world-wide missions.

To begin with, the zeal of the early reformers, as well as of those who came after them, was not evangelistic, but polemic instead, was anti-Catholic, theological, ecclesiastical. Such was the fashion that had come down from the schoolmen. But further, the fact is well established that, at least in the case of an important portion, missionary fervor was smothered by certain misreadings of scripture, and certain eschatological misconceptions. As they judged, the signs of the times clearly indicated that, not only was the world "very evil," but also, "the times were waxing late." The gospel had already been "preached in all the world for a witness unto all nations," had already reached its extreme limit in terrestrial space, and the end of all things was at hand. The outlying pagan world was not to be converted, but was about to be destroyed. Haste was to be made to gather out the elect.

But serious hindrances of an entirely different sort are

to be brought to mind. It happened that in God's strange providence Protestantism was compelled to engage at once in a most desperate life-and-death struggle with Rome, one whose fury did not in the least abate for five or six generations, and which has continued even to the present hour. The new doctrine and life must with might and main establish a right to existence, must conquer standing-ground, must first define, and then enlarge to the utmost the boundaries of the Reformation in countries already Christian. So that as yet there was neither much leisure nor vitality left to expend upon the vast and even more benighted regions beyond. In Babylon, out of which with horror they had lately fled, the reformers found a foe ever-present, wily, unscrupulous, and most determined to crush the pestilent Lutheran heresy, and commonly with the ruthless civil power in close league and co-operation. The horrid enginery of the Inquisition was steadily at work, and the Jesuits were plotting night and day. All Germany was in perpetual chaos, social, political, and religious. Recall the unspeakable desolations attending the almost constant "religious" wars of those dark days; how the Huguenots found no rest from persecution, and finally were slaughtered by the wholesale, impoverished, imprisoned, and driven from France. For the better part of a century little Holland bent to the utmost her almost miraculous energies to save herself from utter destruction by the diabolical schemes of Phillip II. of Spain. And as for England, in the persons first of the Lollards, and later of the Puritans, those who would have none of Rome suffered manifold afflictions from Henry VIII., Bloody Mary, Elizabeth, and the four Stuarts, for one hundred and fifty years in all; nor was the fearful stress finally over until happy 1688. Therefore, it is not to be counted in the least strange that the dreary and bloody sixteenth and seventeenth centuries witnessed no evangelistic crusades to speak of aimed at remote Africa, America, and the Islands of the Sea.

But besides this warfare, open and remorseless, between Protestantism and the Papacy, there was another conflict going on at the same time within the ranks of the reformed. The theological and ecclesiastical strifes which began from the Reformation, esteemed one and all by the combatants "wars of the Lord," were almost as bitter, as exhausting, and even more interminable, than the fight for life against Rome. And, indeed, the task was herculean, full of difficulty, demanded the utmost of wisdom and skill to separate Bible truth from Romish error, with which for more than a millennium it had become worse and worse intermingled. The lamentable heresy and apostasy extended to a multitude of matters pertaining to both belief and practise. The reformers of necessity resorted to the Scriptures anew and investigated for themselves. The human mind now just set free from age-long and galling tyranny, of course was altogether unused to untrammelled exercise, and so not strangely ran riot sometimes, and occasionally went to the other extreme of license, lawlessness, anarchy. Sects sprang up by the score, all manner of hobbies got upon their feet and performed their antics before high heaven. While to beliefs and customs some would bring the least possible change, others would reject these to the utmost, and thus be as unlike as possible to the infamous harlot of the Seven Hills! But the most temperate and conservative were compelled to fashion fresh creeds and forms of worship. And, should ecclesiastical rule be monarchic or aristocratic as aforetime, or democratic rather, or at what point between? And the confession, should it be of the Augsburg pattern, or of the Helvetic, or the Gallic, or the Belgic? Which was verily nearest to God's Word, the Heidelberg, the Westminster, the Thirty-nine Articles, or the Savoy? The spirit of war filled the air in all regions to which the Reformation had come, in all realms fighting, at least with the tongue and pen, was the chief business; and hence Luther was hot against Zwingle, and both against Calvin, and all three could by no means tolerate in the least the wicked errors of Arminius, Servetus, and the rest. In England for long, it was not only Protestant always and everywhere against Catholic, but it was also war to the knife between the Established Church and the Presbyterians, the Puritans, the Independents, the Baptists, the Quakers, etc. Nor, in the nature of things, could it be any light matter, a short and simple process, to escape altogether from the intellectual and moral night of the Dark Ages, to return fully to the truth as it is in Jesus; or for Protestantism to come thoroughly to itself, to a knowledge of its sublime mission, and as well to fashion the instrumentalities needed to accomplish the tremendous task assigned.

Mention must also be made of the essential part performed in the educating and spiritualizing of the Protestant world by the translations of the Scriptures into the vernacular. It was only in this way that the Word could be made accessible to the multitude, and so be popularized, and be able to operate most directly and most mightily upon the largest number. For a thousand years Christendom had been poring devoutly over the lucubrations of the fathers, the schoolmen, the monks, and the decrees of councils, and as a result had become filled with gross misconceptions concerning God, and man, and the Church, and Christian virtue, and the world to come. But now a return was to be made to the very fountain-head of divine knowledge. Celestial wisdom was from henceforth to flow direct to the mind and heart from the pens of psalmists, prophets, apostles, as well as from the teachings of the Son of God. With eyes thus opened, all things taught and practised were to be proved, the false and foolish were to be rejected, while the pure gospel was to be faithfully applied to character and life.

A further obstacle, as good as insuperable, was found for centuries after the Reformation in the fact that everywhere Church and State, the spiritual therefore and the material, were closely united, and so long had the relation existed that now it seemed to most to be not only eminently proper, but also necessary. This was another portion of the evil inheritance received from Rome, and as a result religion had come to be largely a political affair to be managed in cabinets by kings and statesmen and generals, by them to be fostered, guided and defended. Force was in common use to advance orthodoxy, to punish opinions and convictions which by theologians, philosophers, or even politicians, were adjudged to be pestilential. Such a wretched caricature of the spirit and methods of the New Testament as resulted was not worthy of universal diffusion. *Non tali auxilio, neque istis defensoribus!* The nations that sat in the darkness of paganism must needs wait until under the hand of God this unchristian alliance, this profane mingling of the things of God with the things of Cæsar, is brought to an end, at least is on the sure road to the final catastrophe.

And then in addition, as yet, in any realm, nothing of importance was ever undertaken and prosecuted by the individual of his own motion, or by the masses, from an impulse abounding within; but every movement was by prescription, by the authority of pope, king, bishop, and was under the direction of certain orders, and companies, and guilds. The blessed day of voluntary associations was not yet—was far in the future. The benighted people were nobodies, were but cattle to be driven, or clay to be molded, only instruments to be played upon by the few enjoying the divine right to originate, and shape, and manage. As we shall presently see, what little was done to carry the gospel abroad was devised wholly, and was engineered in every case, by royalty and privileged corporations. In those days kings were nursing fathers, and queens were nursing mothers, in a way that was full of evil. All which was as far as possible from the glorious days of the apostles and their successors, when missionary effort was mainly individual, voluntary and spontaneous, and when the entire body of Christ was instinct and overflowing with celestial aggressive force. No world-wide progress could be made until such ignoble and enfeebling bonds were somehow broken, and, if need be, through violent civil and ecclesiastical overturning, and the rude shock of war. The English Revolution with the sublime outburst of the Puritan spirit must precede, the American Revolution, yes, and the French Revolution, with the terrible throes and destructions included of the Reign of Terror and the Napoleonic campaigns, to terminate a great host of old abuses, to teach priests and nobles a much needed but unpalatable lesson in humility and modesty, and to exalt the rights and privileges of the many. And above all, the religious world was waiting for the rise of a great people beyond the Atlantic, untrammeled by tradition, God-fearing, intelligent, each one trained to think and act for himself, with democracy in the State reacting upon the Church, a people loving liberty better than life. Then at length the gospel, free as at the first, left to itself to do its appointed work under the inspiration of the Holy Ghost and the guidance of the Word, and with reliance upon spiritual forces alone, could enlarge itself indefinitely on every side, and spread finally around the whole earth.

There was yet another obstacle to the re-beginning and development of missions which was well nigh prohibitory, and was resident in the fact that, for generations after the Reformation, Protestant peoples possessed no point of actual contact with the heathen world. Hence the existence of any extended and deplorable moral darkness was not brought home to their senses, was a mere matter of hearsay and untested theory. Navigation to distant parts, commerce, colonization, were in the hands of such servitors of Rome as Portugal and Spain. Because Catholics beheld pagan realms with their own eyes they also felt, and sent out missionaries in troops. It was not until after the marked decline of those two powers that Protestant Denmark, Holland and England stepped suddenly forward as rulers of the sea. And the first Danish missions were planted in Danish Greenland and at Tranquebar. In like manner the first Dutch missionaries touched heathen soil in Dutch Java, Ceylon, and the West Indies. Eliot also, and Brainerd were stirred with evangelizing ardor only toward the Indians to be found at their very doors. And where did Carey and Vanderkemp, among the very first of Englishmen to carry forth the glad tidings, make their attempts to rescue the perishing, but upon the Ganges and at Cape Town whither British authority, and British settlers, had already gone? And the first three British societies to be formed with missionary aims had no look other than towards British colonies in the New World and elsewhere. And when the naval and commercial hegemony passed finally into Protestant hands, it was the Lord's sure token that the pure Gospel was about to fly abroad. In due season followed other and more astounding victories for the rising faith of Luther, and chiefly through British valor and aggressive enterprise. It was nothing less than one of the greatest epochs in history, especially in relation to all English-speaking people, and to the publishing of the message to mankind, when almost in the same year Clive conquered at Plassey (1757), and Wolfe at Quebec (1759), and thus eventually by the hundred million Hindus were brought under the care of English Christians, while the French were driven from this continent to make ready for the rise of a "Greater Britain," which should fairly rival the mother country as an ardent evangelizer, and continually provoke her to good works.

One more step of a somewhat similar character remained to be taken, nor was it long delayed. Since the generation which followed Columbus and Magellan and the Cabots and Drake, there had been a strange and long-continued apathy with regard to carrying forward to completion the discovery of unknown regions. Little progress had been made in that direction save by a few like Barentz, and Tasman, and Behring, until Captain

Cook's three famous voyages (1769-79). In particular, he turned the attention of the civilized world to such continental land-masses as Australia, New Zealand, and New Guinea, and brought to light in the hitherto untraversed expanse of the Pacific the South Seas of a century since, islands innumerable, the Society group, the Friendly, the Sandwich, etc. We can scarcely understand the prodigious stir that was made, the boundless enthusiasm that was kindled by his achievements. The explorations of our Livingstone and Stanley were received coldly by comparison. And the impulse given to missions was immediate and very great. Two facts in evidence of this must suffice; it was the reading of Cook's narrative that first set Carey's soul on fire with longing to "attempt great things for God" in heathen lands, and his original plan was to devote himself to toil in "Otaheite" (Tahiti). And the London Society, at whose organization such a remarkable wave of religious zeal arose and spread all over Britain and to the Continent, was formed expressly to carry the tidings of salvation to the South Seas, and in Tahiti its earliest representatives first touched land and opened their work.

A final step remained in preparing the way for successful missionary undertakings. A mighty and widespread outpouring of the Spirit of the Most High had been the chief desideratum. From various causes operating in conjunction during the latter part of the seventeenth century, and extending far into the eighteenth, a sad and dark eclipse of faith had befallen the Reformed churches, a serious decline of vital piety, a lapse into frigid formalism and rank rationalism. The only zeal left was for an orthodoxy which was stone dead. " Never has there been a century in England so void of faith as that which began with Queen Anne and ended with George II., when the last Puritan was buried and the first Methodist was not born." The Pietists of Germany, with Francke among the leaders, were possessed of the true evangelical spirit. In 1722, when the renewed Moravian Church came into being, cheering evidence began to appear that divine grace and mercy were not clean gone forever from His apostate people. And not much later began to descend those marvelous showers of heavenly blessing, through the fervid and tireless labors of the Wesleys (1738-91), Whitefield, and our own Edwards (1734-49), whereby were supplied to many thousands a love fiery and vehement, a faith hardy and venturesome, like that which enkindled and uplifted the church in the pentecostal age. Without this almost unparalleled anointing from above modern missions could never have begun to be, but now it was possible for the kingdoms of this world to become the kingdoms of our Lord and of his Christ.

Closely akin to what has just been mentioned, and in great part as a result of the operation of the same spiritual force, the heart of Christendom began to be mysteriously touched and melted, and filled with compassion for the millions who were suffering and dying— that is, the spirit of humanity, of philanthropy, the Good Samaritan, which is inherent in the gospel, was everywhere active in the early days, but which had long since been almost quenched, was revived. Even Christian souls had been for ages in an unfeeling frame, reflecting thus the old pagan and barbarous times. The laws were cruel and savage. Sorrow and woe and pain found slight sympathy. When the general case was so forlorn, and only the few were intelligent and free, little heed was paid to the misery of others, and especially if of a different nation, out of sight, at a distance. But a marked change in this regard was at the door. John Howard had started on his journeys to abolish the grievous wrongs inflicted upon prisoners; Wilberforce and Clarkson were lifting their voices in denunciation of the sin of slavery; and Raikes had opened his first ragged school. And this was but the feeble beginning of an era of moral reforms which constitute one of the most characteristic features of the passing century, as well as one of its best claims to be remembered with gratitude in centuries to come. Our missions are to be regarded as in no small degree the outcome of the philanthropy to which the gospel has given life and vigor.

This brief glance at the Protestant Christian world, extending from near the beginning of the sixteenth century to near the end of the eighteenth, is sufficient abundantly to demonstrate that the long failure of the Lord's host to go up and possess the whole world for Christ, though in no inconsiderable degree to their shame and their sin, and because of their indifference and unbelief, was also, in yet greater measure, their misfortune, the result of evil environments for which they were not responsible, and which they were compelled to endure. Moreover, those same tempestuous and most trying years were not by any means wholly wasted, but on the contrary were an all-important and indispensable period of extensive seed-sowing in preparation for the magnificent missionary harvest to follow. At length the time was fully ripe. Rome was now so badly battered that no longer need any live in mortal fear, lest either by guile or open assault she should recapture lost territory, and therefore Protestant Christianity could well afford to face some other way than towards the Tiber. Freedom both ecclesiastical and civil had extensively become the sure inheritance of the masses; and also to them the public school and the printing-press were fast bringing intelligence to fit them for evangelistic thought and action. There were no more lands to be discovered, and the railroad and the steamship were soon to bring near, and make easily accessible, the very ends of the earth. And finally, in the nick of time, a few at least, in loving obedience to the last command of their risen and ascended Lord, were ready and eager to go into all the world, and preach the gospel to every creature.

CHAPTER VIII.

PROTESTANT MISSIONS BEFORE CAREY.

THOUGH so little was accomplished, or even undertaken, by Protestant Christians during the first three centuries after the beginning of the Reformation, and that period was one mainly of preparation, for the removal of obstacles, for laying foundations deep and broad, yet after all, a few attempts were actually made, some fruits were gathered in, souls redeemed in pagan lands; and best of all, some undying names appear in the record of men who for earnestness, self-sacrifice and consecrated zeal have never been surpassed, and have been anew to each generation since the source of astonishing inspiration and evangelistic ardor. But be it remembered that the principal value of those three hundred years is found in the fact that during their course, and largely in non-religious realms, a continual process was going on of exalting valleys, making low mountains and hills, making crooked places straight and rough places plain to prepare the way of the Lord, and make straight in the desert a highway for our God.

The narrative of what was attempted for the redemption of mankind is so brief as to be humiliating and painful. Just before his death, in 1536, Erasmus published a work on the Art of Preaching, which has been termed a "missionary treatise," which in passages reads "like a modern missionary address, and might be placed side by side with the appeals of Carey, Duff, and Livingstone." But it fell upon deaf ears, and hearts without feeling. In 1556, at the request of the great Protestant Admiral Coligny, Calvin despatched fourteen pious men, of whom only two were clergymen, to Brazil. But they went for the sake of a proposed colony rather than as heralds of good news to the heathen, and besides, the "mission" soon met with overwhelming disaster. And it was not in the least the churches sending their representatives, but the statesman making request, and the theologian choosing and bidding God-speed. In 1559, Gustavus—the king, and not the Swedish church, or the Swedish Christians—was moved to send the gospel to the pagan Lapps, and his successors carried on what he had begun. Churches were built, schools were opened, and in later years religious books were published in the vernacular, but only the slightest spiritual results ensued. And the reason becomes evident when we learn that all services were held in Swedish, which the people did not understand, and that in the winter months by royal edict the population was gathered to pay tribute *and* to be indoctrinated into the faith. For such were the methods in those days, when the Church was scarcely more than a department of the State. Within the narrow limits of this paragraph is contained the substance of the entire narrative of what was done in the sixteenth century for missions.

And the record of the seventeenth century is not much more creditable, except that in it we discern the promise, the potency, and the preparation for vastly brighter days to come. But even yet, what we find of good omens is for the most part upon the secular side of human affairs. Tremendous revolutions both political and commercial were at hand, which were destined in due season to open wide the door for the introduction of a pure gospel into remotest continents and islands. As we have already seen, for a full hundred years after the stunning achievements of Columbus and Vasco da Gama and Magellan, Spain and Portugal, both devoted to the Papacy, had enjoyed a monopoly of discovery, and trade, and colonization, in all the vast new-found regions. No other nation had been sufficiently venturesome to presume to trespass, scarcely even to land for purposes of traffic, upon the shores either of the East Indies, or of the New World. So that to the very wisest of that day, or of any generation for centuries after, if he had canvassed the question it must have seemed that providence designed Protestants to have no part or lot in the world outside of Europe. But at length and almost the same time, three Protestant nations began to bestir themselves, to build navies and merchant ships, and to voyage whithersoever they would, north, south, east, west, in spite of papal bull, or prohibition from the Iberian peninsula. And the change which resulted has continued to this day, and with results steadily increasing constitutes one of the most striking of historical phenomena; judged by its effects being greater far than the famous sending of Solomon's ships to Ophir or the voyages and settlements of the Phenicians, and in its relation to the universal spread of the gospel every way worthy to be classed with Alexander's conquests in remotest Persia and India, and the countless campaigns of the Roman legions. The earlier outcome was only commercial, political, military; supreme power simply passed from Roman Catholic to Protestant hands. But the deep divine meaning was nothing less than the world-wide spread of the fundamental ideas and principles of the Reformation, and later and more especially, the world-wide and unparalled dominion of God's most highly honored missionary agency, the Anglo-Saxon race.

The Dutch were the first to poach without conscience upon the Portuguese preserves in southern Asia. They had maintained their independence against the utmost that Philip of Spain could do, and he having united in his own person the sovereignty of the two peoples beyond the Pyrenees, and in order to punish these doughty Netherlanders whom he could not conquer, forbade their ships to enter the port of Lisbon, the both entrepot and depot for the spices and all other precious products of the East and West. Now the Hollanders had long been the ocean carriers for all Europe, and thus were threatened with commercial ruin utter, and without remedy. Nor, driven to such desperate straits, were they long in coming to the sensible conclusion that if not allowed to purchase what commodities they wanted nearer home, they would procure them in their native clime, and also at first hand. The annihilation of the Spanish Armada is 1588 supplied the golden opportunity. After three unsuccessful attempts to find a north-east passage by way of Nova Zembla and Behring Straits, in 1596, just when Van Linschoten, after fifteen years' acquaintance with the Portuguese and their commerce in Lisbon and the East, had published a work full of information, containing maps and charts, giving routes, laying down currents, rocks, harbors, etc.; the Houtman brothers doubled the Cape of Good Hope and a few months later appeared in Sumatra waters. In 1602 the Dutch East India Company was organized under a charter which specified as one of the objects to be sought the carrying of the Reformed faith to the heathen. In 1605 Van der Hagen, while en route for the Spice Islands, made a lodgment upon the Malabar Coast in the vicinity of Goa, the Portuguese headquarters in India, and then sailing on to Amboyna, one of the Moluccas, captured it. Now followed almost a century of Dutch conquest. Batavia was founded in 1619. By 1635 Formosa had become subject to the States, Malacca by 1640, while in 1651 fell the last Portuguese stronghold in Ceylon, and by 1664 the entire Malabar Coast had passed into Dutch hands. Also in 1650 a colony had been planted at the Cape of Good Hope, as a sort of half-way house on the road to the East.

But we search almost in vain for any display of missionary zeal in these movements. The Company was purely commercial and political in its designs, and its desires were fastened on something other than evangelists and converts. To be sure, ministers in considerable numbers were sent out, especially in the earlier years, and some of them were truly godly men, in earnest to do good. The gospel was preached in the vicinity of the factories, the Scriptures were translated into Malay and Cingalese, and printed at the expense of the Company. Pagan temples were closed, and Catholic churches were turned to Protestant uses, while an end was put to the celebration of both Buddhist and Romish rites. But, let what occurred in Ceylon and Java stand for the spirit and methods of Dutch evangelization, which at length prevailed. And note the subordination of the religious to the political. It was given out by the highest civil authority that no favors could be expected from the government by any who did not accept the

Helvetic Confession and receive baptism. However, as an easy preparation, it was only required that the candidate should master the Ten Commandments and the Lord's Prayer, and in addition, undertake to pray morning and evening, and say grace before and after meals! And behold, eager crowds pressed into the churches. By the end of the seventeenth century there were 300,000 "Christians" in Ceylon, which number had increased to 425,000 in 1725. In Java 100,000 received baptism under similar impulses and upon similar terms, and both process and results were of the same order in Formosa, Celebes, the Moluccas, etc. Of course the gains to Christianity were but slightly, if any, beyond those which followed from the missionary labors of the Jesuits in the same regions. But the best outcome was to appear later. The Dutch conquests in the East made vast populations known to the Protestant world, and eventually made them accessible to the heralds of a pure faith. The Hollanders were explorers and pioneers. Nor in India and the Spice Islands alone, but in the New World as well. For the Dutch West India Company was organized in 1607; two years later Hudson made his advent into New York harbor, and ascended the river which bears his name; and about the same time settlements were made in Surinam and Brazil, where, at least in some slight measure, gospel work was done.

Protestant Denmark was performing in the meantime her portion of the work of preparation, which though but insignificant in appearance at the time, and its relation to missions long entirely hidden, may not improperly be esteemed of great value, and in a sense even indispensable. In 1616 certain Danish traders made their advent upon the eastern coast of India, and in the same memorable year, building for the kingdom of heaven how vastly better than they knew, or desired, founded factories at both Tranquebar and Serampore. Such was the Lord's mysterious way of setting forces in operation which, ninety years later, should locate in the one the first Protestant mission properly so called, and one hundred and seventy-seven years later should provide for the first band of English-speaking missionaries in the other a safe abiding place, where in spite of the utmost that the British East India Company could do, they were able to maintain themselves, and to carry on their magnificent work.

But within this same period English sailors also had learned the same watery road to the East, and after long and resolutely trying in vain to discover a north-west passage to Asia, at length turned southward and followed the courses struck out by Gama and Magellan. In 1577-9, Drake made the circuit of the globe via Cape Horn, traversing the East Indian Archipelago and the Indian Ocean; Stephens penetrated to the region of the Spice Islands in 1579-82 by way of the Cape of Good Hope, and Cavendish followed in 1586. The East India Company was formed 1598-1603, under a charter granted by William III., and at once sent out the first of a long succession of fleets to trade and fight, as well as to found factories and colonies. Nearly a century followed of war with the Dutch for a share of the islands, and of the traffic in cloves, cinnamon, pepper, etc. In 1614 at Surat the first factory was opened in India, in 1630 the site of Madras was occupied, in 1642 the Hoogley was entered and the seed was planted out of which Calcutta grew, while in 1661 Bombay was transferred from the Portuguese to the English. But no prophet of the time was gifted with foresight sufficient to perceive in the least the importance of the doings of these selfish, and mercenary, and often conscienceless traders as touching the religious future of the many millions of this continental peninsula. And from near the opening of the seventeenth century until near the close of the eighteenth, English Christians were stone-blind to their duty and privilege, and did nothing whatsoever for the introduction of the gospel into southern Asia, and this, though the charter of their great Company expressly required that a plentiful supply of chaplains should be maintained at all its stations, and it was made obligatory upon all these to learn the language of the natives in their vicinity, and to give religious instruction to such of them as were in the company's employ.

Our point of vision passes now to the New World where other momentous beginnings are in progress at the same time, and though belonging to the other side of the globe, are yet in closest connection with those we have just been considering. In the history of modern missions Jamestown and Plymouth will always be words to conjure with, and the dates 1607 and 1620 will take rank with the few that mark the opening of eras. In all the early voyages to America under the lead of Raleigh and others, the conversion of the aborigines received no inconsiderable mention. Upon the seal of Massachusetts colony was represented an Indian with extended arms, and the legend " Come over and help us." As early as 1636 Plymouth took legislative action looking to the evangelization of the pagans dwelling hard by. In 1644 the General Court at Boston ordered the county courts "to have the resident Indians instructed in the knowledge and worship of God," and thus became in the phrase of a competent historian "the first missionary society of Protestant Christendom." But as yet it was not churches, or individual Christians, that moved in this great matter, but corporations, and courts, and legislatures, instead. In 1642 the Mayhews began their apostolic labors upon Martha's Vineyard and the neighboring islands, to be continued in the same family for five successive generations, and in 1646 John Eliot preached his first sermon to the red men in their own tongue, while by 1663 he had completed his Indian Bible. The labors of this gifted and godly man continued until the close of his life in 1690. By the end of the century several thousands had become Christian in name, and thirty churches had been gathered. It was to assist the New England colonists in these labors of love that twelve ministers petitioned Parliament, and as a result in 1649 the Society for the Propagation of the Gospel in New England was chartered, and for years substantial financial succor was bestowed. There were a few Englishmen of eminence in that generation of the spirit and deeds of Robert Boyle, who for thirty years was the president of that society, and contributed £300 to its funds, nearly £1,000 for various translations of the Bible, and at his death left £5,400 "for the propagation of Christianity in infidel and unenlightened nations." It was in this period, too, that Cromwell devised his scheme, which though futile was yet grand, for uniting all Protestant peoples in an effort to evangelize the whole race, parcelling out among them the entire heathen and Mohammedan world.

Two or three almost fruitless attempts on the part of

individuals will complete the missionary history of the seventeenth century. In one of the earlier decades, inspired by Grotius, seven young men of Lübeck were moved to endeavor to rekindle the light of New Testament truth in the midst of the corrupt Oriental churches. One set forth for Jerusalem, but lost his faith while upon the journey; another pushed his way into Turkey and seems to have met death by violence; while a third, Peter Heyling, after several failures, is heard of in Abyssinia in 1634, and for years lifted up his voice in witnessing for Christ. Then in 1664 Von Welz, an Austrian baron of Ratisbon, his heart burning within him, published two impassioned pamphlets in which he called upon Christians to rouse themselves and make haste to seek and save the lost of the race, and proposed the formation for the purpose of a Jesus-Society. But for his longings he found no sympathy. His was a voice crying in the wilderness which found none to listen. The mass of the Lutheran Church regarded his schemes as preposterous, so far as they received any attention. One so learned and pious as Ursinus "distinctly stigmatizes his appeal as a dream, rebukes its self-willed piety, its hypocrisy, its Anabaptist and Quaker spirit, and deprecates the proposed Jesus-Association in these words: Protect us from it, dear Lord God!" This great theologian concludes that the gospel is not meant for barbarians like Greenlanders, Tatars and Cannibals. "The holy things of God are not to be cast before such dogs and swine." Exciting thus only opposition and ridicule in Germany, at length Von Welz took his departure for Holland, gave up his title to nobility, bestowed some $9,000 upon the object so dear to his heart, was ordained, and sailed for Surinam, where he soon died.

Thus ends the second century of Protestant history. The missionary dawn is still almost a hundred years away in the future, but we have now reached the vicinity of certain cheering tokens that the morning will not fail to appear. What must be regarded as distinctly a new stage in the development of missionary activity comes into view in the first years of the eighteenth century, with Denmark and the Lutherans as the actors. And further, as the fashion was, with the king and his court to lead. The fact seems to be established that it was by his chaplain Lutkens that Frederick IV. was stirred up to send forth the message of salvation to the various distant dependencies of the Crown. Searching about earnestly for suitable persons to despatch on this gospel errand, not one could be found within the bounds of the kingdom, and therefore recourse was had to those almost solitary centers of evangelical fervor, Halle and Berlin, and to the renowned pietists, Francke and Spener, so much spoken against by the formalists and rationalists of their time. At length two young men were chosen and found ready to go to the far off regions of darkness. But great opposition was encountered in Germany, on the ground that missions to the heathen were neither necessary nor proper; and so difficult was it found to establish their orthodoxy before a court of Danish theologians, that ordination was secured to the candidates only at the imperative command of the king. But finally, and after a tempestuous voyage of forty weeks, in July of 1706, these pioneers for the kingdom among the teeming millions of India, Ziegenbalg and Plutschau, stepped on shore at Tranquebar, a Danish settlement on the south-east coast, and began their arduous labors. Incredible difficulties were in waiting, and not only from the idol-worshipping natives, but even more from godless Europeans, and from the unbelieving and jealous Danish governor, who set himself to put every possible hindrance in their way, and went so far as to cast Ziegenbalg into prison, where he lay for four months in confinement, and forbidden the use of pen and paper. But in spite of all they held on, mastered the language, translated the Scriptures and other books, opened schools and preached here and there without ceasing. It is estimated that before the end of the century not less than 50,000 converts had been made. The peculiar glory of this mission lies in the fact that it was the first Protestant undertaking in India, or in any remote heathen country, and also that for almost a half-century (1750-98) it was blessed with the presence and magnificent services of Schwartz, whose name belongs among the first half-score of eminent apostles to the pagan world.

In 1714 this same Danish King Frederick established a college of missions, and two years later under his auspices the gospel was carried to Lapland. Just at this time it was also that in northern Norway the soul of Hans Egede was pondering a mighty question night and day. For thirteen years the Macedonian cry had sounded in his ears; he had read of a colony which centuries since had been planted in Greenland, but from which no message for centuries had been received; he longed to undertake something for the relief of his countrymen imprisoned in that land of ice, and sought eagerly in every direction for means to betake himself thither. He petitioned Frederick for aid, and in 1717 resigned his pastorate in Waagen, and made his way to Copenhagen. Finally by sheer persistence, having conquered every obstacle, he set forth in 1721 to enter upon a fifteen years' course of disappointment, and of suffering both physical and spiritual, and with but the slightest measures of success attending. No settlers were found, but only a handful of sordid and most degraded Eskimo. With only his heroic wife to lend comfort and hope, with storm and frost, famine and pestilence, to endure, he held resolutely on until other missionaries came, and he was fairly compelled to retire.

And now the Christian world was to behold yet another step forward in the sublime march of missionary progress. And this likewise was closely connected with Denmark, King Frederick, and the pietist Francke. The renewed Moravian Church had been formed only ten years, and numbered but some six hundred souls, when Zinzendorf, who had felt profoundly the evangelical movement which centered in Halle, paid a visit to Copenhagen at the coronation of Christian VI. While there he heard that the settlements which since Egede went out had been maintained in Greenland, being financially unprofitable, were to be broken up and the missionaries called home (again we see religion placed at the mercy of political and financial considerations), and he also saw two Eskimo converts whom Egede had baptized. Moreover it came to his knowledge that the sister of a negro whom he met was a slave in St. Thomas, and with other wretched bondmen was famishing for the bread of life. This tiny mustard seed of knowledge fell into soil most fruitful and was destined to bear a plentiful harvest. The story was repeated in Herrnhut, and within a few months five intrepid messengers of peace were ready and eager to endure all and risk all, whether at the frozen north, or under the tropics, and in the latter case expecting success only at the cost of themselves being sold into slavery, but glad to suffer this, or even to die, if only able to save a single soul. Such was the inspiring and most extraordinary genesis of Moravian missions. Nor from that day to this has the spirit changed, nor has a halt been called. This little church went on in faith and love to start "more missions in twenty years than all the Protestant churches together had in two hundred." Dr. Warneck justly deems Francke and Zinzendorf "the fathers of the modern mission to the heathen." And further, he declares of the latter that " he is the first in modern times on whose heart lay day and night the desire that all the ends of the earth might see the salvation of God." Think of the marvel, six missions founded so far apart in six brief years: 1732 in the West Indies, 1733 in Greenland, 1734 among the American Indians, 1735 in Surinam, and 1736 in South Africa.

We come now to a great gap, extending from Zinzendorf to Carey. For full sixty years not a single new missionary undertaking was set on foot. True a few societies were organized in England, whose object was at least semi-evangelistic. Among them was the Society for the Promotion of Christian Knowledge, dating from 1698, and which through this period supplied Ziegenbalg and his successors with the sinews of war. And the Society for the Propagation of the Gospel in Foreign Parts, chartered by King William in 1701, and which afterwards sent John Wesley to Georgia. The Scottish Society for Promoting Christian Knowledge followed in 1709, one of whose missionaries in later years David Brainerd became. The few honored names can be mentioned of those who undertook to carry on the work which Eliot and the Mayhews had begun during the century preceding. Such as Horton, who labored among the Indians of Long Island. And Sergeant, who in 1734 resigned a tutorship in Yale College, and removed to Stockbridge to gather the scattered Mohegans and preach to them the gospel, whose successor Edwards became (1750-6). In New Jersey and eastern New York Brainerd was in evangelistic labors abundant and greatly blessed (1744-7), as well as Kirkland among the Oneidas from 1764 onward. In 1766 when Occum visited England in behalf of Mr. Wheelock's school for Indians, he easily raised £12,000 among the churches. But all things considered, the phrase "apostle to the Indians," whether for length of service or for toils, sufferings, and mortal perils endured, clearly belongs to the Moravian David Zeisberger, who for sixty-two years (1746-1808), devoted himself without stint to the Delawares in New York, Pennsylvania, Ohio, Michigan and Canada.

A few sentences will suffice to tell of the great changes in the political world which had an intimate bearing upon missionary movements about to begin. The territorial growth of Great Britain was astounding during the eighteenth century, and both in the east and the west. The Seven Years' War was of slight significance to the powers of Europe engaged, as compared with its tremendous outcome for the spread of the Gospel. For it gave to Pitt the peerless opportunity to end forever, at Quebec in 1759, the dominion of Catholic France in the New World, and in India in 1757 at the battle of Plassey to lay the sure foundations for British dominion in southern Asia. The Dutch were also largely expelled from their eastern possessions, losing Ceylon and Cape Colony in 1795. In 1787 Sierra Leone was occupied as a place of refuge for liberated slaves. Along with this material preparation for missions, for fifty years the glorious Wesleyan revival had been rising and spreading, that greatest effusion of the Spirit since Pentecost, scarcely less important to Christendom than the Reformation itself. In the momentous campaign about to begin against heathenism throughout the whole world, not German and Scandinavian, as hitherto, but Anglo-Saxon Protestantism was destined to lead, and in the bones of William Carey the holy fire had already begun to burn!

CHAPTER IX.

THE CAREY EPOCH IN MISSIONS.

The closing years of the eighteenth century constitute in the history of Protestant missions an epoch indeed, since they witnessed nothing less than a revolution, a renaissance, an effectual and manifold ending of the old, a substantial inauguration of the new. It was then that for the first time since the apostolic period, occurred an outburst of general missionary zeal and activity. Beginning in Great Britain, it soon spread to the Continent and across the Atlantic. It was no mere push of fervor, but a mighty tide set in, which from that day to this has been steadily rising and spreading. Hitherto all similar undertakings had been isolated, spasmodic, and lacking in reliable support. Spurts of vigor were certain to end in fatal relapse. Excepting in the case of the noble Moravian work, every attempt had thus sooner or later come to failure. But from this time forward it is no more to be after this discouraging fashion. Or the fact may be stated in this way. Hitherto the churches, ministers and people together, had been indifferent to the spiritual condition of the pagan world. Whatever had been done was the achievement of some single earnest soul, or some monarch, and usually in that case politics entered largely as a directing force. Only a little circle had been aroused and moved to co-operate, while all about was a dead mass of apathy. And so, naturally, the project ended with the originator. But with Carey was ushered in a more excellent way. A few elect spirits were touched, and from them the flame was diffused to Christians of other names in all the dissenting churches, and to the great Establishment as well ; that is to the most intelligent and spiritual in each. It was the plain people, the masses, that now began to pray and give and go, not tarrying in the least for king or prelate to hoist the signal. Or this form of expression will fairly well complete the setting forth of the change which now transpired, so radical and sweeping as to amount to a revolution. Here and now was the beginning of missionary organization. From henceforth as never before, emotion, desire, holy purpose, were to be incarnated in constitutions and by-laws, in memberships and anniversaries, in treasuries and systematic giving, the continual offering of littles by each one in great multitudes. And Carey's Baptist society, which originated in his brain, was the model for the scores and hundreds which followed after. Thus was ushered in the happy day of voluntary societies, organizations sustained by such as are interested in the promotion of the objects sought.

And the year of grace 1792 is *annus mirabilis*, the famous date from which to reckon backward and forward. Well may it stand side by side with 44 A. D., when the Holy Ghost said, "Separate me Barnabas and Saul for the work whereunto I have called them." Or 53 A. D., when in vision Paul was bidden to lay the foundations of the gospel in Europe. Whatever has been accomplished since can be traced to forces which began to operate a hundred years ago. And Carey is not only the chief figure in the matter, but also the supreme personal force—yes, under God the efficient cause of the wondrous changes which have been brought to pass. We may speak of the "Carey epoch" with every whit as much propriety as of the Luther Reformation. We may as fitly term him the apostle of modern missions as Paul the apostle to the Gentiles, or Ulphilas the apostle to the Goths, or Augustine apostle to the Britons, or Boniface apostle to the Germans.

A glance at such incidents of Carey's life as relate to this sublime re-beginning is next in order. In 1761 a babe was born in central England gifted among other things with a measureless and inextinguishable hunger for knowledge, and a capacity seldom matched for endless plodding and hard work. And a will-power was present able to push and persist without limit, but which could not by any means be allured or driven from the pursuit of any chosen object. To such royal qualities were joined later a stalwart faith, and a zeal for righteousness so fervid and all-consuming that no difficulties or discouragements could quench it. At seventeen we find him a shoemaker's apprentice at Hackleton, nine miles from his birthplace. Already he had commenced the diligent study of birds, eggs, insects and plants, and ere long had begun to delve deep into the mysteries of Latin, Hebrew, Greek and French. And, early and often, he was called to take lessons in the stern discipline of life. When about twenty he was married to one who was "querulous, capricious, obstinate," and without sympathy with his most exalted life-aims, all this perhaps in large part because of a predisposition to mental disease. He passed also through a protracted season of ill health, and besides for years was burdened by the woes of extreme poverty. And further, when the voice of the Lord began to call in clearest tones, "Go preach the Gospel to the whole creation," year after year he stood almost utterly alone in disposition to obey.

It can not but be interesting and profitable to take note of the various steps in the wondrous unfolding of the Divine plan. This future hero for the kingdom of heaven was well on towards manhood before his spiritual nature was effectually and savingly aroused, and then, reared as he had been in the Established Church, hearing a sermon from the text "Let us go forth unto him without the camp bearing the reproach," he made a direct personal application to himself, and with characteristic decision and practical energy, went and joined a little company of Baptists, *because* theirs was a faith despised. Nor was it long before acceptable preaching gifts began to appear. In 1785 he became a member of the Olney church, by which he was called to the work of the ministry, and two years after was ordained as pastor of the Moulton church, ten miles from Northampton, upon a salary of but £15, of which £5 came from London. To eke out a living, school-teaching and shoe-making were added to his occupations. It was while here that his attention was first fixed upon the moral desolations of the pagan world, and his heart began to be deeply moved to hasten relief. The fact is established that it was the reading of the voyages of Captain Cook which brought this weighty theme to his notice, "though if ever an idea was originated in any man by the Spirit of God, it was this idea of the evangelization of the world." From boyhood books of science and history and travel had been his delight, and now from investigating the world's physical features, he turned with all his might to an examination of the religious condition of mankind. When Fuller once visited

Carey's shop in Moulton he saw upon the wall near where he sat at his work a roughly sketched map of the world, upon which had been set in order all manner of facts and figures, to picture to the eye what needed to be done for the diffusion of the Gospel, the redemption of the race. Already also had fuel been added to the heavenly flame by a sermon of Fuller's upon "The Gospel Worthy of all Acceptation," which convinced him that in spite of any hyper-Calvinistic teaching to the contrary, it was the duty of all men to believe, and what was even more to the point just now, the duty of Christians to go everywhere telling the glad tidings to all. A third impulse was supplied by a pamphlet of Jonathan Edwards', published in 1747, and recently reprinted in England, which exhorted God's people to union in "extraordinary prayer for the revival of religion and the advancement of Christ's kingdom upon earth." As a result of reading this, the Baptist ministers in Northamptonshire set apart an hour for prayer on the first Monday of each month, that the power of the Cross might soon be displayed in the most distant parts of the habitable globe. When with his brethren he could not but speak frequently upon the all-absorbing theme, but found few to listen with interest, while as for most he seemed to be a dreamer, a teller of idle tales, one gone daft, his conclusions irrational, his plans impracticable, his longings such as never could be met. Meantime his ministry had been removed to Leicester. It was a crisis in his career, that day at the Association, when having been urged by the moderator to name a subject for discussion, after endeavoring to shun the responsibility, he finally propounded this question, "Whether the command given to the apostles to teach all nations was not obligatory on all ministers, to the end of the world." And the reply of the aged Ryland did but express the indifference and unbelief of Christendom; "Sit down, young man. You are a miserable enthusiast to ask such a question. When God wants to convert the world, he can do it without your help; and at least nothing can be done until a second Pentecost shall bring a return of the miraculous gifts." As yet no one had begun to suspect that here was a "young man" already actually possessed of the substance of that old-time enduement, even to the speaking with tongues!

However, not in the least shaken in his purpose by this rebuff and rebuke, the heroic subject thereof is presently found engaged upon the task of arguing and proving his case with his pen. That is, he put on paper with remarkable clearness, fulness, and cogency, a tabular statement of the size, population, religious condition, etc., of the various countries in the Old World and the New, and then went on to prove that the Lord's command and commission were perpetual, to recite the efforts which in each century had been put forth, and to demonstrate the practicability of making further attempts. This memorable presentment, so novel and so purely original with Carey, which one of his biographers pronounces the "first and still greatest missionary treatise in the English language," closed with an appeal for united prayer, and besides, since petition without suitable effort to match would be but mockery, the gift regularly from each one of a penny a week was suggested. As another token of the current spiritual blindness and apathy, for sheer lack of means to print, this pamphlet lay for six years in manuscript and unread. But that the precious leaven of missionary desire was spreading is shown by the fact that at the Association meeting held in 1791 the two preachers, Sutcliff and Fuller, chose kindred themes; the former taking for his text I. Kings 19:10, "I have been very jealous for the Lord God of hosts," and the latter from Haggai 1:2, "This people say, The time is not come that the Lord's house should be built." Noticing how deep and solemn was the impression produced by these discourses, Carey, with whom action, as a matter of course, must needs follow hard upon the heels of knowledge and conviction, proposed to begin at once to plan and to organize for vigorous endeavor. But for the others the vision of privilege and obligation was still too dim, and the objects aimed at were too indefinite and out of reach. And so another year passed in inaction.

• But May 31st, 1792, a date to be memorized by every lover of the kingdom, came the life-opportunity for this irrepressible agitator for the opening of a world-wide evangelistic campaign. For the Baptist ministers are found together again at Nottingham, and Carey has been chosen to preach. Judged by its momentous and far-reaching results his sermon must be considered one of the very chiefest in Christian history, perhaps second only to the Sermon on the Mount. With Isaiah 54:2-3 for a text, he proceeded to unfold the two matchless and immortal subdivisions, "Expect great things from God," and—eminently Carey-like from first to last—joining untiring works to stalwart faith, "Attempt great things for God." In that never-to-be-forgotten hour the conclusions, the convictions, the longings of years first found full expression, and so, not strangely, the emotions of those who listened were aroused to somewhat of sympathy. But nevertheless, though hearts were swayed, and some tears fell, the audience was about to separate without open definite commitment to any "attempt" in behalf of the fervid speaker's "great things." So in an agony of desire mingled with fear, Carey siezed Fuller by the arm and exclaimed ; "Are you going to again do nothing?" And it was then, as the latter admits, "to pacify him and also to gain time," that it was decided to organize at a meeting to be held five months hence, and Carey was counselled to publish his pamphlet in the meantime. In due season came forth from the press "An Enquiry into the Obligations of Christians to use Means for the Conversion of the Heathen, in which the Religious State of the Different Nations of the World, the Success of Former Undertakings, and the Practicability of Further Undertakings, are considered by William Carey."

In due season also, at Kettering in the back parlor of the Widow Beebe Wallis, was formed the "Particular Baptist Society for Propagating the Gospel Among the Heathen." How utterly insignificant were the actors for number, or station, or gifts ! Only twelve, belonging to a feeble and despised sect, and unheard of outside of the interior counties in which they lived. Only one London clergyman gave countenance to the movement. Kings, statesmen, church-magnates cared nothing, knew nothing. And they made a subscription on the spot for the world's conversion, which amounted to £12 2s. 6d., over which the brilliant Sydney Smith made merry years after, for its preposterous inadequacy when the souls of 420,000,000 were concerned. Indeed, how sublime was that act of faith, that venture far beyond the realm of sight. How exceedingly remote were the heathen, and what an uncounted host. The undertaking was vast beyond conception, and the issue exceedingly doubtful. It was like crossing the Rubicon, like nailing the theses to the church doors, putting forth from Palos upon the untraversed sea, or burning the ships to make retreat impossible. However, it was easy enough to resolve, and to adopt a constitution and by-laws, and not so very difficult to subscribe, but after that came the real tug of war. The pertinent and very practical question was next to be answered, "Who shall be sent forth, and whither in all the pagan world shall they journey?" Carey offered himself as a candidate on the sole condition that a companion be found to go with him, and his thought had long been centered upon the South Seas and the Society Islands as the most eligible spot for a beginning. A committee was chosen to investigate and decide, and was not left long to wait, for the pillar of fire soon began to rise and move forward. By "accident" a certain John Thomas, surgeon in the employ of the East India Company, in Bengal since 1783, converted there and led to engage in evangelistic work in behalf of the Hindus, had recently returned, and was now in London endeavoring to raise money for further efforts. He was heard of, and was sent for, and finally was invited to return under the auspices of the new society with Carey as associate. Thus did the divine hand guide this master-missionary to make assault, not upon one of the comparatively unimportant outworks of heathenism, but directly upon one of the mightiest of its central strongholds.

• But trials and tribulations in plenty were yet in store. The Leicester church was loath to lose its beloved pastor, and touchingly alleged, "We have been praying for the spread of Christ's kingdom among the heathen, and now God requires us to make the first sacrifice." Next Carey's wife, having no sort of appreciation for his life-aims, utterly refused to share the risks and hardships involved in carrying them out. And though the idea cost pain unspeakable, for weeks imperative duty appeared to compel him to set forth alone, leaving her behind, at least for a season. Then too India was 15,000 miles away; the East India Company was in full possession, no Englishman could land upon its shores without a license, while as for missionaries, they were held in fear and abomination, the gospel being "a contraband article" in those climes. After the utmost of influence had been brought to bear upon the directors, it became evident that no license was to be obtained; and therefore, recalling that the apostles did not wait for permission from Cæsar, or any earthly authority, our hero resolved to set forth without the consent of the Company and take the consequences. Then the climax of embarrassment and discouragement was connected with Thomas. In most respects he was but a weak vessel, and among the rest, had an amazing proclivity for being always overwhelmingly in debt. Through his influence with the captain, passage had been surreptitiously engaged upon one of the Company's ships, the fare had been paid, and the baggage put on board. But delayed long by storms under the Isle of Wight, one of Thomas' creditors hearing of their design to proceed to India without leave, sent a communication to the captain threatening exposure. Hence the missionaries were put ashore, with the loss of the bulk of their passage money. But fortunately a few days after a Danish East Indiaman lay in Dover Roads (here again did Denmark through her settlements in the east unwittingly do an important service to Christian missions), upon which transportation was secured, and at the last moment visiting his erratic wife, Mrs. Carey consented to accompany him, only stipulating that a sister might also go.

It was June 13th, 1793, that the departure was finally made, and they set sail upon a voyage so pregnant with consequences to Christianity unspeakably great, and five months later landed in Calcutta, and on the 9th of November.

Of course the passage of these events produced scarcely a ripple upon the surface of the social, or political, or even religious world, were almost altogether unnoticed and unknown. And not many historians even yet make the slightest mention of them. In those days the tremendous stir over the American Revolution was quieting down, but only to be succeeded by the vastly more fearful commotion from across the English Channel. It will be instructive to set down a few dates which locate what many would still deem the notable happenings of the period. In 1789 first burst forth the volcano of the French Revolution, and July 9th the Bastile fell. June 20th, 1791, King Louis XVI. fled from Paris. August 18th of the next year, a few weeks after Carey's immortal sermon, the Invasion of France by the allies began, and the next month followed the September Massacres, and the Republic was proclaimed. January 21st, 1793, the king ascended the scaffold; March 11th the Revolutionary Tribunal was set up and the Reign of Terror was inaugurated; and June 2nd, a fortnight before Carey sailed, the Girondists fell; and as he was nearing his destination the hapless Marie Antoinette met her fate, the Girondists following hard after. As God, and angels, and glorified saints estimate human affairs, who will dare affirm that the Hackleton cobbler's part in history is not in every way worthy to be compared with that of Chatham and Napoleon, George III. and Burke, Mirabeau and La Fayette?

CHAPTER X.

THE GREAT MISSIONARY REVIVAL.

BEFORE proceeding further with the thrilling story of the notable renewal and expansion of missionary endeavor, which set in almost from Carey's sublime venture, it will be of value to put in a paragraph a summary of what the whole of Protestant Christendom was doing at that date for the whole of heathendom. And first as to the religious condition of the earth's population, quoting the language of his famous "Enquiry": "The inhabitants of the world amount to 731,000,000; 420,000,000 of whom are still in pagan darkness; 130,000,000 the followers of Mahomet; 100,000,000 catholics; 44,000,000 protestants; 30,000,000 of the greek and armenian churches, and perhaps 7,000,000 of jews. It must undoubtedly strike every considerate mind, what a vast proportion of the sons of Adam there are, who yet remain in the most deplorable state of heathen darkness, without any means of knowing the true God, except what are afforded them by the works of nature; and utterly destitute of the knowledge of Christ, or of any means of obtaining it. In many of these countries they have no written language, consequently no Bible, and are led only by the most childish customs and traditions," etc., etc. Now, to meet and improve this most lamentable and appalling condition, what endeavors can we discover? Well, the Moravians were carrying on missions with some fair degree of success in Greenland, Labrador, in the West Indies, and Surinam, had once begun work in South Africa, had been driven out, and in the year of Carey's great sermon had sent another force. Besides Zeisberger and a few associates were still toiling under incredible hardships and discouragements among the Delawares, and after various removals, and one wholesale massacre of their innocent converts, were now for safety in Canada. The Danish-Halle mission had pushed in all directions from Tranquebar, had received cheering support from Denmark, Germany and England, had enjoyed a period of prosperity, but at present for several reasons, was in the midst of a steady and lasting decline. Schwartz had before him yet six years of life. In 1757 Kiernander had gone thence to Calcutta to open a mission in that city and was still doing his utmost to advance the Gospel among both natives and Europeans. As other earnest Christians, whose hearts were engaged and whose hands were busy, may be named Mr. Udney, Charles Grant and David Brown of the East India Company, the latter a chaplain. Scarcely a trace was left of Eliot's work for the Indians except his Bible, the last of five generations of Mayhews was ministering to a feeble remnant of a single tribe. On account of the excitements and passions resulting from the French War, and the Revolution, missionary toil for the aborigines had almost entirely ceased. And finally, as recently as 1786, Coke, while on a voyage to Nova Scotia, having been driven by a terrible storm far to the southward and making land first in Antigua, was led to start a mission upon that island. Something such was the situation, and the outlook, when Carey and Thomas left England behind, and turned their faces resolutely towards India. But note the sublime audacity of faith which prompted this dauntless apostle to write while in mid-ocean: "I hope the society will go on and increase, and that the multitudes of heathen in the world may hear the glorious words of truth. Africa is but a little way from England, Madagascar is but a little further. South America and all the numerous and large islands in the Indian and China Seas, I hope will not be passed over." And this also a few months later when the very blackness of darkness seemed to have settled down: " Well, I have God, and his word is sure; and though the superstitions of the heathen were a million times worse than they are, if I were deserted by all, and persecuted by all, yet my hope, fixed on that word, will rise superior to all obstructions, and triumph over all trials. God's cause will triumph, and I shall come out of all trials as gold purified by the fire."

With such a spirit inspiring and propelling the leader, no wonder that something great in the way of results began presently to appear. But nevertheless, these words of George Smith are true: "The first two English missionaries to India seemed, to those who sent them forth, to have disappeared forever. For fourteen months no tidings of their welfare reached the poor praying people of the midlands, who had been emboldened to begin the enterprise." But July 29th, 1794, letters arrived for Ryland, of Bristol, who read them and sent at once for Dr. Bogue, of Gosport, an Independent clergyman, and Mr. Stephen, to rejoice with him. First they all gave thanks and prayed for a blessing upon the Baptist Society, and then the two latter called upon Mr. Hey, a prominent minister, and it was determined to begin immediately to agitate for the organization of a similar society, though with a much broader ecclesiastical basis. Suiting the action to the word, Dr. Bogue prepared an article, which in September appeared in the *Evangelical Magazine*, addressed to "Evangelical dissenters who practise infant baptism," urging all such to bestir themselves; arguing that the time had fully come to begin; expressing the conviction that many would be found willing and eager to assist, if only a few would step forth to lead, and that funds sufficient could be gathered to support at least *twenty or thirty* missionaries. So Carey's letters and this article in God's hands proved to be the "little fire" which kindled "how great a matter."

The effect of this clarion call was immediate, and profound, and wide-spread. The next month it was further stated in the same periodical that, if a society should be formed upon a large scale, and a basis so broad as to unite Christians "without respect to different denominations, or repulsive distinctions arising from points in dispute between Calvinists and Arminians," one man stood pledged for £100, and another for £500, to equip the first six volunteers for a mission to the South Seas. Some weeks later appeared the suggestion over the signatures of eighteen Independent, seven Presbyterian, three Wesleyan, and three Episcopal ministers, for a meeting for consultation, urging that in the meantime local and district gatherings be held to excite interest, collect funds, and choose delegates. In July, 1795, another article reached the public from the glowing pen of "T. H." [Haweis, a Church of England clergyman, whose influence through the years next ensuing was unequalled in raising enthusiasm and moving to effort,] "showing the very probable success of a proper mission to the South Seas," giving a long, and glowing, and intensely rose-colored setting-forth of the situation in those remote parts, proving conclusively the islands to be a very terrestrial paradise, and the people thereof the loving and lovable innocent children of nature!

Then at length, all things being ready, September 21st, the illustrious meetings began in London. At the outset subscriptions were made by the country ministers amounting to £750. Many encouraging letters from all parts of the island were read; it was announced that several men were ready to offer themselves as pioneers in the work; and the vote was unanimous to organize at once. This "fundamental principle," which still remains in the constitution of the London Society, was adopted: "The design is not to send Presbyterianism, Independency, Episcopacy, or any other form of church order and government (about which there may be difference of opinion among serious persons), but the glorious Gospel of the blessed God to the heathen; and it shall be left (as it ought to be) to the minds of the persons whom God shall call into the fellowship of his Son from among them to assume for themselves such forms of church government as to them shall appear most agreeable to the Word of God." Through three full blissful days the meetings continued, with two sermons each day from eminent divines upon pertinent themes, and to audiences "immensely great." It seemed like a new Pentecost "with Christians of all denominations for the first time in the same place, using the same hymns and prayers, and feeling themselves to be one." Two hundred ministers sat together in the galleries; and Dr. Bogue said: "We are called together for the funeral of bigotry; and I hope it will be buried so deep as never to rise again." Whereat "the whole vast body could scarce refrain from one general shout of joy . . . Such a scene was never, perhaps, before beheld in our world ; and it was a foretaste of heaven. . . . We shall account it through eternity a distinguished favor, the highest honor, that we appeared here and gave in our names among the founders of the society. This will be ever remembered by us as the era of Christian benevolence."

The heavenly flame thus kindled in the metropolis quickly spread throughout all Britain, and it followed, of course, that money in abundance began to flow in from all quarters. One church in Southampton subscribed £270, and from Market Harborough came £83 1s. 7d., with this word : "No event in life has given me more pleasure than this glorious attempt to send forth the gospel." The children in a boarding-school, unasked, gave £1 9s. 6d. Scotland also caught the evangelistic fervor, missionary societies were soon formed in Edinburgh and Glasgow, and before many months had passed, some £12,000 had been forwarded to London. This novel idea of missions to the whole wide world took such complete possession of Robert Haldane that he planned a vast mission to Bengal, of which he was to meet the entire cost, proposing to go out himself and securing Dr. Bogue as an associate. And when the East India Company refused their consent to the scheme, turning his beneficence into channels nearer at hand, with his brother James he formed the Society for the Propagation of the Gospel at Home, and within twelve years expended in connection with it the princely sum of £70,000. Nor did the tide of holy zeal fail to cross the Channel and arouse the saints upon the Continent, whose contributions ere long rose to

£1,500. It came to pass that by the end of October the directors had £3,000 in hand, which was more than doubled three months later, and in June of 1796 they report the receipts as £10,000. Missionaries had also offered themselves in encouraging numbers. By midsummer it was decided to purchase a ship and to open missions at once in Otaheite, the Friendly and Pelew Islands, and the Marquesas, with projects besides looking towards Madagascar, the West Indies, and the north shore of the Caspian! So great was their faith, and so enlarged were their ideas and longings. And thus early the prophetic hope was expressed that this uprising for the world's redemption "will spread to every Christian bosom, to the Dutch, German, American, and all Protestant churches, till the whole professing world shall burn with fervent love, and labor to spread in every heathen land the sweet savor of the Redeemer's name."

Accordingly, the *Duff* was purchased at a cost of £4,875, and was furnished for her voyage to the antipodes at an additional expense of more than £7,000, several years' supplies for the missionaries included. A profit of £5,000 was expected from freight to be brought upon the homeward trip. A call was made and nobly responded to, for books, tools, cooking utensils, instruments, seeds and other supplies; and one poor man expended £2 2s. upon six spades, nine hammers and four thousand sixpenny and tenpenny nails. July 28th the twenty-nine persons who had been chosen as missionaries were solemnly set apart to the high calling— six of them being married, *only four of the number ordained*, one a physician, two children, and the others artisans. Thousands joined in the novel and most impressive service, and no less than ten clergymen, representing Episcopalians, Presbyterians, Independents, Seceders and Wesleyans, joining in the public exercises, "showing that affection is increasing between ministers of different denominations, who, previous to this institution, had neither fellowship nor intercourse." In reference to the religious situation it was written soon after: "In no instance in the limits of our recollection has such a spirit of prayer and supplication been poured out upon the churches, or such general approbation been discovered. The greatest kindness has been displayed in all departments of the government. Neither the Council Board nor the Custom House would accept fees." Wednesday, August 10th, 1796, at five A. M., the *Duff* dropped down from Blackall to Gravesend, a vast multitude beholding, and came to anchor at Spithead the Tuesday following. The East India convoy having already sailed, she was compelled (since the French wars were then raging) to wait six weeks at Portsmouth for the *Adamant*, a fifty-two gun ship. September 22nd found her at St. Helen's. The day after her anchors were finally hoisted, and her sails were spread for the ends of the earth. Thus the great undertaking followed in Carey's path, indeed three years and a half later than he, and yet in some respects at least, far outdoing that peerless founder and pioneer. It was at this juncture that one moralized with altogether pardonable exaltation of feeling: "It is highly probable that since the Lord and the apostles, the bosom of the deep has never been graced with such a vessel," or one "in which so many thousands of Christians embarked their hopes and followed with their prayers."

What remarkable growth may be discerned during the brief period under view. How different all this, for the number and variety and standing of those interested, for magnitude of operations and for eclat, from the deed of those twelve obscure Northamptonshire Baptist ministers with their ridiculously inadequate subscription, and the almost insuperable obstacles which to the last moment hedged up the way of Carey and Thomas. For nearly two years, until May, 1798, not a word was heard from Captain Wilson and the tremendous venture made by faith. Leaving the *Duff* to battle for weeks with fearful storms off Cape Horn, and then, baffled, facing about to beat her way past the Cape of Good Hope through 262 degrees of longitude, let us glance at certain steps of progress meantime taken at home. Measures were immediately taken to start a second mission in the Foulah country, some two hundred and fifty miles from Sierra Leone, for which Edinburgh and Glasgow offered to supply two men each, and the London Society was to add the same number. Plans were also laid for a mission in Cape Colony, which had recently been transferred from Holland to Great Britain. In January, 1797, it could be affirmed concerning the religious fervor resulting far and wide: "Christians in every corner of the land are meeting in a regular manner, and pouring out their souls for God's blessing on the world." And again: "The efforts most successfully made to introduce the Gospel to the South Seas have had a most powerful tendency to unite the devoted servants of Christ of every denomination in the bonds of brotherly love, and to awaken zeal to help the perishing multitudes in our own country, and also the Jews." So early was the discovery made that the best possible way to forward the work of evangelization at home is to push missions abroad with all ardor and energy. Month by month came tidings of both local and district movements to raise missionary funds, and to multiply toilers, both at many points in the heathen world, and in every destitute region where the gospel is already known. For this purpose scores of organizations were formed in every denomination. Similar interest sprang up in America; in Massachusetts and Connecticut, in New York and Philadelphia, and in various other parts of the Union. Nor was the enthusiasm less upon the Continent, for in Germany, Holland, Sweden, and Switzerland societies were organized. With all these, as well as with various individuals of influence, the directors of the London Society, the main center and source of the unprecedented outburst of faith and love and good works, opened correspondence for mutual instruction and encouragement. Among the rest Von Schirnding, a German nobleman, was delighted to hear of the evangelizing projects on foot; for years he had been cherishing similar schemes, and would aid liberally with money and men. And Vanderkemp, in Holland, a famed soldier, scholar, and physician, and aforetime a pronounced sceptic, offered himself as a messenger of glad tidings to the heathen, though past fifty years of age, and proceeded to organize the Netherlands Missionary Society. By the sudden death of his wife and only child by drowning he had forever lost his infidelity to the last fraction, had come across a copy of the report of the great London meeting containing the sermons and addresses, etc., and one text, "Curse ye Meroz," entered his soul. Falling on his knees he cried: "O Lord Jesus, here am I. Thou knowest I have no will of my own since I devoted myself to thy service. Prevent me only from doing this great work in a carnal, self-sufficient spirit, and lead me in the right way." Inspiring letters came too from Basle, which since 1771 had been the seat of a wide-spread movement " to maintain evangelical doctrine and piety." Certain devout German brethren sent their congratulations couched in these glowing words: "It is like the dawn promising the beautiful day after the dark night. It is the beginning of a new epoch for the kingdom of God on earth. Your undertaking and its success fills our hearts with joy and our eyes with tears. The history of Great Britain is sanctified by this unparalleled mission. What harmony among different persuasions! You call on the wise and good of every nation to take interest in the work and bear a part. Such a call was never heard of before. It was reserved for the close of the eighteenth century to be distinguished by it." And thus it was that the tide of zeal rose and spread abroad.

The first tidings from the precious missionary ship arrived in May of 1798, in a letter from Captain Wilson written at Canton six months before, and in July following the *Duff* lay at anchor in the Downs. Now naturally came the climax of exultation and buoyant hope. "Never, perhaps, was an undertaking more completely accomplished. Fifty-one thousand miles have been traversed without the least material loss or damage. The winds conspired to waft them safely and swiftly to their desired haven. Everywhere they were received by the natives with reverence and delight. All are settled in the islands they preferred, and apparently in the greatest safety. At Otaheite a most fertile district was bestowed upon them, and a commodious building." In a public address to Captain Wilson, Dr. Haweis did not fail to surpass the most fervid and fanciful in his portrayal of the past, present and future of the mission.

But the directors well understood that something besides pæans of gladness were in order, and therefore, immediately after a day of special thanksgiving had been devoutly observed, they met to plan both how to maintain communications with the brethren already sent out, and also to open other fields for toil. Their faith and courage hesitated not to scan an evangelistic campaign in behalf of the kingdom as extensive as this: " Hindustan, the Sandwich Islands, and other groups of the Pacific; the Creek Indians, Canada, the Bermudas, and any West India islands, and any coasts of America or Asia." And presently they notify the churches: " We must have an enlarged supply of money and men. We expect a body of German missionaries, and we plan to engage a great company and teach them both theological knowledge and also occupations adapted to the islands." But just now all their energies were concentrated upon preparing for a second voyage of the *Duff*, with Captain Robson in command. By November 13th forty-six were in readiness—nineteen single men and ten married, with seven children—and were separated for the work whereunto they had been called. On the 20th the *Duff* dropped down the Thames, and ten days later weighed anchor. But December 8th found her with seventy ships at Spithead, where on account of fogs she lay over two Sundays; on the 21st a south-west wind was so fierce that the fleet put into Portland Roads, and a day or two afterwards was off and out of sight under convoy of the frigate *Amphion*. In the same company sailed the *Hillsborough*, bearing some hundreds of convicts bound for New South Wales, and also Dr. Vanderkemp and three companions, en route to preach to the Hottentots in South Africa. These devoted men preferred to voyage on this ship filled with the worst of criminals, in order that during the five months of the passage they might have opportunity to labor for their salvation.

Hitherto, for five years together, the flood of good feeling and expectation of large results had been steadily swelling with scarce a refluent wave. Not a threatening storm-cloud had crossed the sky. But, of course, such encouraging conditions could not always continue. God's way with his kingdom is not after this fashion. As might have been expected, and as was on every account best for all concerned, a series of trials and searching tests now ensued in the shape of serious reverses, and failures apparently most disastrous, coming from various quarters, of divers kinds, and dropping down in quick succession. The current emotion, though mainly noble and Christian, contained also not a little of unhealthy excitement. Zeal was all aflame, but was not wholly according to knowledge, while many of the expectations most fondly cherished were unreasonable, and without basis in fact. The Millennium had not yet dawned, the victory over heathenism and savagery, even in the charming South Seas, was not to be won without a fight long and most arduous. It had already been noticed, and with deepest solicitude, that scarcely a clergyman, and not one of note and influence, had offered himself to go wherever the Lord through the Society should please to send him. Those who volunteered were, with few exceptions, laymen from the humbler walks of life, without learning, of but common gifts and attainments. And even these had not been sifted with sufficient care, quite a number proved incompetent, and some even morally unworthy. Trouble broke out in the company which had been despatched to the Foulah country. They separated in alienation, some died, and war breaking out among the savages, others left and so the mission came utterly to grief. Next, early in August, 1799, the directors were stunned with the intelligence that the *Duff* had been captured by a French privateer when off Rio Janeiro, and had been taken to Montevideo and sold as a prize. The missionaries would be sent home, but the money loss was £10,000. Then on the heels of these evil tidings, came the further calamitous news from Otaheite that most of the missionaries who had been left there had fled the island, their lives seeming to be in danger, and by a chance vessel had been carried to Port Jackson in New South Wales, this long journey also entailing large expense. Likewise at Tongabatoo catastrophe had befallen, for some had died, some had fallen into shameful lewdness with the natives and had been cut off from fellowship, and finally civil war had broken out, in which the brethren had been first robbed, and then expelled. Only from Vanderkemp and his Hottentots arrived words of cheer. He was able to write that he had made a beginning, and that a "singular interest" had appeared. The "Spirit had begun a good work in some of the most abject and uncultured of the race." But there was no flinching or turning back in consequence. Without a moment's hesitation, either on the part of directors, or of the Christian public, the task was resolutely taken up of repairing the damage, and of sending reinforcements to the South Seas and to South Africa. By May of 1800, a contingent of sixteen men had been forwarded to the front.

The thrilling story will for the present be suspended

of the London Society, whose beginnings were so glorious, as well of such incalculable importance both to Christendom and to the whole heathen world. It was not long after the hopes of so many of the earnest-hearted had been so rudely hurled from the zenith to the nadir, that they began again slowly and steadily to rise. Only the South Seas proved to be no sinless, stormless Eden, and their inhabitants turned out to be exactly of a piece with savages elsewhere. Many reverses were yet in store, and long and tedious waiting for the precious fruits of toil was to be required. Early in this century India, China and the West Indies were entered, Madagascar, that shining marvel among missions, in 1818. And these immortal names among others are found upon the list of those sent out by this honored society: Ellis and Livingstone, Morrison and Milne, Medhurst and Moffat, Vanderkemp, and John Williams the martyr of Erromanga.

No mortal can tell just how many missions, both in the Old World and the New, owe their birth either directly or indirectly to that astonishing evangelistic revival in the last decade of the eighteenth century, which under God originated vastly more with Carey than with any other man, and of which the London Society was not only one of the most remarkable effects, but also in no inconsiderable measure the cause. As we have seen, in its organization several denominations were heartily united, and it seemed to some that the end of bigotry and sectarian division had arrived. But presently the process of withdrawal began, and continued until the Independents were left practically alone. The Episcopalians led the way in 1799 by forming what **now is the Church Missionary Society, one of whose** fundamental rules has been from the first: "A friendly intercourse shall be maintained with other Protestant Societies engaged in the same benevolent design of propagating the Gospel of Jesus Christ." One of the most serious defects in the period is seen in the fact that for many years no clergymen of the Church of England offered their services, and the only missionaries to be obtained were German Lutherans from the training institutions of Berlin and Basle. Among the earlier societies to be formed substantially upon the pattern set by Carey these may be named: In 1804 the British and Foreign Bible Society; in 1810 the American Board of Commissioners for Foreign Missions; the Baptist Missionary Union in 1814; the Basle Society in 1815; the Wesleyan Society in 1816; the Paris Society in 1822; the Berlin Society in 1824; and the Church of Scotland in 1829. The number has increased at the average rate of nearly three a year, until now, a century after the Deed of the Twelve in the back parlor of Widow Beebe Wallis, if all be included, whether denominational or individual, general or special, it surpasses **three hundred.**

CHAPTER XI.

THE GENESIS OF MISSIONS IN AMERICA.

WITH all this kindling of interest, and enlargement of effort for the world's redemption in Protestant Europe, what was there in the meantime to match upon the other side of the Atlantic? Some two hundred years ago a tide of colonization had set this way, and by the last decade of the eighteenth century several millions were found settled within the limits of the United States. But in the main, in the midst of wilderness depths, interminable and appalling, with a vast continent to subdue, including forests, soil, wild beasts, and savage tribes. Emigration is always, and of necessity, a step towards primitive rudeness, if not barbarism. The early generations endured poverty, severest toil, great exposure to the elements and to mortal peril, and wide-spread demoralization resulted. The settlements were small, widely scattered, stretching along the coast for a thousand miles. The population was divided up into colonies which were distinct, independent, with little in common, and often jealous rivals. Besides, wars had been frequent with the Indians, the French, and finally with the mother country, and attended with measureless excitement of evil passion, and deadening of spiritual fervor. Then too a profound reaction was in progress against the stringency of Puritan belief and practice, while the churches were suffering, like Protestantism in the Old World, from rationalism and dead orthodoxy, to which was added near the close of the century the further blight produced by French infidelity.

To complete a survey of the situation, it is necessary also to recall the fact that American Christians had no immediate contact with the heathen world through colonies and resulting commerce, but were widely isolated. To be sure, there were a few thousand Indians at their doors, and to these at the first the gospel had been carried, with at least some measure of earnestness; but after some generations of experience of the tomahawk and the scalping knife, hate, or at least indifference, had taken the place of love, and in addition these troublesome pagans had largely disappeared from the region lying to the east of the Appalachians. And finally, as emigration began to the Great West, the burning religious question related to home missions. Great populations were in the greatest spiritual destitution, and these were their brethren, their dear friends, their sons and daughters. Naturally, and not improperly, their first thought, and the bulk of their beneficence, were bestowed upon the needy frontier. And surely, upon no other body of churches was so appalling a task ever imposed as upon those of the United States, which must needs help to subdue a continent, and spread over it the social and political institutions of a mighty Republic, and also diffuse and maintain a pure gospel throughout all the boundless spaces from ocean to ocean. And, whatever the causes may have been, the fact is patent that at the time Carey was agitating and undertaking in Great Britain, the churches in America were utterly idle and asleep as touching any form of evangelizing effort for the great world lying in wickedness. Eliot and the Mayhews were still held in loving and reverent remembrance, as also Edwards for his work for the Indians at Stockbridge. His stirring call to a monthly concert of prayer had had a wide circulation, and churches not a few had met at stated times for united supplication. The life of David Brainerd by Edwards was a source of continual inspiration to thousands. But just now in missions, as in so many other realms, the old had passed away, old ideas, old methods, old instrumentalities, and the new and better which were to take their place were just coming into being.

At the beginning of the present century the idea of world-wide missions, the evangelization of the entire race, had not begun to dawn upon the consciousness of American Christians. Though for sixty years the Moravians had been bearing the glad tidings to distant lands; though Ziegenbalg, and Schwartz, and Carey, and Vanderkemp had been preaching Christ to the perishing in India and Africa; and though already in Great Britain several missionary societies had been formed, still on this side of the Atlantic, even among the most earnest-hearted, to not a soul came overwhelming solicitude, conviction, and longing, in keeping with the Lord's last command. Hitherto the best efforts had been individual, unsystematic, sporadic and transient. As yet there had been no attempt at coming together in combination and co-operation, to fashion some comprehensive and far-reaching scheme to carry the light far and wide through all the desolate lands of darkness. The nearest approach to the founding of a foreign mission had been made in 1774, when Ezra Stiles and Samuel Hopkins, New England Congregationalists, laid before the Presbyterian Synod of New York a proposition to send two natives of Africa, who had been converted and were now in the College of New Jersey, "on a mission to propagate Christianity in their own country," and requesting approval and assistance. The Synod replied: "We are ready to concur and do all that is proper, since many circumstances intimate it is the will of God." The Presbyterians of Scotland were similarly appealed to, but this promising undertaking to carry the gospel to the Dark Continent, in which three divisions of the Christian Church were ready to unite, was prevented by the breaking out of the Revolutionary War. In 1802 the Massachusetts Baptist Missionary Society was organized "to promote the knowledge of evangelical truth in new settlements of the United States, or further, *if circumstances should render it proper;*" and two years later the Massachusetts (Congregational) Missionary Society changed its constitution so as to read: "Among people of newly settled and remote parts, among the Indians, and through more distant regions as circumstances invite and ability admits." The horizon is evidently receding, the spiritual vision has a broader sweep, but for some years to come almost all movements towards organization will be but local, or bounded by state lines. The real Union, the nation, had not come into existence.

The fact is patent that missions in America were an outgrowth almost direct from missions in Great Britain—though of course at the same time various causative forces, mighty although less visible, were operating throughout Christendom—so that William Carey was the father of the former as well as of the latter. In spite of the violent sundering which had recently taken place between the colonies and the mother country, the relations still existing were at many points most intimate, and especially upon the intellectual and religious side. Great movements starting across the sea were quickly known and deeply felt here also. Consequently, when the English Baptists launched forth in their sublime endeavor, and when soon after Carey sailed for Calcutta, the New World also was looking on with wonder and admiration. In particular, the Baptists of this country were eager watchers. Dr. Staughton, later a pastor in Philadelphia, had heard Carey's famous sermon, and like all the auditors was stirred to the depths; he was present too at the organization in Kettering, and into the collection cast a half-guinea *borrowed* for the purpose, ever after declaring that he "rejoiced more over it than over any other sum he ever gave in his life." Letters and missionary reports sent by English Baptists were quite extensively circulated. And, since Carey with all his stalwart faith in God, was also a stanch believer in the efficacy of vigorous and uninterrupted good works, and hence among the rest was a most indefatigable letter writer, information and exhortation were poured forth in all directions from his prolific pen. Thus communications not a few reached New England and the Middle States, were read with interest, and as a result, considerable sums of money were forwarded to Serampore. In 1806-7 he acknowledges the receipt of $6000, and says: "The Lord has wonderfully stirred the whole religious world of every denomination to favor our work and contribute to a large amount; and our American friends have special claims on our gratitude in this respect." And further in 1811, through the action of the Boston Baptist Association, $4650 were contributed by persons of different denominations in eastern Massachusetts, to aid in carrying forward his numerous translations of the Scriptures into Asiatic languages. Hence the assertion is abundantly justified that "we are indebted to those pioneers for the example which gave a powerful impulse to missions by arousing the interest and embodying the efforts of all denominations."

But an impulse vastly greater was imparted three years later, when the London Missionary Society leaped forth suddenly into vigorous life. Says Rev. Kiah Bailey: "In 1797 Rev. Alexander McLean, of Bristol, Maine, received from Scotland the sermons of Dr. Haweis and others preached at the organization, was charmed by reading them, and loaned the pamphlet to me. I took the pamphlet to Newburyport, where it was soon reprinted and read with avidity by various others, and among them by the Rev. Samuel Worcester, who thus caught the sacred flame. And so was started the rill which led to the river" (the formation of the American Board). In 1796 a society was organized in New York in which Presbyterians, Baptists and Reformed (Dutch) were united, and monthly meetings were held to pray that "the God of grace would pour out His Spirit on His Church and send the Gospel to all nations." By 1807 five societies had been established in Massachusetts alone to propagate Christianity, and similar ones in all the New England States, with some also in the Middle States. During the first five years of the century these periodicals were started, and combined to gather and to scatter missionary intelligence from the Old World: the Connecticut Evangelical Magazine, the Massachusetts Missionary Magazine, the Massachusetts Baptist Missionary Magazine, the Panoplist, and the (Presbyterian) Religious Intelligencer. In 1804 the Massachusetts Society chose the president of the London Society an honorary trustee. It was during this same period that Melville Horne's "Letters on Missions," and Claudius Buchanan's "Star in the East" were published and produced a surprising sensation. In addition, the churches began to be moved by missionary discourses as never before. Upon the General Assembly in 1806 Dr. Griffin " urged the claims of the heathen and the greatness and excellence of missionary work with an eloquence and earnestness seldom, if ever, surpassed." The next year, Parish, before the Massachusetts Domestic Missionary Society, dwelt upon " the growing conviction of the value of Christianity ; and so it was a good time to send missionaries to every nation." In 1808 the General Assembly appointed a day of fasting and prayer to beseech " God to bless the efforts of His people to Christianize the heathen and to extend the Gospel." The same year, in Cambridge, Holmes hailed "the approaching day when idols would be cast to the moles and bats, and all false faiths be superseded by the glorious Gospel of God." Only a few days before the American Board came into being, at the annual meeting of the Massachusetts Society, Norton had the boldness to inquire : " Is the expectation visionary and unfounded that the time is not far distant when from the United States, missionaries will go forth to every region of the globe, accompanied with the fervent prayers of thousands?" Finally, as early as 1806, Norris, of Salem, had given $10,000 to found Andover Theological Seminary, and declared, " My object is the foreign mission enterprise, for we must have ministers if we are to have missionaries." Thus it becomes abundantly evident that the Spirit of the Most High was working upon many hearts, and that something notable was at hand.

These were but some of the preliminary and preparatory steps, and such were some of the significant signs of the times. Hitherto evangelistic zeal had been only general and indefinite, destitute of specific object and aim; but now we begin to come upon desires and convictions burning in the bosoms of godly and heroic men, which cannot at all be contained within the realm of thought and emotion, but must leap forth and incarnate themselves in action. "With such feelings and utterances among the elders, it is not strange that from among the young men some should catch the spirit and purpose actually to engage in missions." At this point, in the person of Samuel J. Mills, there begins to come into very prominent view one who without doubt may properly be termed the American counterpart of William Carey. If there were need of offering proof of this assertion, it would be sufficient to set forth the distinguished and essential part he afterward played, not only in the organization of the American Board, the Cornwall Mission School and the mission to the Sandwich Islands, but also of the United Foreign Missionary Society, the American Bible Society, the American Colonization Society, and the school in New York for the Education of Africans. Like the Hebrew Samuel, from his birth Mills had been lent to the Lord—not to serve in the tabernacle, but to make living and life-long sacrifices in pagan lands. When but a child he "accidentally" heard his mother mention to a neighbor the fact of his having been given to the work of missions, and he never forgot it, but was continually inspired and impelled thereby to his dying day. She often also told him stories of Eliot, Brainerd and others. Converted in 1802, at the age of nineteen, his controlling purpose was already so clear and strong that he could say to his father: "I cannot conceive of any course in life in which to pass my days that would prove so pleasant as to go and communicate the gospel of salvation to the poor heathen." And even then his longing was to be a missionary, not to the Indians near at hand, but in some far off foreign country. Entering Williams College in 1806, his heart was too much aflame with another master-passion to allow him to excel in his studies. The story is familiar how a few kindred spirits were soon found, or fashioned, and at once they began to pray, and ponder, and plan. There is no occasion to dwell upon the memorable meeting under the haystack when the great decision was made, or upon the secret society with its solemn pledge to the foreign work, or the careful and judicious canvass of ways and means for furthering the momentous project they had so fervently at heart. The object of the organization was "to effect in the person of its members a mission to the heathen," and the constitution was drawn up in cipher, "public opinion being opposed to us," and "lest we should be thought rashly imprudent, and so should injure the cause we wish to promote." They proceeded to make the acquaintance of various clergymen of influence, and opened a correspondence with others. They secured the publication and distribution of various sermons and other works on missionary subjects. They visited a number of colleges, or wrote thither, to kindle the holy flame in the breasts of other young men. And surely here was found a remarkable combination of fervent zeal with knowledge of men and affairs. With all their indomitable resolution and boundless ardor, anything approaching dangerously near to fanaticism would be hard to find. The spirit which lifted them up and bore them onward may be discerned in the reply of Hall when later he was importuned to take a Connecticut pastorate: "No, I must not settle in any parish in Christendom. Others will be left whose health or pre-engagements require them to stay; but I can sleep on the ground and endure hunger and hardship. God calls me to the heathen. Woe to me if I preach not the gospel to the heathen."

In 1809 the scene shifts to Andover, the doors of that institution having been opened for students only the year before; and the little band from Williams was reinforced by Nott and Newell, and a few months later by Judson, coming each from a different college, and each also having arrived independently at the dominant conviction. Judson had read Buchanan's "Star in the East," and "the evidences of divine power manifested in the progress of the gospel in India fell like a spark into the tinder of his soul." "I could not study; I depicted to myself the romantic scenes of missionary life; I was in a great excitement." A few months sufficed to bring him to the fixed purpose to devote his life to a missionary career. And though several with whom he counselled thought the idea was irrational, and though at a latter date he was called to the pastorate of an important church in Boston, nothing could change his determination, but he wrote to the London Society with reference to sending him out, and thus began to move before he knew of any other who was like-minded. The meetings of these young men to strengthen one another in their purpose and planning to extend the bounds of the dominion of their dear Lord has been likened to that striking scene in the chapel at Mont Martre, where nearly three hundred years before, the seven founders of the Society of Jesus met to exchange their vows. Though wholly of one desire and determination, they were as yet also wholly without knowledge as to who would authorize them to go and send them forth, as well as to what particular portion of the wide world they should direct their efforts. Consulting the seminary faculty, and their designs finding favor, at length a conference with several clergymen was arranged for June 25th, 1810, and they were advised to petition the General Association of Massachusetts to move in the matter, as that body was to meet at Bradford the next day. The petition was duly prepared and presented, signed originally by the entire six; but lest the large number should strike some timid souls through with terror, two names were taken off! This decisive document set forth that their " minds had long been impressed with the duty and importance of personally attempting a mission to the heathen," and inquired if they could expect "patronage and support from a society in this country, or if they must commit themselves to the direction of a European society." And it was as the direct result of such urgency and agitation on the part of this consecrated company that the American Board of Commissioners for Foreign Missions came into being, the first of the kind on this side of the Atlantic, whose aim was nothing less than to go into all the world and preach the gospel to every creature. And thus it was, therefore, that American missions were born.

It is believed that at this date not less than eighteen or twenty persons had been seriously considering the personal claims upon them of missionary work, and of course more or less of interest had been excited in the minds of a much larger number. But even now only a few ministers, and of laymen fewer still, had attained to any considerable measure of interest. The Prudential Committee were thoroughly persuaded that a considerable time must elapse before they could hope to sustain a mission on a promising scale in any land. One of their number, a successful Boston merchant, was opposed to sending out any men at all unless a fund of at least $60,000 was in store for use in case of inadequate receipts; and an effort, which fortunately was fruitless, was actually made to raise a large sum for investment, while but one was found venturesome enough to insist that they should go forward just as soon as an eligible field was found, fund or no fund, holding that the Lord's hand was evidently in the matter, and that therefore the way would be opened in due season, if only they bestirred themselves with vigor. The young men were counselled to pursue their studies meanwhile and wait in patience for developments. Recourse was had to the London Society to see if the candidates could not be sent out by the two bodies in co-operation, and Judson was sent to England to confer concerning this project. Through a kind providence, however, nothing came of his mission, and hence all concerned were compelled to rely wholly upon God and their own exertions.

And, verily, those were the days of small things. At the end of the first year the receipts had reached but $999.52, and when the next year was well advanced the treasury contained only $1200. Hence with a minimum of sight for a foundation, upon which faith might stand and plume itself for loftier flight into the realm of the unseen and unknown, it is not in the least strange that there was general hesitation about making the supreme venture. But, behold, now in this the hour of their helplessness, and as if to mock the extreme lack of material resources, it came to pass that, without warning, they found themselves caught in a corner and compelled to act. Either the signal to advance immediately must be raised, or else the fact be published that they had no courage or confidence in the divine promise. For word was brought from Philadelphia that in a few days a vessel bound for India would sail from that city, in which the missionaries might take passage, an opportunity not likely to occur again for a period indefinitely long. Then a little later came intelligence that about the same date and for the same region another ship would set forth from Salem. With this golden opportunity for making the voyage on hand, and with four men ready and waiting, most eager and urgent to be sent forth, what should be done? But, to add to the already sore perplexity, what should happen but that a fifth petitioner appears in the person of Rice, importunate to be ordained and despatched with the others! The mettle of the committee rose most grandly to the height of the momentous occasion, and they determined to make the venture, and take the risk. Mingling discretion with valor however, it was stipulated that Rice should secure for himself the wherewith for his outfit and passage to the field; it was suggested that the four wives would better be left behind for a season in order to reduce expenses to a minimum, and further it was intimated that if the worst befell, a portion of the number, or even all, might be transferred to the London Society. Nor did the outcome fail superabundantly to justify this notable act of faith. A ringing call for the money required was issued straightway, and arrangements were set on foot for the ordination services. Fortunately, too, the date of sailing was postponed for a fortnight. And now enthusiasm began to rise in fine fashion. So many hearts were opened, and so great was the eagerness to give, that by the end of the three weeks more than $6000 were in hand, Philadelphia alone contributing more than $1000. Thus it became possible for all to depart, the wives included, and with salaries paid for a year and a half in advance! On February 19th, 1812, Judson and Newell sailed from Salem, and on the 22nd, Hall, Rice and Nott followed from the City of Brotherly Love. As the event soon proved, this beginning was made in the very nick of time, for in June war was declared against Great Britain, and thus for years communication with the East was practically closed. Moreover, as if to reward the Prudential Committee for their course, a bequest of $30,000 to the Board was presently announced.

The instructions drawn up in haste for the guidance of these pioneer American missionaries, though on the whole surprisingly wise, both in what they contained, and in what they omitted, have yet some passages which read strangely in the light of what by experience has since been taught. Thus, taking the hint from Carey, they were enjoined to adopt as soon as possible "some plan of polity or social order," that is, a sort of family or communistic arrangement, such as the disciples entered into just after Pentecost. And still further, "to lighten expenses, apply yourselves to the most eligible ways and means of support, agreeable to the example of the English missionaries, and even of the apostles." For, the ruling idea then was that the stock of the Lord's money was so limited that only sufficient could be counted on to transport the missionaries to the scene of their labors, and to sustain them until a foothold could be gained, and that after that they must rely, at least largely, upon their own resources. But a few years were sufficient to demonstrate that neither of those methods of procedure were called for, or could be profitably reduced to practice. Moreover, in those days primeval, as well as for more than a generation later, the conviction was prevalent that to send women to countries heathen and savage was of more than doubtful propriety. Not only was the matter of delicacy, modesty, and even of greatest danger of gross ill-treatment involved, but since they could not help in the work of evangelization, they would prove a serious encumbrance! But somehow it has happened that to this day, and in numbers increasing at a most astonishing rate, the weaker sex has contrived to get itself commissioned of both God and men to proclaim the glad tidings in darkest and vilest lands.

Ever since the organization of the Board the burning questions had been, first, concerning finances, and second, concerning the most eligible location for missions. The bulk of the vast world was yet unknown, and much of the remainder was inaccessible. During the early conferences of the student originators, "sometimes we would cut a path through the moral wilderness of the West to the Pacific and sometimes to South America, the object always being the salvation of the heathen." The London Society suggested the Indian tribes of America and "Hindoostan." For long months the committee had waited for the rising and moving of the pillar of fire. In 1811 they reported that "scarcely any portion of the world is more important and inviting than Burmah," and that "providence points to Canada and the Caghnawaga tribe;" to the latter since they know of a pious native who longs to carry the gospel to his people, and is getting an education for the purpose. But the war with Britain closed the door of entrance in that direction. India was looked upon with favor, and was finally selected because of the presence there of Carey and his associates, though Burmah, being outside of the domain of the crotchety and jaundiced East India Company, seemed to be a more desirable field.

When, in February of 1812, the grand stroke for the founding of a mission was heralded by the sailing of the first five men for southern Asia, this is the language employed in reference thereto: "The magnitude of the event, if estimated by the probable consequences, is such as to form an era in the history of the American churches, though the immediate consequences may be such as to disappoint"—words profoundly wise, and prophetic as well. Up to this point the work had been only that of putting the hand to the plow, and next were to follow long and wearisome years of painful seed-sowing, and anxious waiting for the harvest. Just ahead, though mercifully wholly hidden, were in store disheartening struggles against obstacles numerous, multiform, and well nigh insuperable. The very first message which was received from the missionaries was to the effect that by the despotic and gospel-hating Company they had been ordered to leave the country at once; and the next, in some respects even more alarming, was that two out of the five, Judson and Rice, had withdrawn from the service of the Board, had gone over to the Baptists, and had been immersed. As was quite natural, the surprise and consternation which followed this radical revolution in sentiment was not unmingled with indignation and disgust, though on the whole, the humiliating set-back was borne with commendable forbearance and resignation. These words with reference to it appear in the next annual report : " The committee has no disposition to impeach the sincerity of these men, but they regret that the subject was not examined before so late a day. Nevertheless, the foundation of God standeth sure. We repose our hopes on this in spite of the instability which we regret to record, but against which no human foresight could provide. Let it rouse a holy zeal ; and should it be overruled and bring an accession of strength, it will be a joyful event." Yes, overruled, and nobody now doubts that thus it soon came to pass.

In noting the most impressive series of additional afflictive providences which ensued, we are reminded of the case of the London Society during the dark days after the *Duff* was captured. After a voyage of four months, Judson and Newell had arrived at Calcutta, June 17th, 1812. At once an order was served upon them to return to America in the ship that brought them thither, nor without them would the *Caravan* be permitted to sail. Later it was concluded that they might take their departure for any region not within the Company's jurisdiction. Presently information was received which "decisively deterred" them from entering Burmah ; and as no door either open, or likely to open, appeared in that direction, at their wits' end, their eyes were turned westward towards Bombay, and possibly

Africa. On August 4th, Newell and his wife took passage in a vessel which could accomodate but two, leaving the Judsons to follow when they could. And, behold, only four days after, the *Harmony* arrived, bringing Hall, Nott and Rice. They too were bidden by the authorities to be off at the soonest. A passport was therefore procured from the police by the two former, passage was engaged and their belongings were on board, when an order came for them to depart for England in the fleet about to sail; but, notwithstanding, they went on board the vessel they had chosen without the knowledge of the officers and made their escape. Judson had already been baptized in Serampore, and Rice put himself into the same company a few weeks later. Meanwhile the Newells were enduring wave upon wave of trouble and sorrow. For a month they were beaten up and down in the Bay of Bengal, Mrs. Newell being very sick of a fever, and then in distress the ship put in at Coringa, and lay for a fortnight. It was November before they reached the Isle of France, and on the last day of that month this heroic soul breathed her last. As the event proved, it was thus that she accomplished far more for the cause for which she exultingly laid down her life, than would have been possible by the longest term of most devoted service.

After a voyage of eleven weeks, on February 11th, almost a full year since leaving their native land, Hall and Nott landed in Bombay. But knowledge of their movements had preceded them thither, and they were met with a command to depart forthwith for England. Appealing to Governor Nepean, fortunately a man large-hearted and thoroughly Christian, he promised to do the best possible in their behalf, and wrote privately to Calcutta to intercede for them. They began at once to study the language. To greatly increase the complication, just now arrived the news of the declaration of war between Great Britain and the United States; for as was to be expected, the missionaries became objects of suspicion as possible spies. In August they learned that their names were down on a list as passengers in a vessel which was to have sailed at once, but on account of a leak was long delayed. In September they asked permission to depart for Ceylon where Newell now was, but consent was withheld. A few weeks later, learning that a ship was to start in a few hours for Cochin, and to go thence to Ceylon, they went on board, leaving Mrs. Nott behind, and a letter for the governor explaining why they had left without authority from him. Delayed at Cochin, letters arrived ordering them to be returned to Bombay. On December 22nd they must certainly sail for England. As a final effort, a most solemn memorial was addressed to Sir Evan Nepean as a man and a Christian, protesting against the serious offense of deporting them, when their sole object in coming was to preach the Gospel to the perishing heathen. But preparations were also made for departure, goods were packed and labelled, coolies and boats were engaged. About to set forth, the captain applied at the pay-office for their passage-money, and it was refused; and not long after came a message granting permission to remain in the city. Newell soon joined them, after ten months in Ceylon, and at once the foundations began to be laid.

At the annual meeting of the Board, held in Salem September 20th, 1815, in the sixth annual report, this is the language chosen to set forth most fittingly both the achievements hitherto made and the current situation:

"The last two reports had recitations of the pilgrimages and adventures, perils and deliverances, discouragements and consolations of our missionaries in the East, seeking a door of entrance, but obstructed, disappointed, and in continual anxiety and suspense. But thus have been showed the faith and patience, the firmness and prudence, the fortitude and devotedness of the brethren, and proofs, affecting and animating, of the wisdom and goodness, the faithfulness and mercy, the almighty protection and overruling providence of God. This report has less striking narrative and affecting incident, and because they have found an open door and a resting place, though even now they have scarcely commenced their public labors." The glad announcement was also made that, after three years of war, peace had returned. During all this protracted period of sore trial, so well had the faith and patience of the saints at home endured, that now, a brighter day having dawned, the way was open for an enlargement of the work. Five men, who had long been waiting for the opportunity, were despatched, some to Bombay to reinforce the mission there, and the others to Ceylon to break ground for a second station. The next year, various hindrances which had hitherto prevented, having been removed, a mission was started among the Indians of northern Georgia. It is in the annual report for 1817 that for the first time several distinct fields could be named. The information is given that $2200 had been sent to Bombay with which to open schools, and that a house of worship was much needed in that city. In Ceylon the government had granted the use of certain old Roman Catholic churches, with their glebes and manses. Among the Cherokees Mr. Kingsbury found much encouragement. Also a mission school had been founded at Cornwall, Conn. And this significant item appeared with reference to the first mission of the London Society: "The late glorious events at the Society Islands—particularly at Otaheite and Eimeo—make our hearts burn with desire to witness the same triumphs of the cross at Owyhee and Woahu [Hawaii and Oahu]. From all accounts this field is white for the harvest."

In 1819 details are given concerning no less than seven missions; Bombay, Ceylon, Palestine, among the Cherokees, the Choctaws, the Indians of Arkansas, and in the Sandwich Islands. And behold, what God had wrought in so brief a space. "The first, only six years ago, was struggling for a place and even for existence, the last just ready to embark, and in all extending from east to west more than two-thirds around the globe." In the north Pacific the way of entrance had been wondrously prepared by the advent into this country of Obookiah, his *quasi*-adoption by Mills, his conversion and education with other Hawaiian youths at Cornwall, and their letters home telling of the Christian faith; and perhaps even more, by the news carried by sailors that the idols had been cast out in Otaheite, as well as by the return of certain Hawaiians after their conversion in the Society Islands. It was a memorable event in the history of the American Board when, in 1819, Bingham and Thurston and twenty others—by far the largest missionary family that had yet been gathered and sent forth at one time—set sail in the brig *Thaddeus*, bound via Cape Horn for the remote recesses of the Western Sea, to proclaim to the perishing the unsearchable riches of Christ. But little came directly from the projected mission to the Holy Land, from which so much was fondly anticipated, and about which had gathered so much of enthusiasm and fine religious sentiment; though indirectly and more remotely it led to the opening of the Board's most important work among the Oriental churches of the Turkish Empire, which now consumes one-third of its income, and embraces one-third of its converts. "So Messrs. Parsons and Fisk were chosen, and sent upon an extensive tour among the churches as missionaries to Jerusalem, whereby a wide and lively interest was excited, and a distinguished liberality of contributions was the result."

In 1820, after ten years of most careful planning and most arduous toil, this is the summing up of tangible results. The cost in money had reached nearly $200,000. From $1000, the receipts of the first year, the annual income rose to $12,266 in 1814; fell to $9494 the year after, on account of the war, and then climbed steadily to $37,521 in 1819. At the end of the first decade in all 110 missionaries had been appointed, of whom 62 were men; and of the 88 still in service, or on the way to their fields, 28 were men ordained. Of the entire force 44 were laboring among the Indians, 25 were in the East, 17 in the Sandwich Islands, and 2 in western Asia. As to fruit-gathering, even yet the report is: "We cannot reckon up much of tangible results." The years following were devoted almost wholly to the development of fields already occupied, rather that to the founding of additional missions.

Thus far we have been dwelling upon the evangelistic designs and doings of the American Board and the New England Congregationalists. And the fact is that for a number of years the bulk both of money and men, was derived from the children of the Pilgrims. Williams College, Andover Seminary, and Massachusetts General Association, were called of Providence to play the foremost part in arousing and organizing the forces which laid the foundations, and began to rear the superstructure, of American missions. It was from accident however, rather than from deliberate design, was the result of circumstances, that of the first eight commissioners chosen, five were from Massachusetts, and the others were from Connecticut. But no statement of the origin and growth of missions in the United States would be at all complete, which did not make mention of the hearty sympathy and generous co-operation of various other denominations, and as well as of other missionary societies to which, directly or indirectly, the work of the Board gave rise. We have already seen what liberal contributions were bestowed by the Philadelphia Presbyterians when the first men were sent out in 1812. The same year by the secretary the General Assembly was invited to form a similar society to co-operate with the Board; but that body in reply expressed the conviction that foreign missions would be best served by a single organization, and added that "their churches rejoiced in the American Board and would sustain it to the best of their ability." And for a generation that pledge was kept. It was not until 1837 that the Old School branch began to establish missions, while the other branch remained in closest connection down to 1870. In order to secure increased denominational comprehensiveness, at the second annual meeting an addition of thirteen commissioners was made to the corporation, of whom eight were Presbyterians. In 1832, out of sixty-two corporate members, thirty-one were Presbyterians, twenty-four were Congregationalists, six were (Dutch) Reformed, and one was Associate Reformed, and the missionaries were ordinarily chosen in about the same proportion. The German Reformed Church also assisted regularly with money-gifts for twenty-five years (1840-65.) The (Dutch) Reformed did not withdraw until 1857.

Especial mention must be made of the second organized movement started in this country, whose beginning constitutes one of the very strangest passages in mission history. This society came into existence through what seemed to multitudes to be a piece of human frailty. Out of disappointment and sorrow, out of apparent failure and disaster, issued almost unparalleled success and enlargement to the kingdom. It was evidently the Lord's doing, and even yet is marvelous in our eyes. Of course the reference is to the famous change of opinion with regard to baptism on the part of Judson and Rice, soon after they had reached India. We have already seen what impression that revolution in sentiment made upon the Prudential Committee. In their astonishment and deep perplexity over it Hall and Nott wrote home as follows: "What the Lord means by thus dividing us in sentiment and separating us from each other we cannot tell. The Lord seeth not as man seeth, and it ill becomes us to be dissatisfied with what he does. We hope and pray that it will not damp the missionary spirit, but that it may burn with a brighter and purer flame." That hope was well founded, and that prayer was not unheard. The work already begun in America was not weakened in the least, except for a very brief season of dismay, while presently, as the direct result, an entire denomination was fairly set on fire with zeal for the world's evangelization, and ever since has maintained the impulse then received. So that among the fruits of that stupendous "failure" we are to reckon the almost unmatched victories of the gospel over heathenism among the Karens in Burmah, and in our day also among the Telugus of eastern India!

As soon as the decisive step had been taken, the two chief actors therein wrote to the American Baptists of what had come to pass. Carey also wrote, and their letters all reached Boston by the same mail in February of 1813. Before he left, with not the least thought that it would ever be of any personal concern to himself, Judson had suggested the formation of a Baptist society, but nothing came of the counsel. But now all of a sudden, unsought, undesired, unlooked for, they find two missionaries in the foreign field, who at terrible cost had joined their fellowship, and were fairly thrust upon them for support. Here were straits even greater and more embarrassing than those in which the American Board had found itself with five men on its hands and an empty treasury. Here also moreover was a question without a negative possible, save one which involved disgrace and almost infamy. Hence as might be expected, a local organization was formed without delay, and circulars were sent out looking to a gathering which should be national in its proportions, and thus unite the entire denomination, a consummation which as yet had never been achieved for any purpose whatsoever. The proposition was made to the Baptist Society in England (America still fearing to undertake to walk alone, and much inclined to lean upon the strong arm of Britain) to receive the two men into its India mission, their support to be supplied from this side of the Atlantic; but the sagacious Fuller wrote in reply, and exceedingly fortunate for the Lord's work in all the world: "Late events point to the origin of a distinct Baptist society in America." Concerning the outcome the following has been written: "The intelligence [concerning Judson and Rice] spread with electric rapidity, and gave to benevolence and Christian obligation a depth and fervor never before experienced. One sentiment of deep thanksgiving prevailed. The providence was too plain to be mistaken. The way had been opened, the field had been prepared, and the true-hearted must enter and prosecute that to which they had been summoned." In May, 1814, a preliminary assembly was held in Philadelphia, attended by twenty-six ministers and seven laymen, representing eleven states and the District of Columbia. Arrangements were made to establish the General Convention of the Baptist Denomination in the United States of America for Foreign Missions [and as if not satisfied with the length of this name, in 1821 were added the words,] "and other important objects relating to the Redeemer's kingdom." In 1845 the name was changed to American Baptist Missionary Union. Much fuel was added to the flame when, in September, Rice reached home and straightway began to tell what marvelous things he had seen and heard. "Here was one who had actually stood among the temples of heathendom and beheld the cruel abominations," something almost outside of the experience of most men in that early day. His was an imagination most ardent, and his pictures were painted in colors most vivid. "He reproduced the rapt predictions of the prophets of the Old and New Testaments, and the thrilling exhortations of the apostles concerning the kingdom of heaven, and multitudes hung on his lips and followed his footsteps with an enthusiasm seldom known since Whitefield." Nothing could withstand the swelling tide of zeal which now set in. For the time at least, before it indifference and prejudice were completely swept away.

And what of Judson meanwhile? For months with no human arm to lean upon, but with unswerving confidence in the protection and guidance of his unseen Master, he looked forward wholly bent upon the accomplishment of the work to which he had been called. Ordered to depart for England by the East India Company, he yet managed by a remarkable train of circumstances to escape to a ship bound for the Isle of France; after three months he returned to Madras, was immediately refused permission to remain, and as the only resort took passage in a vessel with Burmah for its destination. And thus it came about that July 14th, 1813, some seventeen months after his departure from the New World, he was landed at Rangoon, in a region to which he had originally been assigned, but into which while in Calcutta the door of entrance seemed to be hopelessly closed. Here, just on the threshold of his distinguished career, it is necessary to leave him for the present, the story all untold of the years of incredible toils and perils, sufferings and afflictions, as well as the surprising successes, which even in his lifetime began to appear. His name will ever stand high in the illustrious list of Christian heroes.

Only the briefest mention can well be made of the missionary operations of the Methodist Episcopal Church, whose first representative did not reach the foreign field until 1833. From the outset this had been eminently an evangelizing body, and had been unsurpassed in efforts to plant Christian institutions at every point throughout the boundless, and ever-shifting, and appallingly needy frontier of this rising Republic. And therefore not improperly work for the heathen at home took precedence. In the call to this is seen a peculiar ordering of providence, which lends to the narrative an element of romance. As so often happens, it was but a plebeian and commonplace incident, a mere accident, that started a movement of first-class importance. At Marietta, O., a drunken negro, Stewart by name, while in the desperation of shame and remorse on his way to drown himself, was arrested by the voice of a Methodist preacher calling sinners to repentance and promising salvation. By the sermon he was converted, and not long after, in a vision, as he stoutly held, was divinely bidden to set forth westward and northward to preach the gospel to the perishing. Making his journey through the forest, he at length appeared among the pagan and savage Wyandots upon the upper Sandusky River. A revival ensued, assistance was sent, the mission was continued, and later, the facts coming to the knowledge of Nathan Bangs and others in New York, their hearts were so stirred that they proceeded to set up an organization which should systematize and develop the work of missions at home and abroad. This important step was taken in 1819. It was nineteen years later that Melville D. Cox was appointed missionary to Monrovia on the west coast of Africa. The career of this first of American Methodists to bear the message of salvation to distant lands was exceedingly brief. Reaching his destination March 7th, on the 21st of July following he breathed his last, falling a victim to the terrible African fever, but not until he had uttered that ringing challenge to Christendom, whose echo has not yet in the least died away: "Let a thousand fall before Africa be given up!"

The Protestant Episcopal Church was the next to organize. As early as 1817 the English Church Missionary Society (Britain again lending a missionary impulse to America) had urged the founding of an organization here, and in 1820 the Domestic and Foreign Missionary Society came into being. But it was not until ten years later that missionaries were sent out, when two were despatched to Greece, and five years later still that the mission to China was opened. The Free (Will) Baptists commenced work in eastern India in 1833, the Lutherans (General Synod) sent a representative to the same country in 1841, the Southern Baptists set up for themselves in 1845, and the Southern Methodists the year following, while the work of the United Presbyterians dates from 1858. One after another the various denominations have fallen into line, until almost every one of any considerable strength has begun to heed the command, Preach the gospel to every creature. And at length it has come, or is rapidly coming, to this, that the supreme test of loyalty to Christ is found in the answer to the searching question: How abundant in labors, how liberal in giving, how earnest in prayer, is the individual, or the church, or the denomination, for the redemption of the world?

CHAPTER XII.

THE PHENOMENON OF MISSIONARY EXPANSION.

THE chapters just preceding have presented in outline the narrative of the remarkable revival of missionary zeal which occurred during the three decades immediately following the organization of the Baptist Missionary Society in England, and the sailing of Carey to begin the final assault upon heathenism in the vast peninsula of southern Asia. And what astounding progress has since then been made, and how utterly changed is the outlook to-day. The contrast is exceedingly striking at every point, and is full to overflowing of good cheer and ground for hope in years to come. It will be well to note next, some of the forces which have wrought mightily for the furtherance of world-wide evangelistic efforts during the passing century, taking these as specimens of the encouragement the Lord of the vineyard has vouchsafed to his servants who have been enduring the heat and burden of the day. But meanwhile, bearing in mind that at the best, the last hundred years have been in the main for missions only a period of exploration and pioneering, of laying foundations and trying experiments, of gaining experience, and fashioning needed instrumentalities for securing the best and most enduring results. Languages by the hundred have been learned and reduced to writing, and into them the Scriptures have been translated and a host of other books, so creating from nothing a Christian literature. Buildings of all sorts have been constructed, and all manner of institutions, educational, social and religious, have been planned and brought into being; all of which are of the greatest possible value, and indeed indispensable to the solid prosperity of the kingdom. Then several generations, taken out of the depths of pagan degradation, have been trained up into Christian intelligence and virtue, Christian customs, ideas and tastes. Christian homes by the ten thousand have been created, and an army of native preachers, pastors, evangelists, bible-readers and teachers have been enlisted, drilled and introduced into their work. And best of all, some millions of converts have been taught to adorn the gospel in all things by godly characters and lives. Such preliminary and preparatory work is necessarily of the hardest, slowest and most discouraging kind, but it needs not to be repeated, and answers for all time. We are to count this century then as more especially one of seed-sowing. From Carey's day to the present the earnest-hearted have labored thus, while those who come after will enter into their labors and reap the glorious harvest with songs of rejoicing.

Thus viewed, the achievements already made, though as nothing compared with what remains to be done, are yet of surprising magnitude, multitude, and variety. Then missions had been planted almost nowhere, now they are to be found almost everywhere. The countries which are altogether unoccupied are rare exceptions. From numbering a few scores, the stations and out-stations have gone on steadily increasing until now more than 12,000 can be named (not aiming at exact figures, but endeavoring to keep carefully within the limits of fact), and each one a blessed center of gospel light and joy.

Not counting the hundreds who have died at their posts, there are yet living and in the midst of their toil a host of 5000 men sent forth from Christian lands, of whom some 4300 are ordained. And to these are to be added as many women, including some 2500 who are unmarried and filling the callings of zenana-workers, physicians, teachers, etc. Associated with these 11,000 men and women from Europe and America, are found upwards of 40,000 native Christian "helpers," 4200 of them ordained, a portion of the Lord's army upon whom more and more the task of winning victories and holding conquered territory is to fall. A total evangelizing force therefore of at least a round 50,000 is in the field, and practically all raised up since the century began. As to contributions of money to sustain and enlarge the aggressive campaign, it is estimated that a hundred years ago all Christendom was giving for the redemption of all heathendom not more than at the rate of $200,000 a year, a sum which is more than quadrupled by the income of each one of several societies. The annual receipts now reach an aggregate of more than $15,000,-000, and if we include, as we properly may, the receipts of bible societies, tract societies, etc., with the cost of training missionaries in colleges and theological seminaries, the amount will approximate to $16,000,000. A miserable pittance, indeed, as compared with what is needed and what lies within the ability of the churches to bestow, but nevertheless indicating a marvelous increase in the grace of giving since 1792. And finally, as to results, that is, such as can be expressed by figures, though these are likely to be among the least. Of adherents, those who have cast away their idols and put themselves under the teaching of the missionaries, there are upwards of 3,000,000. In India alone according to the last census there are 2,250,000. No account is taken of at least as many more who are halting between two opinions, almost persuaded to choose Christ, or of the various mass movements in which whole regions are deeply stirred religiously, and entire villages forsake their pagan temples and priests. Dean Vahl gives the number of communicants as 1,100,000. In addition, the 17,000 mission schools are giving a Christian education to over 900,000 boys and girls.

Now this exceedingly rapid development of missions really constitutes one of the chief phenomena of this century of wonders, and one which in the religious sphere at least is unapproached. This is indeed the century of missions *par excellence*. No other phrase will express so well, so much of what is best and most characteristic. These facts so inspiring to faith and courage, and so well fitted to provoke to vigorous endeavor to complete the work so grandly begun, have been presented just here mainly because they supply an excellent introduction to a discussion as to how it happened that such marvels came to pass, or what forces wrought together to produce such wide-spread and magnificent results. For no previous hundred years can be named in which progress so varied, and on such a stupendous scale, would have been possible. It is pleasant to discover ample evidence at every step that the same providence, all-wise and almighty, which in Carey's time, and before, so wondrously opened the pathway for a beginning, has ever since been equally busy raising up in every sphere auxiliaries and allies almost without number, that in our day the whole earth might see the salvation of our God.

It cannot but be instructive to survey the general history of the period in search for changes in the secular or non-religious realm which have added immensely to the volume and momentum of missionary undertakings. Take as an illustration the astounding growth of the United States in area, population, wealth, intelligence and spiritual power. A century ago but 4,000,000, all dwelling east of the Alleghenies in a long, narrow strip bordering upon the Atlantic, but now increased to 65,-000,000, spreading from sea to sea, occupying the continent which they have subdued, and easily holding rank among the foremost of nations. Then general chaos prevailed. Uncertainty, dissatisfaction and weakness were universal. Our institutions were all in feeble infancy, the Republic was no more than a novel and astounding experiment. But now, in both church and state, the fundamental principles then introduced with fear and trembling, have been thoroughly tested and found worthy of confidence, better than the most enthusiastic dared to hope. And what if this nation had been omitted from history? What if Britain had subdued the colonies, or they had been confined to their original area, or by secession the Union had been hopelessly rent in twain? Who can doubt that among the purposes of the God of nations in prospering the work of the founders, the builders and the defenders was this, that in the New World might be gathered and developed instrumentalities, which in due season might be wielded for the conversion of the world. In the same category must be placed the, if possible, more amazing spread of British dominion and political influence into every quarter of the globe. Take the two nations together, and what world-force can for a moment compare with this one? The Anglo-Saxon is the supreme colonizer, and civilizer, and Christianizer under the sun. Protestant Britain holds political sway over some 12,000,000 square miles of the earth's surface, or nearly one-fourth of all the land area, and over some 400,000,000 of the human family; or more than one-fourth of the entire race. And this means, among other things, that so far and wide, at least a beginning has been made in establishing good laws, good order, civil and religious liberty, schools, and all the various concomitants of civilization, and that steady progress will ensue. In aiding in the spread of the gospel in heathen lands, *pax Brittanica* is worth ten-fold more than *pax Romana* ever was in the best of the early centuries. What if England had possessed no navy, no fleet of merchant vessels sailing every sea, and opening traffic with every nation under heaven! What a peculiar providence for the furtherance of missions is connected with the matchless results flowing from English commerce, English conquest, and English colonization. Of course, of the same sort, differing only in degree, are the setting up of the Congo Free State, and the Partition of Africa with its numerous "protectorates" and "spheres of influence."

Or, in measuring the secular forces, the non-religious factors which have played a prominent part in hastening the glorious day of redemption for the race, account must be taken of the triumphs of modern science, of discoveries and inventions too numerous even to mention. Recall what steam has done for travel and trade, to quicken intercourse between the nations by bringing them nearer and making them acquainted. The great ocean steamships, the lines of trans-continental railways, and the Suez Canal are divinely appointed and invaluable aids in proclaiming at the soonest to every creature the saving story of the Cross. How much nearer to salvation are the millions of India since the metaled highways and railroads were there constructed, since the telegraph and post-office began their manifold ministries. How much has the task been lightened of going into all the world since Carey endured such vexations in effecting an entrance into his chosen field, since Vanderkemp consumed five months in reaching the Cape of Good Hope, since Duff in an eight months' voyage suffered shipwreck three times, and since the first missionaries to the Sandwich Islands must needs make their passage in a brig, and via Cape Horn. Morrison journeyed to China by way of New York, being tossed about for three months upon the Atlantic, and after that came four months more of tedious alternations of dead calm and tempest, two hundred and thirty days in all. The mission ship *Duff* was gone two years on her first trip to carry the messengers of Christ to the South Seas, and on her second was captured by a French privateer. And in what dreadful isolation were the first missionaries compelled to spend their lives, without sympathy and counsel, thrown almost wholly upon their own resources, so difficult, so expensive, and so infrequent was communication.

Nor must we by any means forget the remarkable results which have been achieved by scores and hundreds of explorers in all lands. A century ago the bulk of the world was utterly unknown to civilized men. Africa, for example, the second of continents for size, had been touched only upon the coast, and there only at a few points. Of the entire interior as little was known as of the surface of the moon. Mungo Park was the only modern traveler who had dared to undertake to penetrate the profound darkness (1795-1806), and had lost his life somewhere on the upper Niger. Not much progress was made in African discovery until Livingstone in 1849, only forty-four years ago, struck out from his mission station to reach the Atlantic coast, and then recrossed to the Indian Ocean. Nor was it until his life work was accomplished, and that of Stanley, and of numerous other courageous and venturesome men, that the Christian churches were in possession of knowledge upon which to base conviction and evangelistic effort. It was Livingstone's saying that "the end of discovery is the beginning of missions." And in this generation troops of missionaries are to be seen pressing into the Dark Continent from the north, the south, the east and west, up the Nile and the Niger, the Congo, and the Zambezi, and the Shire, and opening stations on the great central lakes.

Closed doors also of another sort have been wondrously opened since the century began. Multitudes are yet living who can remember the strange times when among the chief difficulties was that of finding an entering place, making a lodgment for the gospel. To enter China, Japan, or Corea, was to face certain death. In 1840, and by the iniquities and desolations of the "Opium War," five Chinese ports were opened to missionary residence and activity, and only since 1860, after three bloody struggles with western nations, has it been lawful to preach Christ to the teeming millions of the vast interior. It was in 1854, under the persuasion of Commodore Perry's cannon, that the Sunrise Kingdom began to unbar her gates, and after the revolution of ten years later followed another impulse in the same direction, while the "Hermit Kingdom" maintained her exclusiveness until 1882. Already the story seems incredible that for twenty-seven long years (1807-34) Morrison watched, waited, and prayed, in Canton and Macao, unable to hold a public service, preaching Jesus to congregations of half a dozen or less, baptizing only three or four, and so dying in faith, not having received the promise. And that for eight years more Milné, and Gützlaff, and Abeel, hovered cautiously upon the coast, entering the bays and rivers as far as they dared, distributing Christian books and tracts, and in Singapore and Malacca establishing religious services and schools for the large Chinese population gathered there, hoping that thus in this around-about fashion the empire itself might at length be affected in some measure. Then during much of the same period India was practically shut up against missionary effort. Just before Carey was ready to set forth upon his venture, the East India Company had come to regard Christianity as something dangerous beyond endurance for their possessions in the East. "A band of devils" was preferable to a band of missionaries. And when in Parliament their ideas and policy were severely denounced, they were the more determined to keep the Gospel out of India, and over the Vellore outbreak in 1807 their nervous fear became overwhelmingly great. However, by an amendment to their charter in 1813, they were compelled to tolerate British missionaries, after 1833 missionaries from all Christendom might freely enter, and after the mutiny of

1857, which proved the death blow to the great corporation, the last legal restrictions were removed, except in certain of the native states.

Of course, there was no room for missionaries in the Turkish Empire, or anywhere in Mohammedan realms. This form of hindrance to the Gospel is by no means yet removed, and bids fair to exist for generations to come. But Queen Victoria is sovereign over some 60,000,000 Moslems, and their lives are in no great jeopardy if they would accept Christ. In Egypt, too, where British influence is widely felt, there is a fair degree of religious freedom. The Shah of Persia is in many respects a liberal monarch, while even the Sultan is compelled to wear a humiliating hook in the nose, not being able to do just what he would with his Christian subjects, but in many things consulting the judgment and scruples of foreign ambassadors, especially those representing the moral sense of Great Britain. In like manner, as for Roman Catholic countries one and all, they were closed against the entrance of the word of God as proclaimed by Protestants. Church and State were in hearty league to exclude the pestilent heresy. But presently the South American states, one after another, began to rebel against their European masters, to set up independent governments, and to move forward towards liberty, both civil and religious. Since 1867, the gospel has found free course in Mexico. Though under many damaging restrictions, missionaries are tolerated in Austria, in the ancient home of Torquemada and the Spanish Inquisition! and, wonder of wonders, within the gates of the Eternal City itself! Yes, more than two dozen Protestant churches are doing their purifying and ennobling work within easy gun-shot of the Vatican. And the beginning of this miracle was in 1870, when in the midst of the Franco-German war Victor Emmanuel found his opportunity to appropriate the States of the Church, and to make Rome his capital.

Such are some of the more notable changes in the world of science and politics which have had a bearing most direct and momentous on the great matter of the diffusion of Christianity throughout the whole world. All these are forces favorable to the propagation of the Gospel which are resident, not in its own nature and spirit, but rather in its environment. Coming nearer to realms more distinctively religious, the missionary toil of this century has been wondrously assisted by the printing press, by the astonishing production of copies of the word of God, and of a Christian literature in endless variety, and in quantity beyond calculation. Herein lies no small part of the peculiar privilege and glory of the Church of the present time, and in this fact is found much of the secret of its purity of doctrine and vigor of life. It was not until within a few decades that the art of printing emerged from infancy, and in the fullness of strength and skill, entered upon its beneficent career. No man can estimate how much the kingdom, both at home and in the foreign field, owes to the multiplication of copies of the Scriptures, and their distribution by the various Bible societies. Between the Christian Era and the Reformation, a period of about fifteen hundred years, the divinely given rule of faith and practice was translated into but twenty-three languages, at the rate of one in sixty-five years, and in these of course was found only in manuscript. Between the Reformation and 1804, when the British and Foreign Bible Society was organized, the number of new versions reached thirty-four, or one for every nine years. Between 1804 and 1890, when printing by machinery and the power-press had come into vogue, three hundred and forty-two versions were made and scattered far and wide, at the rate of four a year. In the decade 1881-91, the British and Foreign Bible Society alone undertook fifty translations. In all, from the beginning this society has published no less than 135,000,000 copies of the Bible or portions thereof, the American Bible Society 57,000,000 more since 1816, and if we include all other editions like the Bagster, the Oxford, the Revised Version, etc., etc., at least 250,000,000 copies must have been produced since the modern era of missions began. Add now to the Bibles, the host of missionary magazines, annual reports, tracts and leaflets, books historical and biographical, essays, sermons and the rest, and how much has been accomplished to move Christendom, and heathendom also. The lives of Brainerd, and Martyn, and Judson, and Livingstone, and Harriet Newell, and Ann Hasseltine, and scores of others, have sufficed to kindle boundless enthusiasm and devotion. And the thrilling stories of such successes as were won in Fiji and Madagascar, among the Karens and Telugus, by increasing knowledge have increased interest a hundred-fold. In former days the soldiers of the cross had no auxiliary able at all to match the present might of the printed word of God.

But other invaluable instrumentalities have been contrived, other weapons new, and mighty through God to the pulling down of strongholds, are wielded by the modern missionary. It is Livingstone who reminds us that, however it may once have been, it no longer remains true that the missionary is adequately represented by the picture of a man with a Bible in his hand. While an evangelist beyond anything else, he is also something more. Whatever he does is to be for the Gospel's sake, but he is to civilize as well as to evangelize. So far as is possible he is to minister to every human need, from the highest to the lowest. By the school the intellect is to be quickened and enlarged. There is a legitimate place even for industrial training. The splendid results achieved at Lovedale, and by Mr. Duncan among the Indians at Metlakahtla upon the Northwest Coast, are ample proof of this. The man of God in pagan lands is to feed the hungry in times of famine, and in times of pestilence to nurse and supply healing agencies. The medical mission, when rightly employed, is as purely Christlike as any other agency. The hospital and dispensary often prove well-nigh irresistible means of grace, for they are easily appreciated, and set in striking contrast the love, and sympathy, and benevolence of Christianity, and the selfishness and cruelty of pagan religions. Then it is only in this generation that the length and breadth, the height and depth, of woman's sphere as an evangelizer have been discovered, and so the saving efficacy of missionary efforts has been well-nigh doubled. So long as men only were commissioned, and their endeavors were held in honor, one-half of the world was practically shut out from opportunities to hear of Christ. And it was not until women were despatched by the hundred and thousand to enter the homes, to teach the children, to nurse, to practice medicine and surgery, that the gospel began to have a fair chance to vanquish superstition and false faith. The women, and hence the homes, had been but slightly affected, so that the results were comparatively superficial, and the progress slow.

The gains of the gospel in the foreign field are greater nowadays for another reason. Missionary work has been so long in progress that opportunity has been afforded to select, and prepare, and set to their tasks, a native ministry in numbers relatively large. Until this important achievement had been made, missions were not fairly on their feet. Time was when all the toilers were foreigners, wrestling with the language and struggling desperately to make themselves understood, wholly unacquainted with the idiosyncrasies of the people, their ideas, prejudices, and peculiar modes of thought. But now native preachers, pastors, evangelists, Bible-readers, etc., outnumber the missionaries four to one, and presently the proportion will become ten to one, and fifty to one. There seems to be no divided testimony as to the significance of this phase of the current situation. Japan is to be evangelized by the Japanese, not by Europeans, China by Chinamen, Africa by Africans. Only these can impart to the Gospel a native flavor, only these can speak to the native mind and heart. Add to this another result, closely related, the presence in thousands of communities of natives once in the degradation of heathenism, but now enlightened, ennobled, transformed, a daily spectacle to all beholders proving the matchless power of divine grace to save, and well may the kingdom go forward with rapid strides. Children are able to begin where their parents left off.

More and more is the virus eliminated from the blood and bone. A generation is growing up which was born and reared in Christian homes, at least in Christian communities, never having had instruction, or experience, in the follies and abominations of idolatry. And hence we may not unreasonably expect the increase to be in geometrical progression.

Dr. Warneck suggests that in evangelizing the heathen the work naturally passes through various phases which differ widely. His language is: "It generally happens, so history teaches us, that every mission period has three stages, though of course these are not always sharply defined, nor do they always demand an equal continuance. The first stage is that of sending of the mission and of individual conversions, with the gathering of comparatively small churches; the second is that of the organized work of the native forces and the cultivation of the church-life; the third is that of the Christianizing of masses, which is generally connected with the occurrence of specially great events in mundane history, political revolutions, the acceptance of Christianity by the chiefs, etc." Evidence is steadily accumulating that in fields not a few, this third stage of wholesale turning from the worship of idols to the living God is not only at the door, but has already made its most impressive and significant advent. In Fiji, for example, and Madagascar, and in southern India, in Ongole among the Telugus, among the Santals also, and latest in the Methodist missions in the Northwest Provinces. In cases quite numerous mass conversions are occurring, whole villages putting themselves under Christian instruction, hundreds and thousands coming together desiring baptism. Even in conservative China this phenomena begins to appear.

But finally, such remarkable progress, with all this impressive combination of favoring forces, would never have been made unless unusual measures of power from on high had been vouchsafed to this century. It is the century of missions largely, yes mainly, because it has been also, beyond any other, a century of revivals, of quickened and purified spiritual life. The seasons of refreshing which marked the early decades of the Wesleyan movement both in the Old World and the New have returned with increasing frequency and with added abundance of blessing. In large measure modern missions are the direct product of revivals. The vast accessions of vital force must needs expend themselves in some form of religious activity. And, happily, the zeal of Christendom was turned away from speculation, theologizing and endless debate, to benevolence, philanthrophy, sympathy for the needy of every class. Hence the temperance and anti-slavery reforms, as well as hospitals, asylums, and humane undertakings innumerable, missions at home and missions abroad, among the rest.

CHAPTER XIII.

MISSIONS IN INDIA.

HITHERTO, in tracing the beginning and the unfolding of modern missionary undertakings, our attention has been confined mainly to Christendom, to the quickening among the churches of zeal for the world's evangelization, and to the organization of societies through whose instrumentality the stupendous task might be hastened forward to completion. The point of vision will now be transferred to heathen lands, and in various countries the condition without the Gospel will be presented, as well as the circumstances attending the entrance and progress of the truth as it is in Jesus. And in all fitness India should hold the first and most prominent place, both because it was the first region to be entered by missionaries, and also because it surpasses all others as a field for missionary toil. Within its boundaries more societies are represented, and the working force is greater, than is anywhere else to be found. Here is "the chief scene of Protestant mission work, upon which have been concentrated from all sides its numerous and most powerful agencies." India " is the chief bulwark of the kingdom of darkness," and its evangelization "is perhaps the most stupendous enterprise the church of Christ has ever undertaken."

And, at the outset, something about the country, its physical characteristics, which have an intimate connection with the people. Until within years quite recent the name was Hindostan, the land of the Hindus. In the largest sense both Ceylon and Burmah are included, that is, everything lying between Afghanistan and Siam, everything from the Himalayas to Cape Comorin. Thus defined, India is about 1,900 miles from east to west, and not far from the same distance from north to south. The proportions are fairly imperial and continental, the area being nearly 1,800,000 square miles; or half the size of the United States, equal to all Europe with Russia omitted, larger than the Roman Empire by 200,000 square miles, or fifteen times greater than Great Britain. This vast peninsula, of triangular shape, is divided into three sections which are exceedingly unlike. The Himalaya region is mountainous of course. The Ganges basin, including the valleys of the Indus and the Brahmaputra, is exceedingly fertile and holds a large majority of the inhabitants. The Deccan is a plateau begirt by mountains, the Vindhya range upon the north, with the Ghauts upon the east and west. The Western Ghauts rise near Bombay to an elevation of 4,700 feet, and further south to 8,760, while the Eastern Ghauts maintain an average height of about 1,500 feet, though with peaks reaching an altitude of 4,000, and one near Madras of 7,000. The general slope of the inclosed plateau is everywhere to the east. The coast section is narrow on the western side of the peninsula and the mountains rise abruptly, but on the eastern side is a plain varying in width from fifty to a hundred miles, which constitutes the Carnatic of history. Taken as a whole, India contains almost every variety of soil, climate and physical feature, the dryest and the wettest of tracts, the extremes of arctic cold and of torrid heat. There are deserts where rain is next to unknown, and at least one locality where the precipitation reaches the prodigious average of six hundred inches a year. The greater portion of the country under view lies within the tropics, is exceedingly hot, and consequently, most trying to the health of those of European and American birth.

One reason why the Christianization of India is a task so herculean, is found in the vastness of its population. According to the census of 1891, upwards of 287,000,000 are crowded together upon its acres, or about one-fifth of all the inhabitants of the globe. For populousness only China is a rival. Africa, though nearly seven times as large, has but about one-half as many. The population is equal to that of Europe with Russia omitted. India contains three times as many as the Roman Empire held when at its best. If the United States were as thickly settled, we should have some 600,000,000. In Bengal alone three times as many human beings are found as this republic can number, and twice as many dwell in the Central Provinces. Some Indian areas surpass for density of population all others on the face of the earth. The average for the valley of the Ganges is 500 to the square mile, while 600 are often found, and sometimes 700. And this host is not massed in great cities, but upwards of ninety per cent. are agriculturists, who dwell in 715,000 towns and villages, of which 343,000 have an average of less than 200 inhabitants each, and 223,000 between 200 and 500. The poverty of these hordes approaches to the indescribable and unimaginable, while their intellectual and spiritual condition is in close correspondence.

In order to understand the missionary problem in India it is necessary to subdivide both the country and the people in various ways. Thus while nearly 1,000,000 square miles go to make up British India, or that portion of the peninsula which is ruled directly and absolutely by Great Britain, about 800,000 square miles lie within the limits of the numerous native, or feudatory, or dependent states, which, with certain restrictions imposed by the supreme power, are left in the hands of Hindu or Mohammedan princes. But while the native states have an aggregate of some 66,000,000 inhabitants, British India has upwards of 221,000,000. Then it must never be forgotten that there is no Indian nation or people. The land is a very Babel, the inhabitants by race, color, physiognomy, language, intellectual character, social customs and religion, are sundered as far as are those of Europe; for example, the Britons, Turks, French, Irish, Germans, Finns, Italians, Russians, etc. Some 200 distinct languages and dialects are spoken between the Himalayas and the Cape. First, there are the Aryans, or Hindus proper, most numerous and most intellectual, and numbering 196,000,000. These are mild, effeminate, timid and servile, especially in Bengal. Next come the more than 57,000,000 Mohammedans, and composed of a mixture of Arabs, Afghans, Persians, Tartars, and what-not, who are possessed of greater pride and energy, are luxurious and dissolute, warlike and fanatical, and are impatient of English control. But, from long dwelling side by side, these two sections of the population have borrowed much, each from the other. Next follow the Dravidian races, like the Telugus and the Tamils of the Central Provinces and further south, of whom there are some 53,000,000. And finally there are the numerous bodies of aborigines (hill tribes), some 20,000,000 in all, dwelling each tribe in a district by itself, like the Santals, Khonds, Bhils, Khols, Karens, etc. If we divide by religion, we shall have of adherents of Brahmanism 208,000,000, Mohammedans 57,000,000, and several smaller subdivisions. Sir William Hunter is authority for the statement that there are at least 60,000,000 who are either outside of, or so slightly inside of orthodox Hinduism, or of Islam, that they are easily accessible to the Gospel. And it comes to this, that in this single country are found every grade of false faith and worship from the highest to the lowest, from the Koran with teachings at various points approaching somewhat to Christianity, and the theology and morals taught in the Vedas and the writings of the founder of Buddhism, to the most degrading superstitions of devil-worship. "Here is to be found a form of civilization at some points intellectual and lofty, and then hard by a state of affairs which in the social and religious realm reflects only ignorance and savagery." India contains therefore a confused jumble and chaos of conditions, peoples, ideas, and practices. As Professor Seeley well suggests, it is "not a political name, but only a geographical expression like Europe or Africa. It does not mark the territory of a nation and a language, but the territory of many nations and many languages."

No attempt will be made to present a complete statement concerning the various religions of India, or to set forth the doctrines contained in the ancient books. Some of the salient points, the characteristic features of a few will be given as they appear in the thoughts and lives of the people. Nevertheless, here, as always in matters relating to the land and its inhabitants, such is the endless diversity that general statements, however true, are almost certain to be misleading. The specifications which follow, in the main, will apply only to the Hindus proper, who constitute about two-thirds of the population. When missionaries first entered the country certain phenomena were very prominent, and made a deep impression, which now possess only a historic interest, since, thanks to the resolute action of the British rulers, they have entirely disappeared. Such was the famous, infamous, worship of Juggernaut, and suttee, and certain forms of human sacrifice. Infanticide also, and Thuggism, the latter for ages a legalized form of murder, practiced with the accompaniment of religious rites, and the dedication of one-third of the spoil to the goddess especially interested in such affairs. Hook-swinging, once common as a form of ascetic self-infliction in order to win salvation, though forbidden by law, even yet occasionally occurs. The fakirs, sometimes Hindus and sometimes Mohammedans, are as numerous as ever. One recently appeared in Bombay who for years, in order to free himself from sin, had worn upon his body iron chains weighing six hundred pounds. A prominent part is played in Indian society by the nautch girls, a numerous class of prostitutes, whose presence as dancers on all occasions of ceremony is considered to be essential, the highest English civil dignitaries also accepting the custom without protest.

Among the enormities is to be named the systematic and extensive pollution of girls and married women in the temples, and all in the name of religion, to please the gods. Polygamy is practiced by Moslems and Hindus alike, with the accompaniment of the seclusion of women in zenanas, their abject ignorance, and slavery. Child marriage too is dreadfully common, and works a world of sorrow and degradation. Girls are forced into marriage in tender years, and if the husband dies, the woeful lot of the widow is theirs for life. The pious Hindu holds animal life sacred, and it is at least in part to scruples at this point that we are to attribute the astounding passiveness and unconcern with which the ravages of tigers and venomous serpents are endured. It sometimes occurs that public highways are effectually blockaded for months by tigers, and villages are depopulated. The cobra destroys an average of 20,000 human lives a year. In 1875-80 no less than 1,073,546 snakes were killed by British influence, while 103,000 Hindus perished from their bites.

But last, strangest, and constituting the greatest hindrance to the introduction of the gospel, is India's peculiar institution of caste. Nor is this an integral part of original Brahmanism; it is not enjoined in the Vedas, but is of a later growth. The Brahmans, constituting the highest of the four principal social divisions, are the priests, number some 20,000,000, affect an awful sanctity, and are most haughty in their bearing towards the multitude. Being the learned men after the Indian fashion, they possess great influence, and as vice-gerents of the great divinities, at many points make themselves indispensable. Of late however, since occidental ideas have invaded India, and the power of the Gospel has been felt far and wide among the masses, this sacerdotal order has sadly fallen from its former high estate. Especially in the crowded railway carriage the Brahman is liable to be profanely jostled, and, when reduced to poverty, is compelled to labor for a livelihood like common clay. The subdivisions of caste are legion. Thus the last census took note of no less than 8,363 in all, including 521 kinds of Brahmans, and 957 varieties of the cultivator caste. A single division of the merchant caste, the Wanias, has 411 subdivisions, the carpenter caste has 94 divisions, the blacksmiths 76, the goldsmiths 86, and the coppersmiths 108. To such an incredible extent does this pernicious species of barrier-building between man and man prevail that even the out-castes have their classes, and of the Mahars there are 244 kinds and 154 of the Mangs. Concerning this phenomenon, Monier Williams says: "It is difficult for us Europeans to understand how pride of caste as a divine ordinance interpenetrates the whole being of the Hindu. He looks upon caste as his veritable god, and those caste rules which we believe to be a hindrance to the acceptance of the true religion, are to him the very essence of all religion. They influence his whole life and conduct." Probably the condition of the pariahs is as deplorable as that of any portion of the human family. They are held in contempt by all above them, have no social or civil rights which others are bound to respect, the public schools are closed against them, the public wells and tanks would be fatally polluted by their use, and in general they are doomed to the deepest poverty and ignorance, and to the worst of moral and sanitary conditions. It is the last triumph of grace, the one convincing evidence of genuine acceptance of the Gospel, when men of different castes will meet, and love, and associate as brethren, without repugnance will sit together at the Lord's table!

A brief outline of Indian history is next in order. The introduction of this peninsula to the civilized world occurred as far back as 327 B. C., when Alexander penetrated into the Punjab. But for unknown centuries before that date, and ever since, invasion and conquest have been the lot of well-nigh every generation. For, though upon the north India is marvelously well protected against outside enemies by gigantic mountain walls rising to heaven, upon three sides the exposure is great to attack from the sea. And also, at both the northeast and the northwest, by way of certain passes down gorges cut by the Brahmaputra and Ganges through the Himalayas, a hostile entrance is by no means difficult. And it was by the Khyber Pass—one of the most important natural highways upon the earth's surface, as well as one of the mightiest forces in the shaping of Indian history—that most of the conquering hosts have descended. Leaving unmentioned all earlier irruptions, the Mohammedans began their long series of assaults in the year 664. Among the most effectual of their attempts at conquest were the twelve campaigns of the Afghan, Mahmud of Ghazni (997–1030), who pushed his dominion far to the east and south of the Indus. Timour the Tartar was crowned at Delhi in 1398, and Baber, the fifth from Timour, led his irresistible followers down the passes in 1525. Akbar, the founder of the Mogul Empire, flourished during the reign of Elizabeth of England (1556-1605). The greatest of that line was Aurangzeb (1658-1707), though a fatal decline of power had already set in. Thus, for seven or eight centuries, host after host of semi-savage Moslems poured in to ruthlessly burn, pillage, and slaughter. About the middle of the last century, within twenty-three years, no less than six such destructive incursions occurred.

The Portuguese were the first of Europeans to enter India, making their advent from the ocean, and coming merely for purposes of trade. Goa was their commercial center. It was nearly a hundred years later before any of the Protestant powers ventured to follow in their footsteps. We have already seen, in an earlier chapter, how the Danes, building far wiser than they knew, the full import of their deed not appearing until nearly two centuries had passed, in the same year (1616), founded both Tranquebar and Serampore. The Dutch dispossessed the Portuguese of Ceylon in 1651, and five years later opened a factory at Chinsurah, on the Hoogly and some twenty-five miles above Calcutta. The English, never dreaming of the imperial dominion in store for them, first touched Indian soil at Surat in 1614, and between 1630 and 1661 established trading places at Madras, Calcutta and Bombay, with forts and a handful of troops for their protection. It was almost a hundred years after that circumstances began to thrust upon this astonished company of merchants the possession of large territories, and civil authority without limit. Two forces in particular conspired together to compel the East India corporation to decide between meddling with energy and decision in the political affairs of the country, and withdrawing altogether from trade with the natives. First, all matters relating to government and civil authority were in utter chaos. A few years after the death of Aurangzeb the vast empire reared by him fell to pieces, and generations followed of rebellion, revolution, and armed strife, unusual even in Indian experience. Between the "Home of Snow" and the Southern Cape, scores and hundreds of upstart rulers were crowding their purely selfish schemes, with universal disorder and violence as the result. Besides, Frenchmen had entered the land as traders, and had occupied several localities, some of them in the vicinity of Madras. From time immemorial Briton and Gaul had been rivals and antagonists, and were often at war. About the middle of the eighteenth century, and while the Seven Years' War was raging, Dupleix was found at the head of French interests in India, a man of consummate ability in the realm of statecraft, and full of ambition and far-reaching plans He soon perceived that the Hindu, trained by European officers, would make a reliable soldier. And further, that in the prevalent anarchy, with troops thus secured, by siding with certain native aspirants for political power, he could advance his own interests most effectually. And then, almost of necessity, he came into collision with his British neighbors. How marvelous the coincidence, by the crushing defeat of Montcalm on the Plains of Abraham in 1759 Catholic France was forever driven from North America, and in the year following, by another as disastrous at Wandewash, she was driven from the Indian peninsula, from henceforth leaving British influence supreme, and almost without a European rival. And what is especially of importance, the conquerors in this strife never forgot the lesson taught them by Dupleix. Now it is that the East India Company ceases to be simply an incorporated body of merchants, and plays hereafter, often perhaps too thoroughly, the rôle of conqueror and sovereign. But still further, two years before Wolfe's victory had been won, Colonel Clive had made an achievement in the vicinity of Calcutta almost as decisive, and leading to results perhaps fully as memorable. The reference of course is to his overwhelming victory at Plassey over Surajah Dowlah and his hordes of Hindus, a battle fought to avenge the shocking barbarities of the Black Hole. By that single stroke Bengal, with all its teeming millions, became British territory. From that day to this, sometimes it must be confessed with aims and by means utterly without justification, but perhaps oftenest rather under the urgency of a real political necessity, the boundaries of British rule have been steadily enlarging until now nothing is left in the peninsula not really subject to Queen Victoria.

It cannot but be esteemed one of the world's wonders how the almost 300,000,000 of Indians are held in subjection by the about 100,000 Englishmen to be found in the land. So tremendously outnumbered are the rulers —only about one European to 3,000 Asiatics—that as some adept in figures has calculated, if each Hindu should take up a handful of dirt and cast it upon the intruding foreigners, they all would be buried under six feet depth of soil! To be sure, a standing army is maintained, numbering some 75,000 Europeans and 160,000 natives, with a well-drilled police force in addition of 150,000 mostly armed with guns or swords. But besides, 18,000 miles of railroads have been constructed to connect all the principal cities, and a splendid system of public roads, nearly 150,000 miles in all, of which 33,400 are metaled, as well as nearly 40,000 miles of telegraph lines. Millions have been expended upon public works like bridges, reservoirs, and irrigation canals. Of the latter, one stretches through the valley of the Ganges for 437 miles, with 3,576 miles of distributaries, and another is found in the Punjab, 542 miles in length, with 4,385 miles of subordinate canals, while in the Madras Presidency these works, so essential in guarding against famines, are most extensive and costly of all. But far better to strengthen and perpetuate British sovereignty, is the good government everywhere maintained. Justice is secured to all, and peace, absolute freedom from despotic exactions, with safety to person and property. The method of government is peculiar, and varies greatly according to circumstances. While a portion of the population is subject to legal codes thoroughly English and civilized, many are governed much as their fathers were centuries ago. This diversity in the kind and degree of control is found mainly in the native, or feudatory states. These are all nominally under the rule of Hindu or Mohammedan princes, but really only with the help and in accordance with the advice of a British resident or agent. They have no right to make war or peace, or to send ambassadors to each other, or to governments outside of India. They are not allowed to maintain a military force beyond a certain limit. No European is permitted to reside at court without especial sanction. And in case of misgovernment on their part, the penalty of dethronement may be inflicted. But with these restrictions, the native chiefs possess sovereign authority. Some of them, like the Nizam whose dominions cover 100,000 square miles, collect large revenues, and surround themselves with oriental magnificence, while the sway of others is confined to a domain ridiculously meagre. The native state of Kathiawar has an area of 22,000 square miles, and a population of 2,600,000; but is subdivided into 182 separate and distinct states, of which 132 pay tribute to the nawab (nabob) of Junagarh, ninety-six pay tribute to the supreme government, and thirteen pay no tribute at all. So far as possible, consistently with safety and the general welfare, local self-government is allowed and encouraged. Moreover, various schools are maintained, in which the natives are trained to fitness to fill important public positions. An educational system is in vogue which dates from 1854, and comprises a total of 138,350 schools of all grades, in which some 3,700,000 are receiving instruction, while 12,000,000 more are able to read and write. But after all that has been done by the government and by the various missions, it remains that only 19.3 per cent. of the boys of school age are found in the schools, and only 1.8 per cent. of the girls. Normal schools are established in every province, and various medical colleges to train the natives for service in the numerous public hospitals and dispensaries. In general it may be affirmed that, at least for the last fifty years, at the head of affairs in India have for the most part been found only men of the highest intellectual ability and moral worth, able statesmen, and worthy exponents of Christianity, who honestly, earnestly, and effectually, sought to rule in righteousness, and with the utmost of benefit to all classes of the people.

So much for India, the country, its history, its peoples, and their present rulers. We come now to the story of the beginnings of the Gospel, and its progress towards the fulness of strength. The far-off date cannot be given when for the first time the glad tidings crossed the Himalayas. But by the middle of the fourth century churches were found upon the Malabar Coast, and the Nestorians, so long famous for their missionary zeal, may have pushed down through the Khyber Pass, bent on errands of love. Certain it is that the light then kindled has never since been entirely extinguished. Modern missions in the land of the Hindus date from 1706, when the Danish-Halle work was begun at Tranquebar, by Ziegenbalg and Plutscho, and in which so long Lutherans and Calvinists, Danes, Germans and English were so harmoniously united. The number of laborers was always small, and these were usually crippled for lack of financial support, as well as by vexatious interference on the part of the ecclesiastical authorities at home. It was only after great delay that ordination was secured for native ministers. In addition, the well-meant but unfortunate attempt was made to compromise with caste prejudices. These hindrances, with the disturbances connected with the frequent wars of the period, combined finally to bring the mission to the verge of ruin. The career of Schwartz was illustrious in almost every particular, covering nearly a half century (1750-98), and filled with deeds of the noblest and most self-denying kind. Such were his shining qualities of both mind and heart, that he was often counseled with by the British authorities upon important matters of state, and he also gained the absolute confidence and affection of such sturdy and unscrupulous

Hindu-Mohammedan foes as Hyder Ali. At his death a monument was erected in his honor by the Rajah of Tanjore, and another of great cost and beauty was reared in Madras by the East India Company.

As Schwartz was nearing the end of his course in southern India, the God of missions was preparing an instrument even greater than he, and one by whose labors, far more than by those of any other, the whole land was at length to be opened and filled with the gospel of salvation. As was most fitting, this new empire, being an English possession, was to be Christianized mainly by those speaking the English tongue, though the whole Christian world was to presently make ready, and go up together to conquer this vast and populous realm for Immanuel. Carey was the divinely chosen leader, who, landing in Calcutta from the Danish East Indiaman, first set foot on Indian soil November 11, 1793. The way had slightly been prepared for his coming. Thus Kiernander, formerly of the Tranquebar mission, had been transferred from Madras to the Hoogly as far back as 1758, and ever since had been in labors abundant alike for English, Portuguese and Hindus. A few earnest and devoted Christian men were found in the city from among the servants of the Company. Such were Charles Grant, Mr. Udney, and David Brown, chaplain of the Military Orphans' College. As early as 1778 they had commenced to agitate for the introduction of the gospel, and Mr. Grant had offered to give £360 a year for the support of two missionaries. In 1783 John Thomas had come out as a surgeon and had given himself zealously to the task of evangelizing the natives. To secure funds for the enlargement of his undertaking, he had gone home and thus had come into contact with the new-born Baptist Society and with Carey, and thus the latter was providentially led to this portion of the pagan world. Claudius Buchanan (1796-1808), while filling the position of chaplain, rendered invaluable service by tongue and pen, while Henry Martyn, another chaplain (1806-12), kindled a fervor for missions which has not died out to this day.

The situation as Carey found it cannot be understood without some reference to the attitude then recently taken by the East India Company as touching the introduction of Christianity into their domain, and which was in some measure maintained almost to the end of his life. In former times no repugnance had been felt towards missionaries. They had been permitted to enter freely, and without let or hindrance carry on their work, and sometimes had even been granted free passage. Kiernander had taken up his residence in Calcutta at the express request of Colonel Clive, while, as we have seen, Schwartz was held in high favor, and was the recipient of distinguished *post mortem* honors. But a change of sentiment began to appear when Grant and his friends, with Wilberforce for champion, urged upon Parliament to provide for India a complete religious establishment. Party lines were drawn and the debate was acrimonious. The charter of the Company was to be renewed for twenty years in 1793, a few months before the fight reached its fiercest stage, and ended for the time in a victory for the policy of exclusion of all religious effort in behalf of the natives. The opposition to missionary activity was inspired by various considerations. Of course religious indifference, **not to say malignant** hatred to Christianity, played a large part. Too many of the "old Indians" had succumbed to the manifold allurements which had beset their steps, with serious damage to their morals. Then the idea was quite prevalent that the Company was not in the least responsible for the intellectual and spiritual wellbeing of the millions of Moslems and Hindus, and hence was under no sort of obligation to undertake aught in their behalf. They had their ancient religions and social customs, and, whether for good or evil, let these remain as they are. There was an absurd affectation of superior toleration and breadth of sympathy, and a disposition to maintain that Brahmanism, and Buddhism, and the devil worship of the aboriginal tribes were actually better for the people than a faith and practice which they could never appreciate. Hence, on the part of not a few in authority, there was a readiness to excuse and wink at the worst abominations to be found, and even to derive from them a pecuniary benefit. But beyond all this there was something in the evident facts in the case which appealed mightily to the fears of the timid. There was that vast population, most bigoted, and all ablaze with fanaticism. Therefore, how suicidal to British interests to allow missionaries to travel up and down in the effort to make proselytes. It would be only to provoke an explosion, whose result would be the death of every European. The few thousands could continue in the land only by refraining carefully from all lines of action calculated to excite the passions of the multitude. After the mutiny at Vellore in 1806 this morbid fear was still further strengthened.

But, notwithstanding, the moral sentiment of Christian England had begun to assert itself, and temporary defeat only tended to add to its depth and breadth. The discussion went steadily on, with Carey and a few other missionaries barely tolerated in India to lend efficient assistance, and when the charter was, in 1813, to be once more renewed, an amendment was carried, to the effect that "it is the duty of this country to promote in India the introduction of useful knowledge, and of religious and moral improvement, and that facilities be afforded by law to persons desirous of going to and remaining in India, to accomplish these benevolent designs." A bishopric was also provided for, with an archdeacon for each one of the three Presidencies. It was not, however, until after yet another amendment to the charter, introduced in 1833, that the gospel was suffered to have free course throughout British India. The first missionary to enter any of the native states was not allowed the opportunity until 1841, when the Irish Presbyterian Church occupied Kathiawar.

The great Mutiny of 1857 may very properly be taken as the dividing line between the ancient and the modern periods in the history of efforts for the evangelization of the Hindus, and in length each portion is not far from a half century. The first was the time of beginnings, the day of small things. This mightiest fortress of paganism was not to be taken by bold and sudden assault. A protracted siege was required instead, and so an investment must be made, extensive works were to be constructed, and adequate forces gathered, the artillery put in position, and the sappers and miners set to their tasks. That is, the numerous languages were to be mastered, and translations of the Bible made and published. Schools were to be opened, and a generation of native helpers raised up and prepared for their calling. And all this, while at home public opinion was bringing the recreant Company to reason and conscience, and while British authority in the peninsula was receiving steady enlargement and consolidation. The bloody Marathi wars in the early decades of the century brought substantial increase of territory, as well as the two campaigns against the Sikhs in the forties, and the two struggles for mastery with Burmah. In 1850 considerably less than a score of societies were represented in the land by 339 foreign ordained agents, by 21 ordained natives and 493 other native assistants, while the communicants numbered but 14,661, and the native adherents all told, but 91,091.

For various reasons, the sudden and terrible outburst in 1857 of combined race-hatred and religious fanaticism, was of profound significance for India, and was wondrously overruled for the enlargement of Christianity. For one thing, it brought to an end, at once and forever, the East India Company, after a career of more than 250 years. Having long since fulfilled its mission and outlived its usefulness, this mightiest and most famous of commercial corporations went out of existence "unwept, unhonored and unsung." From henceforth the land of the Hindus was to constitute an integral part of the British Empire, and was to be governed directly and completely by Parliament. And, by the unutterable barbarities which attended the Mutiny, there was thrust upon British statesmen, and British Christians, a knowledge of the spiritual condition of the population, and a deep conviction that, at least for Britain's sake, if not for the sake of these degraded millions of subjects, the humanizing, elevating gospel must be carried at the soonest to every community from the boarders of Thibet to the Malabar Coast. A remarkable awakening of missionary zeal ensued, and within a decade or two some hundreds of devoted men and women were despatched to engage in loving, self-denying toil for all classes alike, whether semi-savage hill tribes and pariahs, or Brahmans and Mohammedans, and representing almost every considerable denomination of America and Europe. The supreme government, though scrupulously neutral in religious matters, and allowing the largest liberty to all faiths consistent with good order, is yet resolute at many points in forbidding violations of morals and decency, and in various ways renders indirect assistance to the heralds of the cross. Thus, English courts compel obedience to law, and no more can the native Christian be robbed of all property rights by legal process. Grants-in-aid are freely allowed to mission schools upon certain conditions, and many Englishmen filling important stations in the civil and military service, not only adorn the gospel by godly lives, but also on all occasions act and speak in behalf of the Lord they love. As a result of the wise and patient seed-sowing of the pioneers and founders during the first half of the century, combined with the vastly more favorable environments existing in later years, the ingathering has been relatively very large, and visible progress, all things considered, has been astonishing, and full of encouragement at every point. To-day in every province and in almost every state of India, missionaries of both sexes are to be found, with schools, hospitals, dispensaries, etc., as powerful auxiliaries.

Thousands of zenanas are wide open, inviting Christian women to enter and utter the word of life. And every year the indications multiply, and become more unmistakable, that a new and glorious era is approaching, in which millions will be seen flocking to Jesus for salvation. Already the number of ordained missionaries has nearly reached 1,000 with ordained natives almost as many, and with other toilers native and foreign sufficient to raise the total of the evangelizing force to but little if any less than 10,000. And as standing for the harvest of souls, let these figures suffice: The communicants aggregate about 235,000, and the adherents (native Christians) some 750,000, or if the Roman Catholics are included, 2,500,000. Upwards of 300,000 children are gathered in the various mission schools. How changed from November of 1793 when Carey landed in Calcutta! What hath God wrought!

In pursuing the thrilling narrative of the onward movement of the kingdom of heaven in India, it remains to single out a few of the societies, which were earliest in the field, or which have been especially blessed with abundant fruit, and to present in brief outline some of the more striking phases of their work. Many volumes would not be sufficient to tell all that here has been dared, and endured, and achieved, for Him who commanded, "Go ye into all the world." As a matter of course, we set forth from the Baptist Society, and from Carey and Thomas, "who landed unobserved, coming in a ship which had cleared from a foreign port, but escaped arrest and deportation only because their presence and mission were unknown." For months following, they struggled with all manner of embarrassments, and seriously lacked the very necessaries of life, "enduring hardships unknown to any other missionaries in India before or since." But what stalwart faith was present to sustain, is seen in this record made one day in his diary when the external situation was at the worst (the words are well worth repeating): "Well, I have God, and his word is sure; and though the superstitions of the heathen were a million times worse than they are, if I were deserted by all, and persecuted by all, yet my hope, fixed on that word, will rise superior to all obstructions, and triumph over all trials. God's cause will triumph, and I shall come out of all trials as gold purified by fire." For comfort he reads David Brainerd. Then they removed to Bandel, a Portuguese settlement thirty miles up the river, where Carey was to support himself by farming, and Thomas was to live by the practice of medicine; but some months later both are found located in "the waste jungles of the Sunderbunds, in the tiger-haunted swamps lying to the east of Calcutta." But in the meantime, not in the least neglecting the diligent study of various languages, or any opportunity of offering to the natives the bread of life. So passed the first year, and then the dark skies began to brighten. For a Mr. Udney offered to each a situation as indigo planter, in the Dinajpore district one hundred and fifty miles up the Ganges, with a salary of £250. This occupation was followed for six years, their time being divided between the secular duties of superintendence, and study and translating the Scriptures, as well as teaching and preaching. In 1799 a large reinforcement to the mission arrived, with Marshman and Ward among the rest, in an American vessel, and at the suggestion of Mr. Grant, one of the directors of the Company, passing by Calcutta and ascending the river to Serampore, a Danish possession. Here a cordial welcome was accorded them by Governor Bie, who for years had been under the influence of Schwartz in Tanjore, with an invitation to remain, and a promise of protection and assistance. And when later a demand was made that these dangerous "interlopers" be surrendered, in order that they might be sent back to England, this doughty commandant refused, and declared his determination to shield the missionaries with all the force at his disposal. Next, under a Danish pass, a visit was made to Carey, and though much against his will, he was finally persuaded to fix the seat of the mission at Serampore. What if the Danes had not opened a factory upon the Hoogly in 1616?

Thus marvelously it came about, after seven long and weary years of waiting, that in the first year of the new century something systematic, and substantial, and enduring, could be undertaken in the shape of regular public services, schools, translating and printing. For economy's sake all the missionaries dwelt together, and had all things common. Almost at once, a variety of institutions began to appear and to steadily develop. Before the end of the twelvemonth the first Hindu convert, Krishna Pal, was baptized, over which event, for excess of joy, poor Thomas went insane for weeks. The year following saw Carey installed as teacher of Bengali and Sanscrit in the Company's College of Fort William, with a salary of £700, and raised later to £1,800! From this income so much was saved that, with what Marshman and the others could earn by teaching, etc., the Serampore Brotherhood were able to contribute to the mission in all £90,000 ($450,000). A full third of a century remained on earth for this immortal father of modern Protestant missions, in which to unfold his far-reaching and multitudinous plans, and behold the fruits of his prayers and toils. His direct aim and endeavor took in nothing else than the entire eastern world, with the redemption of its teeming millions. More particularly, he undertook to give them in their own tongues the priceless message of salvation, and applied himself with such boundless energy and skill that he lived to see the Scriptures, or portions thereof, published in not less than forty of the languages or dialects of southern Asia. Besides this, he gave himself with all diligence to the performance of his duties in the college. Though with prudence and caution, yet plainly and with fearlessness, he uttered his protests against the policy of the Company in countenancing the abominations of paganism while putting Christianity under the ban, and happily lived to see that policy overthrown. And finally, all along and without cessation, he tugged away with tongue and pen at the herculean and most discouraging task of arousing the Christian world to earnestness in praying and giving, and in organizing to send their sons and daughters to bear the glad tidings to every land. And here, too, he was permitted to behold wondrous advancement. As to his own mission, by 1813 it had grown to thirty stations in northern India, including Patna, Agra and Orissa, and manned with sixty-three European and native laborers. Aud with what enterprise the work was pushed appears in the fact that it was in Serampore that India saw the first large printing press, paper mill and steam engine set up, the first vernacular newspaper printed in Bengali, and the first efforts put forth for the education of Hindu girls and women.

The London Society was early in the Indian field. Mr. Forsyth was sent to Calcutta in 1798, but located himself at Chinsurah, a Dutch factory, some twenty miles up the river. Here he toiled alone until 1812, and with little apparent effect. The next missionaries were sent to the southern portion of the peninsula, in which also, next to Madagascar, its most extensive victories for the kingdom have been gained. In 1805 work was begun in Madras, the next year in Vizagapatam, far up the coast of the Bay of Bengal in the Northern Circars; in 1820 at Bangalore, and in 1824 at Cuddapah, both some distance to the northwest of Madras. It was in the field last named that, about two decades later, occurred a wholesale renunciation of idolatry on the part of the out-caste Malas. The kingdom of Travancore, a native state in the extreme southwest of India, entered in 1809, with Nagercoil and Trevandrum among the chief stations, has been the scene of large ingatherings. Nearly 300 out-stations are supplied with the means of grace, and about 50,000 native Christians are under religious training. Missionaries were sent to Calcutta in 1817, to Benares three years later, and since to various other points in Bengal. This society is now represented by 95 Europeans of both sexes, as well as by 42 ordained natives and 445 native preachers. Into the 630 schools 34,853 pupils are gathered, while the church members number 9,449 and the native Christians 71,000.

The Church of England performs its part towards the

evangelization of the hosts of the Queen's subjects in southern Asia largely through two organizations, the Society for the Propagation of the Gospel, which is in the hands of the ritualistic party, and the Church Missionary Society, controlled by the evangelicals. Though working separately, and sometimes holding the attitude of rivals to each other, it will be convenient to regard their work as a unit, and speak only of combined results. Before Carey sailed, an attempt, fortunately a failure, had been made to set up the Establishment in India, and so with Parliament to manage missions. So long as Christianity was excluded by law, churchmen sat with folded hands viewing the abominations and woes of idolatry with slight concern. But, soon after the amendment of the Company's charter in 1813, a movement was started to lay foundations for the Gospel in each of the three chief cities; in due season various other subordinate points were occupied, and ever since the work has been spreading in all directions, until now in almost every province, north, south, east, and west, English Episcopacy is found acting upon the aggressive against heathenism with all manner of weapons, and constitutes one of the chief factors in the coming evangelization of the land. In Madras, work was begun as early as 1815, in Calcutta the next year, the year following in Benares and in Ceylon; in Bombay in 1820, etc. Among the chaplains who performed distinguished services may be named such as Claudius Buchanan (1796-1808,) and Henry Martyn (1805-12). Bishop Heber commenced his brief but brilliant career in 1825. The Church work finds the climax of results in the south, with Tinnevelly as the center, where in 1838 village movements to Christianity set in, and within about four years 18,000 cast away their idols. In this district more than 1,000 villages contain true disciples of Jesus. In Madras also the work has progressed so far that it is committed wholly to native hands. The Khols of Chota Nagpore, a province of Bengal, have supplied some 50,000 converts to the Propagation Society and Gossner's (German) Society together. Combining all the missions from Ceylon to the Khyber Pass, we have such large figures as these: The Church of England is represented by 203 ordained missionaries, 249 ordained natives and 890 native lay preachers, 55,000 communicants, and 198,000 native Christians.

As we have seen, the American Board commissioned five men for India in 1812, and after months of greatest uncertainty and embarrassment, work was opened in Bombay. This proved to be a barren field, but work of all kinds was pushed with the utmost vigor of faith and love. In the forties occurred an outburst of Hindu opposition, in alarm over the encroachments of the new religion. The pagan press was employed with such ardor, that at one time ten papers and magazines were in full blast in the effort to save the temples and priests from ruin. In 1847 the Bible was issued in Marathi. In 1831 a mission was opened in Ahmednagar 175 miles back from Bombay, to which several stations have since been added. Ceylon was entered by five men in 1815, and the government was found favorable to their designs. They were allowed the use of certain churches and glebes left behind by the Catholic Portuguese, and the Bible had been translated into Tamil by the Dutch while in possession of the island. Reinforcements came within four years, and for nearly a quarter of a century revivals frequent and extensive were enjoyed. In 1834 the narrow strait was crossed, and to the Tamils on the continent the Gospel was carried. Madura was chosen as the seat of a mission, and ever since has proved a fruitful field. Some years later came a fierce struggle with caste, with a serious falling away for a season, but ending in defeat for those who would maintain between brethren barriers of pride and prejudice. In Madras (1836-51) a large printing establishment was kept busy pouring out a varied Christian literature. This society has now upon Indian soil three missions, with 453 stations and out-stations, manned by 79 American laborers, and 1,279 natives, of whom 301 are preachers. The churches number 93 and the church members 8,259, the native Christians 21,000, the schools 447, and the scholars 19,824.

With the first missionaries of the American Board Judson had crossed the ocean, but before reaching Calcutta had so changed his opinions as to make it necessary to change also his ecclesiastical connections. It was as a Baptist that he set foot on shore in Rangoon in July of 1813. Burmah was then wholly pagan, and the government was one of the most cruel and tyrannical to be found even in the Orient. But for all this, it was a country more tolerable for those who would introduce the gospel than the dominions ruled by the " Christian " East India Company. It was the lot of this gifted, and most heroic, and devoted servant of God to have his path beset almost to the end of his life with appalling difficulties, and perils, and sufferings as great as any ever endured by any herald of the cross in heathen lands.

From among the Burmans proper he saw little fruit from his toils, and this mainly because of the determined and ruthless opposition of the powers that were. He found a people numbering perhaps 8,000,000, and occupying some 300,000 square miles. Buddhism was the dominant faith, but among the numerous aboriginal tribes, like the Shans, Karens, etc., a gross devil worship prevailed. For several years Judson was left to endure alone, that is with only his wife to cheer and strengthen, the famous Ann Hasseltine, a woman for intellectual gifts and spiritual graces, for courage, resolution, and fervor of love, a worthy helpmeet. The tedious time of waiting was occupied in study of the language, preparation of tracts, etc., and in work upon a translation of the Scriptures, meanwhile seeking in vain for the royal permission to begin openly to proclaim Christ to the people. It was during this period that when asked concerning the outlook he replied: " It is as bright as the promises of God." And again, when inquired of in relation to results, the answer was: " Wait twenty years and then look this way again." After six years the first helpers came from America, and the first convert was baptized. In 1824 the first Burman war broke out, and, suspected of being a spy in the interests of Britain, he was arrested, and for two years constantly faced death from fever, heat, hunger, and brutal treatment in filthy prisons; for seventeen months wearing three, and part of the time five, pairs of fetters. During this terrible scene of trial his wife exerted herself in his behalf in every possible way, ministering to his wants and seeking his release, " walking miles in feeble health, in the darkness of night or under the burning sun, much of the time with a babe in her arms." Such was the strain to body and spirit, that not long after her husband was set at liberty and the war was over, a deadly fever set in and ended her career upon earth. During an ensuing period of confusion and uncertainty the mission was moved about between Rangoon, Amherst and Maulmain. In 1827 other missionaries arrived, among them Mr. Boardman, and presently work was commenced among the Karens, a tribe justly famous in Christian annals for its readiness to receive the truth. In 1834 the translation of the Bible was ready for use, and an addition of fifteen was made to the working force. Judson survived till 1850, two years afterwards the second Burmese war befell, forced upon the British by the pride and presumption of the king; with a third conflict produced in a similar way by King Thebaw in 1885, which ended in the annexation of Burmah to India. In these results is to be found the monument to this illustrious soldier of the cross, who risked all for his Master. And who shall say that the achievement is not well worth all the cost? The mission force in Burmah consists of 828 persons, including 158 ordained natives, the schools number 505 with 15,306 scholars, and the churches 580, of which 337 are self-supporting, with a membership of 34,672. The native contributions reach $50,000 annually. The native Christians number some 200,000. The Propagation Society, the Berlin Society, the English Wesleyans, and the American Episcopalians, are also engaged in the evangelization of Burmah, with a total of 16 missionaries, 6 native laborers, and 7,577 communicants.

The English Wesleyans, though so intensely busy seeking the complete redemption of Great Britain, were yet also not strangers to zeal for missions in the broader sense. Coke had been appointed superintendent for all worldwide schemes of propagandizing. Burning with desire to minister to the needs of the heathen, he had offered to give £6,000 to found a mission in Ceylon, and in 1813 the Conference had appointed him and six more to proceed thither. He died upon the long voyage; the others soon fixed themselves at Colomba and elsewhere, gave their energies with fulness of devotion to what their hands found to do, and were rewarded by seeing souls turning to righteousness. In 1817 Madras was entered in the Lord's name, and later Bangalore, Trichinopoly, Mysore and Seringapatam were occupied. Later still missionaries were sent into Hyderabad, the Mohammedan state (Nizam's Dominions); to Calcutta also, Benares, Lucknow, etc., in northern India. At the end of eighty years from the first of the pioneers, this body of believers has in this broad field 150 missionaries and assistants, proclaiming Christ in about 500 preaching places, with a band of 2,083 evangelists, catechists, local preachers, etc. The "full and accredited" members number 7,249, and the attendants on public worship 30,932. The schools number 635 and the scholars 39,452.

It was an event of no ordinary importance for the land of the Hindus when, in 1829, the Church of Scotland appointed Alexander Duff to open work in behalf of the perishing millions. For here was a remarkable personality, a man of tremendous energy, full of enthusiasm and holy zeal. Calcutta was chosen as the scene of his life labors, which continued for almost fifty years. His special design was to open a collegiate institute, in which the youth of India could gain the higher education (a), with English rather than the vernacular as the medium for giving instruction in western sciences, and (b) with the Bible everywhere in the forefront. It was a shocking innovation to many, but he carried his point and succeeded so wondrously that the learned Orientalists owned themselves beaten, and gave up the fight for Sanscrit as the best language for all higher uses. Other similar institutions were founded in Bombay by Wilson, another missionary of great eminence, by Anderson in Madras, and by Hislop in Nagpore, the latter receiving the gift of $13,000 from an officer in the Indian army. In 1843 came the disruption in the Scottish church, whereby the Free Church came into existence, and became heir to all the missionaries then in the field, though the property was retained by the Establishment. A number of the educational institutions were soon duplicated; both divisions pushed forward the work of evangelization with commendable vigor, and, ever since, each has often provoked the other to good works. Probably more than any others, these two bodies have pushed the intellectual phases of Christianity, and as many judge sometimes almost to the exclusion of the spiritual. The Established Church, beginning just when the British nation was awakening to a sense of its obligations to its Hindu and Mohammedan subjects, has expended the bulk of its energies upon them. Twelve principal stations are maintained in various regions between the Himalayas and the Cape, with 14 European and 96 native agents, 862 communicants and 3,903 native Christians, 89 schools and 4,811 scholars. The Free Church is represented by 31 ordained missionaries and 10 ordained natives, and a total force of 475. The communicants number 2,186, the adherents about as many more, the schools 191, and the scholars 13,482.

The Presbyterians of America until 1870 were largely connected with the American Board, but as far back as 1833, the year in which India was opened to the entrance of the gospel, a company of missionaries was sent to the Northwest Provinces and the Punjab, the latter at the time constituting the kingdom of the fanatical Sikhs, with Runjeet Singh the Lion as their ruler. One station after another was occupied until the line stretched over some 900 miles, or from Allahabad to Rawal Pindi, not far from Khyber Pass, and with Lahore, Lodiana and Futtegurh among the important centers. The work was much hindered by the two bloody Sikh wars in the forties, while during the Mutiny not only was much property destroyed, but three missionaries, with their wives and children, were captured and put to death. It was the next year, and as a result of such dreadful experiences, that the Lodiana mission sent out to Christendom a pathetic call to prayer for the world's conversion, suggesting the opening days of January as a fitting period, and thus originated the "Week of Prayer." With all the other instrumentalities employed to rescue the individual soul and to construct all manner of Christian institutions, special prominence has been given to work in zenanas and among lepers. Including Kolhapur, in Central India, so intimately associated with Rev. R. G. Wilder, the mission of the Presbyterian Church, North, includes 35 ordained Americans and 26 ordained natives, 50 lay missionaries, and a total force of 406. In the 30 churches are 1,796 members, and in the 147 schools 8,399 scholars.

It is more than doubtful if the history of missions contains a chapter more remarkable in all its parts than the one which relates to the work of the American Baptists among the Telugus. Of this people there are some 20,000,000, located for the most part in southern India, and the portion now under view are found dwelling to the north of Madras, not far from the Bay of Bengal. The first missionary went out in 1835, but did not undertake work in Nellore until four years after. Obstacles of all sorts, and unusually great, even for India, were met with. So rigid were caste rules that it was scarcely possible to enter the houses. Men, too, were lacking as well as funds, and so the mission long hovered between life and death, while at home more than once, after serious discussion, the decision was imminent to retire from the field. At the end of two decades, only one native assistant could be reported, one church with nine members, and two schools with 63 pupils. After twelve years of discouraging toil, Mr. Jewett came home in 1863 worn out and in feeble health, was informed how the Society felt, and was asked for his opinion. His heroic reply has become historic: "Well, brethren, I do not know what your mind is, but if the Lord restores my health, I am going back to live, and if need be to die, among the Telugus." And this was the conclusion reached: "Then we must send a man over to give you a Christian burial." Two years later Rev. J. E. Clough was on the ground, and found but twenty-five converts after thirty years of endeavor, while four other societies in the same general field were no better off. But presently a change began to appear. A church was organized at Ongole which in ten years had a membership of

2,761, while in the entire mission were 3,832 communicants. Then ensued several terrible years of combined flood, cholera, and famine, the latter so severe as to destroy some 6,000,000 lives. Food was furnished by the government, and extensive public works were constructed to supply labor, and Mr. Clough, who had formerly been an engineer, was put in charge of a portion. By 1878 the wholesale demand for baptism had become irresistible. The applicants were turned away, the day of trial was postponed, and the examinations were made most searching, but in spite of all, in six weeks 8,691 were admitted to the churches, 2,222 in a single day. In one day 1,000 came to the compound of the Ongole station and gave up their idols. And ever since the work has gone on in similar fashion, and the interest has spread in all directions. In 1892 the baptisms numbered 3,398. These hosts of converts were mainly from the lowest of the people, though not a few belong to the higher castes and some are Brahmans. According to the latest returns this "Lone Star" mission has 87 members from America, of whom 42 are men, 66 ordained natives and a total force of 602. The 77 churches have a membership of 54,986, while 7,565 scholars are found in the 632 schools. Evidently, the efforts to evangelize the Telugus are not a "failure."

The American Methodists were somewhat later in entering the boundless Indian field. Though an appropriation for the purpose was made in 1852, it was four years later before Rev. William Butler was ready to break ground. The Northwest Provinces were chosen as the district, and Bareilly as the center. But scarcely had he made a beginning when the Mutiny broke out, and he was compelled to flee for his life. When the terror was over reinforcements came, the first convert was baptized in 1859, and steady progress has ever since been made. In 1870 William Taylor began work in southern India, and since then the entire supervision of Methodist evangelism in all these parts has been placed in the hands of Bishop Thoburn. The women of this church are urging forward such lines of labor as relate to zenanas and hospitals. For three years past the indications have steadily increased that by the thousand and ten thousand from henceforth the Hindus of northern India are to flock to the gates of the kingdom. In 1862 the number of church members was but 96, ten years later it had increased to 758, ten years later still to 3,138, and in 1892 to 15,938, and including probationers to 43,933.

Of the German societies, Basle was the first to despatch missionaries to aid in the conquest of southern Asia, and sent them forth the year after the unwilling Company was compelled to tolerate their presence, that is, in 1834. The district chosen lies far to the south upon the Malabar Coast. A force of 129 Europeans is maintained, with 113 native pastors, evangelists and catechists. The communicants number 5,993 and the native Christians 11,365. In the numerous schools are found 6,453 pupils. Gossner's Society followed in 1845, choosing Chota Nagpore as a field, and the degraded Khols as the objects of self-denying endeavor. For years no fruit appeared, the Mutiny brought much disaster, while in 1869 came a lamentable schism. But before this latter calamity befell, the mission had been visited by a work of grace "overwhelming, and rarely experienced." The converts now number some 30,000. The Leipsic Society fell heir to the Danish Tranquebar mission in 1847, and in that vicinity has ever since been active. Twenty-nine missionaries are found ministering to about 13,500 communicants, and to 4,817 children in the schools.

Especial mention must be made of the missions of certain societies which have begun work in times comparatively recent, or whose working force has been but small. The Evangelical Lutherans (General Synod) entered India in 1842 occupying Guntur in the Madras Presidency. Upwards of 4,000 children are taught in the schools, and nearly 7,000 communicants are gathered in the churches. In 1855 the United Presbyterians of the United States appeared in India, and five years later their ecclesiastical brethren of the same name in Scotland followed, while the two together chose the northwestern portion of the great peninsula as a work field, and have cultivated the same with thoroughness until this day. The toil of the one has been rewarded with 3,894 church members, a Christian community numbering 10,632, and 5,824 pupils in the schools; and the other with 526 church members and 5,413 pupils. The American Reformed (Dutch) having co-operated with the American Board from the beginning, determined in 1858 to engage in independent work, and the Arcot mission in Madras Presidency was turned over to them. Nor has this portion of the Lord's heritage suffered in the least in their hands. The double task of converting and training has been diligently and wisely attended to, and with these results: Communicants 1,981, native Christians 6,504, pupils in the schools 5,517.

No statement of what has been undertaken for the evangelization of India would be at all complete, which did not include some mention of medical missions, and woman's work, in both of which the last two decades have seen a remarkable enlargement. The female half of the population is found in a condition especially deplorable, and utterly inaccessible to all ordinary agencies. As far back as 1835, Miss Wakefield, a missionary sent out by the Society for Promoting Female Education in the East, succeeded in entering two or three zenanas in Calcutta, and other women followed until in 1843 one was appointed for this specific work. After the Mutiny came a marked enlargement. Mrs. Mullens also aroused a deep interest; various societies were organized to carry light and joy to Hindu homes, and now twenty-two are united in the sacred task. In 1890 the number of foreign and Eurasian women employed was 711, with 3,278 native Christians in co-operation; 40,518 zenanas were open with 32,659 pupils; in 1,673 schools, of which 166 were boarding schools, there were 71,500 pupils, or including those in zenanas, 104,159.

It is to the true glory of the government that it has undertaken so much upon the physical side of the public weal, and its abundant good works in this direction inure to the advancement of Christianity in the land. There are in all 1,641 public institutions for the relief of suffering and the healing of disease, in which in 1893 were treated 265,000 in-door and 11,987,000 out-door patients. In 48 hospitals and dispensaries for women, 9 of them being in native states, 412,591 received treatment. There are besides 26 lunatic asylums, and 23 leper hospitals. Vaccination is compulsory, and some

5,700,000 a year are shield d from a disease which carries off about 125,000 annually. In 1885 the Countess Dufferin formed the Association for Supplying Female Medical Aid to the Women of India, and so generous was the response in Great Britain, and elsewhere, to her appeals that a fund amounting to £81,000 ($410,-000,) is now in hand, 103 women with thorough medical training are at work in its 30 hospitals and 20 dispensaries, while 200 more are under training as nurses and physicians in India, and others also in England; and in 1892 nearly 460,000 women, afflicted with bodily ills, received counsel and medicine. The number of missionary physicians is 76, and 28 of them are women. The first woman to enter this calling was Miss Swain, who in 1869 was sent out by her sisters of the American Methodist Episcopal Church, though she had been before appointed to the same work by the Woman's Union Missionary Society, and opened a hospital in Bareilly in the Northwest Provinces. It was not long after that the nawab of Rampore, a Mohammedan prince, bestowed for her use the munificent donation of forty-two acres, together with certain large buildings worth $15,000. The rapid development of woman's work, which is doing so much to hasten the day of redemption to truth and righteousness, appears in the fact that while at the first Conference at Allahabad, 1872-3, the sex was altogether unrepresented, at the second held ten years later, at Calcutta, there were 181 women, to 249 men among the members. However, though two had been appointed to prepare papers, it was not thought proper to have them presented by female lips. But ten years later still, at Bombay, where only 263 men were in attendance, and 276 women, the latter were admitted to full equality in every particular.

These figures which follow will show some of the results accruing at the close of a century from all the co-operating influences and instrumentalities and methods of work. They relate to the facts as these existed at the close of 1890 and were prepared for the recent conference which met at Bombay. The tables have been corrected so as to include the Baptist work in Burmah.

Missionary Work in India.

Societies.	Foreign Ordained Agents.	Native Ordained Agents.	Native Lay Preachers.	Native Christians.	Communicants.
1. Baptist	270	375	853	285,000	85,473
2. Congregational	76	84	582	77,466	13,775
3. Church of England	203	249	870	193,363	52,377
4. Presbyterian	149	64	520	34,395	11,128
5. Methodist	110	116	561	32,381	15,782
6. Lutheran	125	48	365	62,838	24,207
7. Moravian, Friends, and 8. Isolated Missions.	16	10	13	398	114
9. Women's Missionary Societies	—	—	—	150	30
10. Supplement	49	11	155	25,548	11,508
Total in India	998	957	4369	710,000	214,394

Woman's Work in India.

	Female Agents.		Boarding-Schools.			Day-schools.		Zenanas.	
	Foreign & Eurasian.	Native Christians.	Schools.	Pupils.	Orphans.	Schools.	Pupils.	Houses.	Pupils.
Church of England	223	988	60	2599	432	411	15,129	11,109	4361
Presbyterian	112	515	20	788	152	324	12,814	1612	2959
Congregational	38	390	18	662	103	188	9554	11,782	4120
Baptist	108	310	15	705	229	99	5276	3244	2468
Methodist	113	616	32	1738	555	364	11,687	7893	14,858
Lutheran	2	136	10	407	128	18	1859	293	21
Zenana Bible and Medical Mission	56	161	2	47	1	54	2191	3995	3063
Miscellaneous	59	162	9	356	184	49	3904	585	812
Total	711	3278	166	7302	1784	1507	62,414	40,513	32,659

It may seem to some that the results of missionary effort in India are discouragingly and scandalously small at the end of a hundred years, and after the expenditure of so much money, and the toil of such a host of devoted and heroic men and women. Only 710,000 (or only 2,285,000, if Roman Catholics are included). But these considerations must be taken into account. The territory under view is so vast. The Roman Empire was smaller by some 300,000 square miles, and yet that realm of the Cæsars was not conquered until after three centuries. The Queen's dominions in southern Asia approach Europe for area, and that continent required a millennium of most arduous endeavor before heathenism was banished. And even Great Britain was not evangelized in less than ten generations (600-900 A. D.) Then the population is great beyond conception, approximating to 300,000,000, or one-fifth of the human race, or three times greater than that of Rome when at her greatest. In addition, we must remember what a heterogeneous and chaotic mass of races, religions, and languages are found between the Himalayas and the Cape. How herculean the task of mastering these tongues, translating into them the Word of Life, and creating a Christian literature. An ancient and complex civilization was in full possession, and was thoroughly permeated by a religious faith and practice much older than Christianity. Or rather, if possible, made harder to uproot by long contact and struggle with Mohammedanism, one of the very sturdiest foes the gospel ever met. Then there are the aboriginal tribes sunk in the lowest depths of ignorance and superstition, with the pariahs, whose degradation is scarcely exceeded by that of the

Hottentot, or Patagonian. Probably caste presents as formidable a barrier to the advent and increase of New Testament virtues as any social or religious institution to be found upon earth.

As if these hindrances were not enough, India lies mainly in the tropics, the heat is almost unendurable by foreigners, and great loss of life has marked the history of missions. Here is no mean rival to Africa as a cemetery for such as counted not their lives dear, if their Lord might be glorified by the redemption of souls from sin. Moreover, the first half of the century was marked by frequent wars and general commotion, such as the struggles with Hyder Ali and Tippoo Sultan and the ferocious Marathis, the two campaigns against the Sikhs (1841-9) and the three against the Burmese, and the Mutiny. About half of India is yet in the hands of native princes, either Hindu or Moslem; until 1841 Christianity was wholly excluded from these, and has been much opposed and hindered since that date, and even yet is under the ban in some of them. But worse was the insane and unaccountable opposition of the East India Company, which lasted almost to the end of Carey's life, and its effects for evil were felt for two decades longer. Though the representatives of Christianity were "interlopers" subject to imprisonment and transportation, and when their presence was tolerated were shamefully fettered and muzzled, the abominations of idolatry were countenanced and patronized as a source of gain. Suttee was winked at, and infanticide, and hook-swinging, and Thuggism, but one who received Christian baptism might be robbed of his property in the courts, etc. **The spectacle** of the representatives of **a**

Christian nation repudiating and scorning the religion they professed naturally increased the odium and contempt already cherished towards Christianity. It was not until after 1858 that these fearful scandals came to an end. And finally, the entire century just past has been emphatically a period of pioneering, exploring and laying of foundations. How best to evangelize the nations was an art long since lost by Christendom, and costly experiments were necessary before the wisest methods, and the most potent instrumentalities, could be fashioned and put into operation. So that it is only for about a generation that the kingdom of heaven has had a fair chance to reach the millions of India and work its miracles of blessing. Happily, now the supreme government is conscientiously neutral in matters religious, except that while each one may worship as he will, humanity, decency, and good order must be regarded. It is to be hoped that ere long the shame connected with the legal support given to the traffic in opium and intoxicating liquors may cease, that child marriage may be forbidden by law, and the nautch dances be suppressed.

These peculiar phenomena appearing in connection with the progress of missions in this strange land may well be noticed. Not all the multitudinous races are equally susceptible to the regenerating influences which have been brought to bear. The Aryan and Moslem portion of the people seem to be farthest from salvation, while the great majority of the native Christians have come from the lower castes, the outcasts, and the aboriginal tribes. Wherever found, the Mohammedans are notoriously hard to reach with the gospel message, though hundreds have listened, believed, and honored the truth in their lives. One of this class has recently published a list containing the names of about a hundred and twenty converts of distinction, of whom seventeen are ordained ministers, and from northern and central India alone. Brahmans who accept Jesus as redeemer and king are also few and far between. And not strangely either, for these are the priests and *literati* of Hinduism, self-interest is involved, and they represent the scribes and Pharisees of Christ's day. So far back the question was asked, Have any of the rulers or of the Pharisees believed on Him? And it has always been that, not many wise men after the flesh, not many mighty, not many noble, are called, but the humble and lowly multitude have been the ones to receive most gladly the gift of gifts. It is always, and everywhere, from the lower strata upwards, that the gospel leaven works. Nevertheless, in no small numbers Brahmans have humbled themselves to obedience and trust, and are adorning the gospel by godly lives. The aboriginal races (Dravidian, etc.) like the Tamils, Telugus, Khols, and the Karens and Shans of Burmah, have supplied a relatively large number of converts. And curiously, it is the Madras Presidency which has furnished the bulk of the native Christians to be found upon Indian soil. While of the total of 2,285,000, in Bengal only 182,000 are found, and in Bombay but 170,000, in Madras, of which Tinnevelly and Travancore form a part, and which also holds the most of the Telugus and Tamils, almost three-fourths or, 1,584,000, have been persuaded to turn from the worship of idols to the living God.

CHAPTER XIV.

MISSIONS IN AFRICA; MADAGASCAR.

THIS continent constitutes the greatest of all mission fields. That is, it covers by far the largest area, though both China and India contain a much larger population. Besides, no such vast spaces can elsewhere be found upon the face of the earth, so wholly enshrouded in intellectual and moral darkness so dreadfully dense. For to the midnight of utter ignorance, and superstition, and beastly vice, is added the, if possible, darker midnight of extremest barbarism and savagery. Negro, Hottentot, Bushman, have long been synonyms for the lowest conditions in which humanity is ever found. And to crown all, it was in this most benighted and wretched quarter of the globe that the slave trade wrought its horrors and desolations. And therefore, though for these and other reasons possessing peculiar claims upon Christendom for help, Africa supplies the mission field which is difficult and discouraging beyond any other.

After Asia, the Dark Continent is much the largest of the six. The length is not far from 5,000 miles from north to south, and the width is not much less. The number of square miles of surface is estimated to be 12,000,000, or about one-fourth of the land surface of the globe. Asia covers some 17,000,000 square miles, and the two Americas together nearly the same. The United

States added to Australia would be only half as large as Africa alone, while Europe is only a pigmy by comparison, is only one-third as large, containing but 4,000,000. As the most striking, as well as the most unfortunate physical feature, is found the fact that the interminable coast line is so nearly unbroken, is indented by so few bays, and hence affords so few harbors. In this particular the neighbor continent to the north is at the furthest remove. For while the circumference of the one measures but 15,000 miles, the other is longer by 4,000 miles, though the area is only one-third as great. It follows from this that Africa is the most inaccessible of the earth's great land-spaces. While it is true that no good roads exist between the borders and the remote central portions, and the jungles are dense, all travel must be on foot and all carrying is done on the backs of men, and though the tsetse fly is deadly to horses and cattle, and the fever almost as deadly to those of foreign birth, and cannibal tribes abound; yet the serious absence of safe anchorage and of streams navigable from the ocean far inland, supply the chief reason for the long neglect under which the perishing millions have lain. As to general contour the surface has often, and well, been compared to that of an inverted saucer. Next to the sea is everywhere a low-lying rim, which at no great distance back rises to mountain ranges, and these inclose a boundless plateau. The mean elevation is greater than that of either Europe or Asia, and in spite of their Alps and Himalayas. The altitude of South Africa averages about 2,000 feet, and of the north-central portions about 4,000. The plateau is loftiest in the region of the great lakes. Between the two Nyanzas, in a distance of less than 100 miles, the descent is 2,300 feet, or from 3,800 to 1,500. The highest mountain summits are found to the east of the lakes, Kilimanjaro and Kenia rising to 18,000 feet.

Africa has four great river systems which taken together, comprise a large part of the area of the continent. The Congo carries by far the greatest volume of water to the sea, though the Nile is longest, next follow the Niger and the Zambezi, with the Orange not so very far behind. Rising either in the great lakes, or else in the same general region, of the four streams one flows northward to the Mediterranean, two empty their floods into the Atlantic, and the other ends in the Indian Ocean. But these and all lesser rivers, and for precisely the same reason, are absolutely worthless for navigation between the outside world and the vast interior. The bulk of their course is upon the elevated central plateau, from which they must descend to sea level, and besides must break through the mountain barrier which about the entire circumference separates the interior from the coast plain. And so, for a long distance during the lower part of their course, rapids and waterfalls abound. Thus the Nile has its three cataracts, and its Murchison and Ripon Falls farther towards its source, the Congo has 250 miles of broken navigation, the Zambezi has it Victoria Falls, etc., etc. Three immense areas are found from within which no streams make their way to the ocean. One is the famous Sahara, which stretches from the Nile to the Atlantic, and from the Mediterranean to the Soudan, and covers something like 4,000,000 square miles, about one-third of the entire continent, or a space as large as Europe.

Another lies about Lake Tchad, and a third about Lake Ngami.

The remarkable lake system found in east-central Africa constitutes one of the leading physical features, a collection of bodies of fresh water surpassed, or equalled, nowhere except in our own country, and with only our Superior greater than the greatest of the number. Victoria Nyanza has an area of 30,000 square miles to Huron's 20,000, and Tanganyika has an area of 10,000. One other characteristic feature may be mentioned. Stretching ten degrees north of the equator and ten degrees south, and entirely across the continent, say 1,000 miles by 2,500, is a forest great and terrible. Proceeding north or south from this, a broad stretch of open park-like country is entered, and this again shades off into boundless pastures, both towards the Desert and the Cape. Next in order lie barren regions, Sahara and Kalahari, with only the slightest rainfall, and finally, whether in the Barbary States or in the southern portions, agricultural lands are found. It will be noted that the equator crosses Africa at no great distance below the center, and hence the bulk of the continent is intertropical. The climate is so deadly to the unacclimated on account of the extreme heat, taken together with the dense forests, and the exceedingly heavy rainfall.

As to the population, how large it is, nothing whatever is certainly known. All statements made concerning this matter are at best but guess work, and the estimates differ by several scores of millions. Thus, it has been common to set the figure at 200,000,000, and sometimes as high as 300,000,000, while others would diminish the sum by half. The latest calculations made by Wagner and Supan, as competent statisticians as the world contains, give 164,000,000 as the most probable number, though Ravenstein, another practised and painstaking authority, would reduce it to 130,000,000. According to the Statesman's Year Book, whose judgment for years has been thought to approach the infallible, the population is 168,000,000. Dividing the whole into sections, we may give the result roughly as follows: north Africa 20,000,000, the Sahara region 3,000,000, north-tropical, or Soudan, 100,000,000, south-tropical 35,000,000, and South Africa 5,000,000.

It will be profitable to take note of some of the principal divisions existing among the population as to race. Accordingly to the common apprehension all native-born dwellers in Africa are Negroes, than which nothing can be further from the fact. At the north are found millions of Moors, Berbers, Arabs and Turks, and at the northeast other millions of Copts, Nubians and Abyssinians; the latter sufficiently black, but by no means Negroes. The genuine Ethiopian is marked by wooley hair, a flat nose, thick lips, a receding forehead and projecting jaw, a flat foot and long heel, and his home is found only in the Soudan, or north-central Africa, to the north of the Congo, to the west of the great lakes. This part of the continent is most thickly inhabited, and contains nearly half of the population. Further south dwell the great Bantu race, their habitat extending from the Atlantic to the Indian Ocean. Beyond these lies the country of the Bushmen, the Kaffirs, and the Hottentots, who differ radically from all the rest. Dr. R. N. Cust, an excellent authority, gives the number of African languages as 438, with 153 dialects in addition.

If the population be divided according to religion, about 1,000,000 are Jews dwelling largely in the Barbary States. Of Christians there are some 8,000,000, of whom less than one-third are Roman Catholics, found for the most part in Algeria and the Portuguese settlements in Angola and Mozambique; something over one-third Protestants, composed mainly of British and Dutch colonists in South Africa; and the rest are Abyssinians, and Copts in Egypt. Then nearly one-third of the inhabitants are believed to be Mohammedans. These have been steadily increasing and spreading themselves for nearly twelve centuries. Entering from the northeast as traders and slave-stealers they have pushed across the Sahara and up the Nile, across the Red Sea and down the eastern coast, until Islam is known and honored as far as the Congo and the great lakes, in Zanzibar, Mozambique, and even in Cape Colony. Probably 40,000,000, and perhaps 60,000,000, of the dwellers in the Dark Continent are at least nominal followers of the Prophet of Arabia, and have adopted to a greater or less extent the ideas and practices of the Koran. The Arab portion of the Moslems represent the last remnant of the former host of slave-dealers, and their work takes rank among the foremost specimens of existing inhumanity. These pitiless men-stealers make systematic war on region after region, with wholesale burning, slaughter, and capture. The surviving victims are chained together in gangs and started for the coast, across the Great Desert or towards Arabia. Infants, the sick, and feeble, are killed without ceremony, and it is alleged that not more than three or four per cent. is left alive at the dreadful journey's end. Finally, not far from two-thirds of

Africa's millions live and die in the depths of abject paganism. What religion they have is but a degrading superstition. No god higher than a fetish is worshiped; they offer sacrifices to spirits, and wear charms to ward off evil, and to secure the attainment of their desires.

A few words are in order concerning the twin curses under which the Negro, the Bantu and the Hottentot alike have groaned and died for long centuries, and for which Christian lands are mainly responsible. It is estimated that in the four hundred years during which the slave trade lasted, not less than 40,000,000 Africans were seized to be sold into slavery, the woes and torments included of the "middle passage." The bulk of these were taken from about four thousand miles of the western coast. Happily that day of general sin and shame is past. But another form of ignominy and iniquity, whose result to Africa is perhaps even greater for damage and woe, remains and appears to be on the increase. If slavery slew its thousands, rum is leading to destruction its tens of thousands of poor victims. The figures rise to a magnitude which is amazing, and appalling. At one port a single missionary, and 50,000 barrels of whiskey, were landed at the same time. All vessels bound for West and South Africa, coming from Europe and America, stop at Madeira. And this is the list of liquors which passed through in one week! 28,000 cases of Irish whisky; 30,000 cases of brandy; 30,000 cases of Old Tom; 36,000 barrels of rum; 800,000 demijohns of rum; 24,000 butts of rum; 15,000 barrels of absinthe; and 960,000 cases of gin. The natives so ignorant and so weak, are helpless in the presence of this foe. Their evil passions are still further inflamed, and they are dragged down to yet deeper depths of degradation and savagery, while the best that the handful of missionaries are able to accomplish is in great danger of being neutralized. In a few states in South Africa, from which intoxicating liquors are excluded by the strong arm of law, the progress of degraded tribes in all good things is surprising, and many of the chiefs would gladly keep the rum-seller far from their borders if possessed of the ability. On one occasion seventy chiefs united in affirming: "Brandy is a fearfully bad thing. We should become wild animals here if it were introduced."

Before taking up the story of the modern attempts to evangelize this continent, an outline of the course of discovery and exploration will be useful as an introduction. Though, through Egypt and Carthage, Africa is among the oldest of lands, in the Bible narrative sometimes almost rivaling Asia, yet, taken as a whole, it stands among the very newest and least known. Only twenty years ago the Encyclopædia Brittanica could affirm with truth: "As yet the only portions of which we possess any approach to an accurate topographical knowledge are, Cape Colony and Natal under British rule in the south; the French colony of Algeria; the Portuguese possession of Angola; and Egypt and Tunis, dependent on Turkey, in the north." It was effectually shut up against entrance by the desert upon one side, and by the ocean upon the other three. Ancient navigators did not dare to venture so far from home upon such pathless wastes. One of the greatest physical problems for the philosophers of antiquity related to the mysterious Nile, from whence it came, and the cause of its annual overflow, without which Egypt would be absolutely barren of vegetation and uninhabitable, but by whose potent influence almost never failing it was the garden and granary of the Grecian and Roman world. The Arabs appear to have made voyages of discovery at an early date down the eastern coast, as far at least as the latitude of Madagascar. By the middle of the fifteenth century the Portuguese began to creep gradually southward along the western side, reaching Cape Verd in 1446, Sierra Leone in 1463, the mouth of the Congo in 1484, doubled the Cape of Good Hope in 1486, and in 1497 Vasco da Gama explored the east coast from Natal to Cape Guardafui. In 1652 the Dutch founded a colony at the extreme southern extremity of the continent, to which some thousands of Huguenots were added after their expulsion from France. After a hundred and fifty years (1795-1806) Cape Colony became a British possession. In 1787 Sierra Leone was settled under the auspices of a British company by Africans who had gained their freedom in America by the chances of the Revolutionary war, and constituted the first attempt to introduce civilization and Christianity to a region which hitherto had been visited only by slave-stealers in the pursuit of their nefarious occupation.

To Mungo Park (1795-1806) belongs the honor of being the pioneer in modern African exploration. He made two journeys towards the interior, entering from the west through Senegambia, and crossing to the upper waters of the Niger, penetrated as far as Timbuctoo and was killed by the natives. Hence, practically, all that we know of this continent has been given to the world within a hundred years, or since Carey founded the first missionary society and led the way to the world's evangelization.

And further, the great bulk of the explorations belong to the last half of the century. It is almost wholly during the memory of multitudes yet living that, under the love of adventure, or love of gain, in the interests of science, philanthopy, or religion, by the score and hundred, and from all points of the compass, the daring and venturesome have been pouring in. It was as late as 1830 that the Landers took up the task which Park had left unfinished, and traced the Niger to its mouth. In 1857, and again in 1865, Du Chaillu pushed hither and thither through the unknown in the same region. From the south the Dutch Boers migrated steadily further and further back from the coast. In 1817 Moffat began to combine exploration with proclamation of the glad tidings, and entered a field far to the north of the Orange River. Next followed Livingstone (1840-73), the greatest name of all in this connection, and one standing for a marvelous career of self-denial and devotion, of endurance and achievement, consecrated completely to the tremendous task of revealing to the civilized world the horrid secrets of this vast *terra incognita*, and based upon his famous dictum that "the end of geographical discovery is the beginning of missionary enterprise." In 1849 he crossed the Kalahari Desert and discovered Lake Ngami. In 1853-7 he advanced northward to the Zambezi, turned westward to the Atlantic, and then facing about, made his way eastward to the Indian Ocean, descending the Zambezi to its mouth, and among the rest discovering the famous Victoria Falls. In 1859 he ascended the Shiré to its source in Lake Nyassa, returning later to explore the entire circumference of the latter. In 1866-73 he penetrated still further, to Lake Tanganyika and the region lying beyond its western shores, in eager search of the head streams of the Congo. Stanley found him at Ujiji, in 1871; spent five months in his company drinking in his noble spirit, later sent him supplies, and two years afterwards the prince of Africa's benefactors was found dead upon his knees near Lake Bangweolo.

But years before this, Krapf and Rebmann, German missionaries in the employ of the English Church Society, had entered East Africa from Mombasa and Zanzibar, were the first of Europeans to set eyes upon Kilimanjaro and Kenia, and heard reports of the existence of a vast body of water further towards the interior, known then as Uniamesi. In 1847 Burton and Speke penetrated to Tanganyika, and pushed thence to Victoria Nyanza, while in 1860 Speke and Grant proved this greatest of African lakes to be the source of the Nile. In 1875 Cameron crossed from Zanzibar to Benguella, and the year following Stanley entered upon his journey of a thousand days lacking one, which brought him at length to the mouth of the Congo. On account of this and other distinguished achievements, his name must stand hard after Livingstone's among those whose most arduous labors have made possible the coming of the Kingdom in these boundless realms of darkness. And finally, meantime, from the north, yet others were pressing inward towards the centre. In 1849, the same year in which Lake Ngami was discovered, Richardson and Barth set forth across the Sahara for Lake Tchad, but the former died when in the midst of his undertaking, and the latter continued his journeys through the Soudan for seven years. In 1864-7 Rolhfs was in the same region, entering from Tripoli, and making his exit to the southwest, reaching the ocean at the Bight of

Benin. Only a few names from a long list have been given, and in order that, in some measure at least, might be presented the remarkable phenomenon of African exploration upon which this generation has been permitted to gaze. The changes wrought, the astounding additions made to human knowledge are not unworthy to be compared with those resulting from the ventures of Columbus and Magellan. The task accomplished was vastly greater. What appalling difficulties and perils have been faced and overcome, what sufferings have been endured, and how many have laid down their lives. Only about forty years ago Krapf put on paper this suggestion, which, no doubt, to many of his contemporaries wore the look of a wild dream, but which to us has been changed into real matter of fact; and yet, in many respects, what an ancient look it wears. In 1850, giving a view of the great results to which his discoveries might lead, he wrote: "When once the time has fully come that the Hamitic race shall be made acquainted with the gospel, and be received into the family of God's children upon earth, the high roads of Africa will take every observer by surprise. It will then be manifested that the facilities of communication on the African continent are not inferior to those of Europe, Asia and America. God's providence has certainly paved the way for the speedy accomplishment of his sublime designs. The Niger will carry the messengers of peace to the various states of Nigritia, while the Tshadda, together with the Congo, will convey them to the western center of Africa, towards the northern tribes of Uniamesi. The different branches of the Nile will lead the missionaries towards the same center from the north and northeast, while the Jub and Dana will bring them in from East Africa, and the Kilimani [Zambezi] will usher them in from the south. The sources of these great rivers are not so distant from each other as our present geographical knowledge would lead us to believe. Shall we propose, therefore, and undertake the formation of a mission chain, linking together the eastern and western coasts of Africa? or shall we follow up the water courses of the continent, by establishing missions at the sources and estuaries of those great rivers? The Tshadda, the Congo, the Nile and the Kilimani rivers take their rise either from the great lake in Uniamesi, or very near it. And if the communication with Central Africa shall be found so simple and so easy, why should we question the speedy spread of Christianity and Christian civilization in Africa?" This same intrepid evangelist-explorer proceeded to propose to the Gaboon mission the formation of a continental mission-line to connect with his in the neighborhood of Zanzibar. Commenting upon this proposition some four years later, a missionary authority suggests: "The place of meeting would be upon some one of the central mountains which divide the great basins of the Nile, the Zaire and the small rivers running into the Indian Ocean. They may be from eight hundred to a thousand miles from either coast, and Krapf and Rebmann have explored some three or four hundred miles of the eastern portion. Providence is opening wide the door."

Among recent events of exceeding great importance in relation to the redemption of Africa must be named the astounding parceling out, or partition, of the bulk of the continent among the various powers of Europe, a wholesale appropriation of territory entirely without an equal in history. The whole procedure is high-handed in the extreme, and affords ample justification for the severe though witty affirmation of Dr. Cust that, whereas, " in former years Europeans used to steal Africans from Africa, now they are trying to steal Africa from the Africans." And yet, at many points, it cannot but result in benefits unspeakable to the natives. The beginning of the scheme may be said to date from the setting up of the Congo Free State by the imposing Berlin Conference in 1884, when fourteen governments, also four hundred and fifty African "kings" not refusing assent to the same, fixed certain boundaries, rules and regulations, and placed King Leopold II. of Belgium in the seat of supreme power. At divers conventions held since, various "claims" to territory have been considered, allowed, or rejected, with this as the general outcome at the present stage of the business. The South African Republic and the Orange Free State had been in being for some years.

	AREA.	POPULATION.
Great Britain,	2,500,000	40,000,000
France,	2,500,000	10,000,000
Congo Free State,	900,000	17,000,000
Germany,	900,000	5,000,000
Portugal,	750,000	4,500,000
Italy,	320,000	5,500,000
Spain,	250,000	150,000
Total, Africa,	12,000,000	165,000,000
Left in native hands,	2,500,000	85,000,000

One other class of invaluable aids to the evangelization of Africa remains to be mentioned. After the explorers had completed their indispensable work, by banishing the mystery and uncovering the contents hidden from the beginning of time, and after the famous partition had made certain the suppression of the slave trade, and the worst forms of savagery, as well as civil and social order and security to life and property, a further step forward became a necessity. As we have seen, one of the most serious obstacles to the entrance of civilization and Christianity had been found in the unusual paucity of good harbors upon the fifteen thousand miles of coast, and the even more fatal lack of rivers navigable from the sea into the remote interior. These physical barriers alone were next to prohibitory. The task of conquering for the kingdom was well-nigh too great to be undertaken. By some effectual method the way of the Lord must be prepared, and in the desert a highway for our God be made straight, and that so the feet of the messengers of glad tidings might enter, and traverse these boundless realms of darkness. And by a strange providence, in the very nick of time, what was required had been prepared by the science and mechanical skill of the nineteenth century. All unconsciously to themselves, Watt, and Stevenson, and Morse, were missionaries. As a result of what the Spirit of God wrought out through their intellects, already upon the great African lakes, Nyassa, Tanganyika, and Nyanza, several steam vessels are found, and continually moving from shore to shore and from island to island, so that these inland seas are priceless helps to travel, and transportation of goods. Upon the Congo, with its numerous tributaries affording abundance of navigable water extending to the very heart of the continent, the Free State maintains nineteen steamers, seven below the rapids and twelve above, while others are made use of by various missions. The Niger too, and the Zambezi, and the Shirè, are traversed, in the same fashion, for the furtherance of the Gospel. And ere long the terrible endurance, and strain, and peril of months, will be exchanged for a journey unattended with any special difficulty, while with exposure avoided, and the comforts of civilized life secured, the assaults of the deadly fever may much better be resisted. But even more. The locomotive is the matchless vanquisher of time, and space, and physical barriers, and long since began to crowd its way irresistibly from various points upon the seaboard towards the centre. The French are steadily extending the rails through Algeria, in the direction of Lake Tchad and their possessions upon the Gulf of Guinea. The long stretch of rapids separating the lower from the upper Congo will soon be conquered by the iron horse. Another railroad is slowly advancing from Benguela towards Bihe, and the head waters of the Zambezi, while South Africa rejoices in the possession of several thousand miles of track. Still another road will presently be completed between Beira upon the Indian Ocean and the gold fields of Mashonaland, while surveys have been made for one which shall connect Uganda with the east coast. And finally, largely through the superb statesmanship and enterprise of Sir Cecil Rhodes, a trans-continental telegraph line is under construction, to extend from Table Mountain past the great lakes to the mouth of the Nile. And these examples are but specimens; they represent only the insignificant beginning of marvelous good things to come for the redemption of Africa.

The stupendous task of redeeming Africa by the proclamation of the Gospel began under most hopeful auspices as far back as the day of Pentecost, when certain from Egypt and the parts of Libya about Cyrene were present in Jerusalem to share in the gift of the Holy Ghost. Another African, the eunuch of Ethiopia (perhaps Nubia and perhaps Abyssinia), was introduced into the kingdom of heaven not long after by Philip. And, a little later still, we hear of Apollos of Alexandria, so fervid and eloquent. Though it is not known exactly in what way, or by whom, at an early period the entire southern coast of the Mediterranean was dotted with Christian churches, while Alexandria and Carthage became leading centers for the new faith, with such famous names as Clement, and Origen, Cyril, Athanasius, Augustine and many more, as theologians and preachers. Abyssinia was Christianized, after a fashion, about the middle of the fourth century, and ever since the church has maintained its existence in that country, that is, it has had a name to live. But the faith and practice of the African saints were never very pure, and at their best contained large admixtures of paganism. In particular, the Egyptian church went far astray in the paths of false doctrine. As a result, as everywhere else in the Orient, in the fall of the Roman Empire, and later after the campaigns of Islam for world-wide dominion, the remarkable conquests of the truth were well-nigh utterly lost. The Copts however of the Nile valley, though suffering terrible persecutions, and losing multitudes by apostasy to Mohammedanism, maintained their organization, and still occupy their ancient seats. For almost twelve hundred years no Christian voice was lifted to call this continent to repentance.

As to modern missionary work in Africa, the story is one full of deepest interest, with chapters overflowing with passages most pathetic and even tragic. It is a long and sad, but thrilling narrative of heroic undertaking, attended with a world of suffering, sickness, death, and apparent failure. The steps and stages of the divine task were in outline something as follows. It will be convenient to make five divisions of the theme, and to speak of evangelizing efforts begun and carried forward in the following order: In the southern portions of the continent, upon the west coast, in the Congo valley, in the region lying about the great lakes, and lastly on the northern border.

South Africa.

This portion of Africa was naturally entered first by the heralds of the cross, because here first European colonies had been established. And for various reasons missions have been most numerous and successful to the south of the line adjoining Walfish Bay with Delagoa Bay. The latitude is that of the south temperate zone, and hence the climate is healthy and invigorating. Besides, for nearly two centuries and a half, civilized government and society have been steadily extending from the coast far into the interior. The demoralization of the slave trade has happily been absent, though the Dutch scrupled not to reduce the Hottentots to servitude. Many thousands of European inhabitants are now scattered over a wide area, with liberal additions of Hindus, Chinese and Malays, attracted by the rich mines and the fine agricultural resources. To meet the civil needs of this population two British colonial governments have been set up, Cape Colony and Natal; two areas are under native Dutch rule, the Orange Free State and the South African Republic; and there is the roomy domain of the British South Africa Company. Or, if we include the east coast as far north as the lower Zambezi, and the west coast up to the mouth of the Congo, we must add the Portuguese provinces of Lorenzo-Marques and Angola, and German Southwest Africa. Concerning this entire region Dr. Cust is of the opinion that there is no other mission field like it, with so little to fear from climate or people, and he declares that none except the first man to enter it (the Moravian, Schmidt) can lay any claim to heroism, and his antagonists were not pagan Bantus or Hottentots, but Dutch Christians.

The Moravians were the pioneers in bringing the blessed good news, Africa ranking among the most attractive of areas for these queer souls, whose characteristic principle it has been from the first to prefer toil in the midst of environments most forbidding, discouraging, and desolate. And their earliest mission had been located among the degraded slaves of the West Indies. It was nearly a century after Cape Colony was founded, and some twenty-five years before Carey was born, that George Schmidt was dispatched from Herrnhut to make Christ known to the benighted. For years already he had been a great sufferer for the Gospel's sake, having lain for six years in a Bohemian prison, and a portion of the time in chains so heavy that he was crippled for life. Arriving at Cape Town in 1737, he made his errand known, but was met with amazement and incredulity, and afterwards with derision and scorn. That is, not at all by the poor heathen, but by the Dutch, people and preachers together. And because, forsooth, he had determined to cast in his lot with the Hottentots, whom the stanch Calvinists held in measureless contempt, and had enslaved. It was a generation or two later, and by another missionary, that this notice was seen over a church door, " Dogs and Hottentots not admitted." Presently he made his way to Bavian's Kloof, about sixty miles to the east. Being advanced in years, and unable to learn their language, Schmidt essayed to impart instruction in the Dutch tongue. Such love and devotion were not lost on the natives, and in due season a few were baptized who seemed evidently to have turned from their sins to God, but with the greatest offence to the "Reformed" in those parts. The scandal was two-fold. Brutish creatures, whom they had reduced to bondage, had been received into the church, and by one who being a Moravian heretic had no authority to administer the ordinances. After seven years of most faithful and self-denying toil, and when a company of nearly fifty converts had been gathered, the civil authorities gave command to cease from such unlawful business. Returning to Holland to plead in behalf of his beloved Hottentots, permission was refused to enter the Colony again. The feeble flock waited long and anxiously for his return, and little by little were scattered for lack of a shepherd. It was fifty years later before the mission was renewed, and when in 1792, the memorable date of Carey's beginning, three Moravians revisited Bavian's Kloof, only one person was found, an aged woman, who remembered Schmidt. From this time to the present the work has been maintained, and one new station after another has been occupied. In particular Gnadenthal among the Kaffirs is a noted spot. And among the many other Christlike deeds in that region must be named the opening of an asylum for lepers at Hemel en Aarde. Such measures of success have been vouchsafed that the work is divided into the Western and Eastern Province, and includes 26 stations and out-stations, with a force of 33 men and the same number of women, together with a large company of native assistants. The churches contain 3,598 members, while about 14,000 are reckoned as adherents. In the schools are found 2,813 pupils.

The next missionary enterprise in behalf of Africa was begun in 1799 by the London Society, and with the distinguished Dr. Vanderkemp as leader. A graduate of the University of Leyden, for sixteen years he was an officer in the army of the Netherlands, and withal in those days an out and out infidel. Later a course of study was pursued in Edinburgh, followed by years of practice as a physician. Losing his wife and only child by a shocking accident, of a sudden, and with all the fervor and whole-souled determination of Paul, Jesus was accepted as Lord, though past fifty he offered himself as bearer of glad tidings to the lowest of the low that wear the human form, and by choice sailed for the Cape in a convict ship bound for New South Wales with some hundreds of desperate characters on board. The scene of his toil was mainly at Graaf Reinet and in the vicinity of Algoa Bay. It was a time of general disturbance, since Dutch dominion was about to end, and British sway was to follow. Much trouble was suffered from the opposition of the civil rulers, and more from the prejudice and hatred of the Boers. But he gave himself without stint, and with tireless energy, to the betterment of the Hottentots, and with several associates to co-operate, was able to win to a remarkable degree their confidence and affection, as well as to gather some hundreds of converts, whom he trained not only to piety and godliness, but also in the useful arts of industry. After his death in 1811 the work was carried on for a season, but presently on account of various changes of population, etc., was relinquished. In 1818 the same society sent out Robert Moffat, one of the chief of civilizers and Christianizers in Africa, to begin a term of more than fifty years of service, and with Kuruman in Bechuanaland as the theatre for his activity, as well as with Africaner, once a murderer, robber and outlaw, on whose head a price was set, as the most famous trophy of divine grace. In 1840 followed Livingstone to the same mission, to the north of the Orange River, and some 700 miles from Cape Town, though ere long pressing forward further into the interior, and at length entering on his magnificent career as explorer. Not especially skilled or successful as an evangelizer in a direct and personal way, he yet wrought wonders in opening the path for others. His was the rare genius of the statesman-missionary. His view was prophetic. His life-scheme embraced nothing less than the entire continent. He would uncover to the gaze of the world the appalling facts in the case, and so stir men's convictions as to raise an irresistible crusade, against slavery first, but also against the universal paganism and barbarism. And all this he achieved. Other missions have been since founded in Cape Colony, in Kaffirland, and Matabeleland, so that there are now four in all, manned with 16 missionaries and their wives, with scores of trained natives to assist, while the pupils in the schools number about 2,000, the church members some 3,000 and the native Christians 8,000.

The English Wesleyans were the next to enter South Africa, despatching their first representative in 1814, and appointing Barnabas Shaw the year following. The Wesleyan doctrine was in bad repute at the Cape, and he was instructed by those in high civil station that his presence was not needed, or desired, thereabouts. Thereupon he set forth northward to find room for his proclamation beyond the pale of civilization. And it was when on this first journey, and after traveling three hundred miles, that he met a Hottentot chief who had already advanced two hundred miles in search of white men to teach his people. Then together the man of God and the heathen seeker after truth entered Namaqualand where the Gospel call was long sounded out. In addition to his limitless courage and fervor, Mr. Shaw was possessed of unwonted skill to instruct the poor creatures about him to do many useful things. In particular, a plow which he fashioned with his own hands was the cause of the greatest wonder, and on one occasion after watching it in operation, an aged polygamist exclaimed with fine enthusiasm, "Why, it will do in a day the work of ten wives!" The Wesleyan work in the southern portion of the continent is found in the Transvaal and Swaziland, and contains 23 missionaries and assistants and 92 native ministers, 222 native local preachers, 64 chapels and 115 other preaching places, 4,000 church members and 32,000 attendants upon public worship.

The Paris Society (*Société des Missions Evangelique*) entered South Africa in 1829. Receiving no welcome from the Boers of Cape Colony, the missionaries, like so many others, crossed the Orange River to find a field containing no foes to resist except from among the heathen, and at first fixed themselves at no great distance from Kuruman and Moffat. But many vicissitudes were in store, one station after another was abandoned until finally they found rest and prosperity in Basutoland, a small country hemmed in by Cape Colony, Transvaal and Natal. A chief of this tribe, after making the purchase of a gun, was told by the merchant that there was something better to buy, the Gospel to wit, which brings not death but life, and was informed where this doctrine could be found. As a result, he sent a message to the French missionaries, who received it as from God. Progress was slow for a long period, but patient continuance in well doing finally brought reward in rich ingathering. The last ten years have seen the number of native Christians doubled, and the number of pupils quadrupled, so that now of the former there are 8,969, and of the latter 15,460. The work is carried on by 27 European toilers, 3 native pastors and 81 native evangelists.

Three German societies share in the burden of proclaiming Christ in this quarter of the globe, the Rhenish beginning work in 1830, the Berlin following four years later, and the Hermannsburg in 1858, from the call of a Bechuana chief and a letter from the Dutch authorities. The general German method is to secure large tracts of land, gather colonies from home, or from among the natives, and to carry on a large number of useful occupations, and thus, so far as possible, to make the mission self-supporting. How wisely and zealously toil has been bestowed appears in the fact that the combined force of 172 missionaries have gathered upwards of 10,000 pupils into the schools, 30,207 into the churches, and almost 60,000 have put themselves under Christian instruction. The Berlin Society has organized six synods whose names indicate how wide-spread is the work. Transvaal North and South, Natal, Kaffraria, Orange Free State, and Cape Colony. In addition to these, two Swedish societies, and one Norwegian, are represented in South Africa.

In 1834 the American Board laid the foundations for a mission among the Zulus, which has passed through its full share of vicissitudes, from war and various outbursts of superstition and savagery, so that more than once it appeared to be on the verge of destruction, but the supply of men and women of saintly and heroic mould never failing, such conquests have been made that the 31 American laborers occupy 28 stations and out-stations, with a total of 204 natives to assist, the schools have 2,323 pupils, and in the 18 churches are 1,664 communicants, while the adherents number 7,283. Some years since the attempt was made to establish an East African mission far northward towards the Zambezi, but thus far this work has not advanced beyond the tentative and experimental stage. But—to go quite beyond the limits of South Africa proper—in 1884 the West African Mission was established upon the highlands some 200 miles back from the Atlantic coast, and with Bihe and Bailundu as central stations. The outlook is encouraging.

Two Scotch missions remain to be mentioned. And first, the one in charge of the Free Church, which dates from 1821, and was organized by the Glasgow Society, but in 1843 was transferred when it had already reached a flourishing condition. The Kaffirs are the special objects of prayer and labor, and Lovedale constitutes the most characteristic and famous feature. This institution, which so well combines the evangelizing and educational elements, is located some seven hundred miles to the northeast of Cape Town, was opened in 1841, is for the benefit of both sexes, and the courses include general education, industrial training, and preparatory study for teaching and the ministry. A large farm is owned and cultivated, twenty-two buildings are in use for dormitories, dwellings, etc., whose total cost was £30,000, and the annual expenditure reaches £6,000, of which one-third is met from fees, one-third from government grants, and the rest from donations. About 800 pupils are in attendance, of whom not a few come from long distances. The mission field is divided by the Great Kei River into two parts, and taken altogether contains 15 ordained men and a total working force of 284, the 12 churches have a membership of 5,057, and the 85 schools of all grades have 6,196 pupils. A second school, fashioned after Lovedale, has been started at Blythewood in the northern portion of the mission. And finally, the United Presbyterian Church of Scotland also received in 1847 a well developed mission from the Glasgow Society, and ever since has been faithful in caring for the charge. Twelve ordained missionaries are in the work at present with 98 native helpers, while the harvest gathered is represented by 2,400 scholars and 3,356 communicants.

A complete list of evangelizing agencies in operation for the redemption of South Africa would include several additional societies which have entered the field in recent years, or whose methods of work are so peculiar as not to be easy to compare with the rest. As an example of the latter class, the Propagation Society (S. P. G.) has a large force of workers, but is engaged mainly in behalf of European colonists. Some idea may be gathered of what the various churches of Christendom are doing for the kingdom of heaven in the portion of the Dark Continent under view by scanning these brief summaries of facts already given in fragmentary form. The principal societies at work number 12, and they employ 374 missionaries, and 1,724 native helpers. In their schools are found 37,354 pupils, and in their churches 60,858 members. The number of native Christians is 149,700. In addition, should be included the Wesleyan South African Conference, now independent of the society through which it came into being, with upwards of 33,000 native members. After a century of British rule and missionary toil, Cape Colony is clearly to be regarded as both civilized, and Christian. For according to the recent census, in a population of 1,500,000, of whom 350,000 are white, are to be found 206,777 Dutch Reformed; 110,240 Wesleyans; 79,126 Church of England; 39,829 Independents; 23,786 Presbyterians; 14,012 Moravians; 13,159 Rhenish Missions; and 14,012 Roman Catholics. The total number of persons, therefore, with church affiliations of some sort, in this fragment of the British Empire, is 527,689.

WEST AFRICA.

This is a term commonly employed to designate some four thousand miles of the Atlantic Coast, lying between Senegambia on the North, and Angola on the South, and including various subdivisions like Sierra Leone Coast, Ivory Coast, Gold Coast, Slave Coast, etc. Except upon the Niger, the width of the territory under view is nowhere more than from two hundred to three hundred and fifty miles. This phrase is a synonym for sin, sorrow and tragedy. For long centuries this region was the woful scene of the slave trade, which is perhaps the most amazing and shocking example in history of man's inhumanity to man. It is estimated that within a period of four hundred years not less than 40,000,000 of blacks, with the accompaniment of wholesale fire and slaughter, were here seized to be transported over sea and sold into bondage, though probably the greater number perished during the horrors of the "middle passage." And, as if this were not calamity and catastrophe sufficient, the climate is deadly to those of foreign birth almost beyond that of any other portion of the earth's surface. So superabundant is the moisture, and so intense is the tropical heat, the African fever has slain its tens of thousands, "the white man's graveyard" is the gruesome but fitting epithet applied, and the cost of efforts to evangelize has been exceeding great.

The first missions were singularly disastrous. The Moravians were the pioneer bearers of good news, sending two men as early as 1737 to the Guinea Coast. But death snatched away one after another, until baffled at every point it was deemed best to suspend the work. Within thirty years two more attempts were made, with the same result, after nine had laid down their lives. In 1795 the English Baptist Society entered Sierra Leone, but the indiscretion of one missionary, and the ill health of the other, proved fatal to the undertaking. The next year the London, Glasgow, and Edinburgh societies united to open work among the Foulahs, each supplying two representatives, and this effort also came to nothing, through the combined agency of dissension and disease. No permanent work was set on foot until the Church Missionary Society appeared in 1804, and even now long waiting and heavy endurance of discouragement and disaster were demanded. The tide of anti-slavery conviction was then rapidly rising in England under the arguments and appeals of Clarkson and Wilberforce, and in 1807 victory came in the shape of statutes prohibiting the traffic in slaves. Sierra Leone had been purchased in 1787 by an English company, as an asylum for a number of bondmen who had been liberated by the British troops during the progress of the American Revolution, and here they had been set down and left in a condition in every particular most appalling. And to this mass reeking with nameless vices were added from time to time other thousands rescued from slave ships, until *two hundred* African nations and tongues were united to constitute a combination of babel and hell. For years it seemed as though nothing could be accomplished, but at length a wonderful transformation began. But, ah, the loss of life. In twelve years twenty-six had entered the work, of whom fifteen had died. In eight months of 1823 fourteen were cut off from the mission, eleven being either missionaries of their wives, while by 1826, out of seventy-nine, only fourteen remained to carry on the arduous campaign. In 1827 Fourah Bay college was founded, and with the name of Samuel Crowther standing first upon the roll. Since then upwards of eighty Africans have here been trained for the ministry, some of them for stations of special honor and usefulness. The diocese of Sierra Leone has existed since 1852, and since 1862 the native church has been "self-governing, self-supporting and self-extending." In 1843 the Yoruba mission was opened far down the coast towards the mouth of the Niger, with Crowther to lead, and in 1857 a third one some distance up that stream. In 1864 Crowther, the African and ex-slave, was consecrated in Canterbury Cathedral first Bishop of the Niger. After three generations of steadfast endurance and resolute struggle, 20,957 native Christians are found to represent the results achieved for the kingdom of heaven, 8,139 communicants, and 7,677 pupils in the schools. To these ministers a missionary force of 12 ordained Europeans and 32 ordained natives, and 304 other native helpers.

As early as 1769 Dr. Coke devised a scheme for carrying the Gospel to West Africa which proved a failure; but in 1811 the Wesleyans entered Sierra Leone to remain and do valiant and most efficient service in supplanting grossest barbarism with Christian civilization. Of course the early missionaries were compelled to face the same sore trials to which their brethren of the Church of England were exposed. At the end of forty years, of one hundred and twenty-three who had come out, fifty-three had died, and others had returned broken in health. To save life, a period of seven years of service was fixed upon, to be followed by a season of rest and recuperation in a better climate, afterwards shortened to three years and finally to two. But before the terrible lesson of wisest precaution had been thoroughly learned, in the Senegambia mission adjoining more than half found graves in pagan soil. But, for all this mortality, there was no lack of candidates to fill the places of those who fell, and the spirit of many appears in the words of one who declared: "The more I hear of the difficulties and dangers, the more anxious I am to go;" and when his mother protested, "If you go to Africa you will be the death of me," replied, "And if you do not let me go, you will be the death of me!" With such intrepid devotion the ground was held and other fields were occupied, until now there are four principal missions, the later ones being the Gold Coast, Lagos and Dahomey. In all there are 156 chapels in use, with 451 other preaching places, 52 missionaries and assistant missionaries, 74 native catechists, and 600 native preachers; the pupils in the schools number 8,788, the church members 15,821, and the attendants upon public services 62,671.

The American Baptists entered Liberia in 1821, sending two colored men, one of whom, Lott Cary, had been a slave and had purchased his freedom. That colony had just been founded for the benefit of emancipated negroes, and numbers of this class had presently been transported thither. At the end of fifteen years five churches were in existence, with two hundred and fifty members, but all were immigrants from the United States, with not a converted idolater among them. And of ten white missionaries who had come to share the burden of evangelistic toil, all but one had died or taken their departure. Eight more were sent to take their places, but five had soon succumbed to the climate, or had fled to escape death. After a long period of such experiences, in 1856 the mission was suspended, to be in a sense revived in the Congo valley.

The American Presbyterians (O. S.) sent missionaries to Liberia in 1832, and no long time elapsed before the entire six had fallen victims to the fever. After ten years colored ministers were substituted for white, with such excellent results that a presbytery was organized in 1848. Six years before this, however, a second mission was opened to the south of the Bight of Biafra, upon the Gaboon River, and in 1850 a third upon Corisco Island at no great distance. The Gaboon work was organized in 1842 by the American Board, and was carried on until 1871, when it was turned over to the Presbyterians, whose two main bodies had been united the year preceding. Stations have been opened some hundreds of miles up the Ogowe River. The West African field includes 15 principal and 21 subordinate stations, manned by 13 ordained missionaries and 5 ordained natives, 24 unordained Americans and 24 unordained natives. The communicants number 1,611, and 635 pupils are in the schools.

The Basle Society has suffered as much and as nobly, and has gained as many trophies, as any other. Beginning with 1827, eight missionaries were sent in three companies to toil in Liberia, but all either died or were compelled to leave. The next year four were despatched to the Guinea coast, and two more followed a little later, but ere long only one remained, and three times he was brought to death's door. Removing the station to higher ground, better health was secured, and since then the days of extreme darkness have passed away. In 1887, when the colony was annexed to Germany, the missions at Cameroons and Victoria, which the English Baptists had founded, were transferred to the Basle Society. The experiment was tried with considerable success of employing colored ministers from the West Indies. The number of toilers is now 48 men, 38 women, and more than 100 native helpers of all grades. In the schools are 3,600 pupils, in the churches are 5,996 communicants, and in the congregations are 13,662 native Christians.

The American Methodists made their advent into Liberia in 1832, sending Melville Cox as pioneer. Before leaving home he said to an intimate friend, "If I die, you must come out and write my epitaph." "I will, but what shall I write?" "Write, Let a thousand fall before Africa be given up." A few months finished his career, but successors came, and acting upon that noble motto, have pushed steadily forward to success. Of late the work of supervision has been placed in the hands of Bishop Taylor and is carried on by quite a company of missionaries, assisted by upwards of 50 native local preachers. The churches have upwards of 3,400 communicants, and the schools nearly 3,000 pupils.

The Mendi Mission, established in 1842, by the American Missionary Association, had a peculiar origin. Three years before, the slave ship Amistad had been captured, and found in possession of the negroes who had risen up against the captain and crew and overpowered them. After a long and bitter contest in the courts, John Quincy Adams being one of their defenders, the bondmen were declared free, and afterwards by certain philanthropic persons were sent back to Africa, with missionaries to give them the Gospel, and a settlement was made in the Sherbro country, on the coast of Sierra Leone. Later when the mortality became almost beyond endurance, the effort was made to gain a supply of Africans, or men of African descent. In 1883 the whole work was turned over to the United Brethren, who had long been laboring in close proximity. The number of Christians is about 5,000.

The American Episcopalians entered Liberia in 1834, sending two teachers and later a clergyman. Through much tribulation the work has been carried on from that day to this with proportions constantly increasing. At the head is now found a colored bishop, and from seven principal stations the light of truth is diffused through the surrounding gloom. The clergy number 11, of whom 6 are Liberian and 4 are native, whose labors are supplemented by 40 lay-readers, catechists, etc. There are 982 communicants, about 3,000 attendants upon the public services, and upwards of 1,000 pupils in the schools.

The United Presbyterians of Scotland sent missionaries to Old Calabar, lying between the mouth of the Niger and that of the Congo, and in 1846, with the design of manning the mission with Africans. Eight principal stations are sustained by 10 ordained men, two of them being natives, with the aid of 8 other Europeans and 21 natives. There are 465 church members and 905 in the schools.

In 1847 the North German Society sent four men to plant a mission upon the Gold Coast, not far from Dahoman territory, but before a location could be made, only one was left alive. Others came and the same morality continued, so that after forty years, out of one hundred and ten who had volunteered to face deadly peril from the fever, fifty-six had died, and forty had retired with constitutions broken, while out of fifty-six children born in missionary homes only twenty-six survived. At one time, so past endurance seemed the situation, that the work was abandoned, though only to be taken up again in 1853. Keta, then simply a harbor, was chosen as the location for a settlement, while several stations were opened in the vicinity in later years. Divers wars among the surrounding tribes brought disaster. Not until quite recently have any considerable signs of promise begun to appear. Since the climate is so fatal to whites, especial pains are now taken to train up natives to take the burden of toil, of whom some are educated in the mission and others in Germany. Fourteen Europeans are found at the present time engaged in evangelistic effort, with 32 native helpers. In the schools are 350 pupils, in the churches 472 communicants, and the congregations about 1,200 who have put themselves under Christian instruction.

The American Lutherans (General Synod) in 1860

laid the foundations of a missionary settlement in Liberia, securing for their uses a grant of several hundred acres of land. From the families of recaptured slaves forty children were selected and bound out by the government to the mission, to be educated and receive manual training. The culture of sugar cane, rice and coffee is a source of income. The chief hindrance to large progress is found, not in the climate, or in prevalent barbarism or heathenism, so much as in the demoralization resulting from the vast quantities of rum imported from Europe and America. The force employed is but small, consisting of but four persons, with one ordained and several unordained natives to assist. The pupils number about 225 and the church members some 170.

In addition to the societies named must be added the Southern Baptist Convention which has eight representatives and six native helpers, one hundred and fifty members in the churches and about the same number in the schools. Lagos and Abeokuta are among the principal stations. The United Methodist Free Church is also represented on the west coast, as well as the colored Baptists and Methodists of the United States, and the Methodist Protestant Church. It will be noticed that while a few diminutive sections have been quite abundantly supplied with the Gospel, like Sierra Leone, Liberia, and the region lying in the vicinity of the mouths of the Niger, the bulk of the vast stretch of four thousand miles of coast is even yet practically untouched. And also that with few exceptions it is only the seaboard and a narrow strip bordering thereon which have begun to receive the light of life, while the boundless interior remains in the blackness of darkness of ignorance and sin. In making an estimate of what has been accomplished, of course the reduction to writing of some two score languages and dialects is by no means to be forgotten, or the translations of the Scriptures, and the creation of a considerable literature. But, at the very best, after a century has passed since the first missionaries touched the shores with the message of salvation, the redemption of West Africa is yet to be achieved. What are these among so many? The figures which follow will give at least some idea of the spiritual forces at work, and of the visible rewards of toil. Twelve societies are performing the bulk of the evangelizing work with 253 American and European agents and 1,304 native helpers. In the churches are 35,598 members and in the schools 23,894 pupils. The number of adherents is upwards of 130,000.

West Central Africa.

In its present use, this phrase is equivalent to the Congo Basin, or the Congo Free State, including thus the equatorial portion, extending from the Atlantic to the vicinity of the great African lakes. It is in this extensive region, together with the corresponding one stretching from its eastern limits to the Indian Ocean, that within the last two decades a most remarkable development of organized efforts for the evangelization of the Dark Continent has occurred. And whatever has been undertaken is the result primarily of what Livingstone endured and achieved, with Stanley and King Leopold to carry forward towards completion what he so magnificently planned and initiated. As we saw, as far back as 1850, the fervid and prescient Krapf dreamed of a day approaching when a chain of missions should be established along "the high roads of Central Africa" from sea to sea, and this missionary explorer was permitted to live to see his hope and expectations change to visible fact. It was in 1866 that Livingstone crossed the Zambezi to devote the residue of his days to journeys here and there, searching for the head waters of the unknown Congo. And it was not until August of 1877, and after nine hundred and ninety-nine days of incessant hardship and peril, having followed its course for thousands of miles, that Stanley reached the mouth of that majestic stream, and the civilized world began to have knowledge of what treasures, and wonders, and peoples, the immense interior possessed. Next came five years of further exploration of the upper waters, under the direction of the same fertile brain and indomitable will, and the hewing out of a road past the long stretch of rapids, and after that, in 1884-5, the sessions of the famous Berlin Conference, which brought into being the Congo Free State, forbidding the slave trade, promising to end domestic slavery at the soonest, and guaranteeing to all liberty of conscience and religious toleration. Committed to the care of the philanthropic King of Belgium, ever since efforts have been unceasing to establish universal peace and public order, and to encourage the entrance and prosperity of every worthy enterprise. And thus it was that a territory of 1,000,000 square miles, and a population estimated at some 20,-000,000, were uncovered to the gaze of Christendom, and made quite easily accessible to missionary effort.

The story of what has been done to redeem the Congo Basin from savagery and degrading fetish worship is a short one of necessity, so few are the years covered thereby, nor can long columns of impressive statistics be supplied. Up to the present hour the task has been mainly that of choosing and opening stations, learning the language, and carrying all manner of matters through the trying preliminary and experimental stage. It is not at all strange that the important geographical discoveries just referred to produced a profound impression upon the churches, that enthusiasm was stirred, and that not a few were presently found ready and eager to enter in at the door just opened. Indeed, without waiting for all the preparatory steps to be taken, as early as 1878, the year in which Stanley's "Darkest Africa" was published, and hence seven years before the Free State was set up, the Livingstone Inland Missionary Society had planted a station near the mouth of the Congo. H. Grattan Guinness and the English Baptist Missionary Society were active in this movement. By 1884 such energy had been displayed that the one station had increased to seven, of which three were upon the Upper Congo, seventeen laborers were engaged, while a steam launch below the rapids, and the steamer "Henry Reed" above, were in use to facilitate intercourse and enlargement. In that year the mission was turned over to the American Baptists, whose work in Liberia had previously been abandoned. The fatal fever has carried off its victims, the Arab slave-stealer has not yet ceased from his destructive raids, and many are the trials to faith and patience, but men and money have been liberally supplied, and the return for all the expenditure is given in small part in these figures. The missionaries are 27 in number with 15 wives, 8 unmarried women and 3 physicians in addition, as well as 21 native preachers and 42 other native helpers; a total of 109 laborers, of whom more than half are Africans. The 14 churches have a membership of 1,212 the baptisms were 438 in 1893, the scholars in the schools were 1,557, and the adherents may be estimated at about 3,000.

The English Baptists were among the first to enter this new territory, receiving the impulse in part from an offer of $5,000 by Mr. Arthington of Leeds, on condition that a mission be planted at once. A beginning was made in 1878 upon the Lower Congo, and in Portuguese territory. This society has two steamers, and a force of 30 missionaries, distributed above and below the great rapids, has gathered some 500 pupils into its schools, and about 100 members into its churches. The losses by death have been peculiarly afflictive, one entire family of consecrated men and women, the Combers, consisting of two brothers, their wives, and a sister, having laid down their lives.

Of several other undertakings only the names and the dates of entrance can be given. The Swedish Society has three stations with about a score of missionaries on the north bank of the lower river, and for ten years has been sounding out the glad tidings. Bishop Taylor has opened several stations which are based on the principle of self-support. In 1889 the Congo-Balolo mission was established by the East London Missionary Institute, taking for its share of the broad field certain southern or eastern branches above Equatorville. Though the ravages of the destroyer have been fearful in their ranks, and little beyond foundation work has been accomplished, such consecration and readiness to toil and suffer as have been abundantly displayed, cannot fail to tell eventually in the conversion of souls, and the building up of Christian institutions. In 1888 Arnot's mission was located in the extreme southeast corner of the Congo

Basin, so far away indeed as to be most easily reached from Benguela, or even from the east coast.

In all, eight societies have planted stations in the west central portion of Africa, and though in the first ten years fifty-five who entered this field were buried within its soil, the number of survivors is not far from 100, and the number of converts is about 1,500. From the coast the word of life has already penetrated at least a thousand miles towards the center of the continent, and the work is well taken in hand of reducing to writing several of the one hundred and sixty languages and dialects said to exist in this area, and of translating into it God's wonderful message to men. The infamous and desolating slave trade seems to be nearing its end, steamers are steadily multiplying on all parts of the river and its branches, the railroad in a few years will be completed to connect the lower with the upper waters, the sacred task will certainly be carried forward in spite of all obstacles, and will be properly enlarged, the divine blessing will not be witheld, and therefore, only time is needed to make the desert to bud, blossom, and bear abundant fruit.

East Central Africa.

This portion of the continent includes so much of the eastern coast as lies between Abyssinia and the mouth of the Zambezi, the region lying about the great lakes, and the area intervening. For size it surpasses the portion last considered, but the population is very much less. The bulk of missionary work thus far undertaken is confined to the seaboard and the vicinity of the lakes, and because of the difficulties of travel and transportation elsewhere. Though the Portuguese had been for centuries in nominal possession, and engaged in trade with the natives, no perceptible impression had been made upon the universal barbarism and superstition. The high honor of pioneering for the Gospel belongs to the Church Missionary Society, and to Krapf and Rebmann its representatives, and the remotest beginnings were made as far back as 1839 in the extreme northeast. Krapf had landed at Zeila, on the Gulf of Aden, hoping to be able to enter Abyssinia, but failing in that project, after several extensive tours through Somaliland and Gallaland, concluded in 1844 to locate upon the Zanzibar coast, with the especial design of reaching the Gallas from this direction. Two years later he was joined by Rebmann, and for nearly ten years these most devoted, and enterprising, and fearless, servants of God, gave themselves without stint to preaching, teaching, and translating the Scriptures; with all the rest also pushing back repeatedly far from the coast, and gathering a mass of most important geographical knowledge.

The exceedingly fruitful labors of the one continued until 1855, and of the other until 1875. But Krapf, though nominally no longer a missionary, yet returned twice to the scene of his labors, to lead forth companies of Christian toilers, and to aid with his counsels in laying foundations. It was in 1861 that the United Methodist Free Church determined to open a mission in East Africa, and despatched four men with the German apostle as leader. The Galla country was chosen as a field. Sickness and death have visited the stations, in a savage raid one missionary and his wife were murdered, and the forays of the Arab slave dealers have caused much embarrassment; but with no great number of converts gathered as yet, the outlook is full of encouragement. In

1865 a Swedish mission was opened among the Gallas; this also with the advice and assistance of Dr. Krapf. The sacrifices have been great, the exertions have been enormous, the tangible gains have been relatively slight, but eleven Europeans and a larger number of natives continue to crowd on the Lord's work, adding to the usual forms of evangelistic effort a medical mission and the teaching of trades.

But it was not until after the death of Livingstone, in 1873, that the grand impulse was given to missions in East Central Africa; and it is not too much to affirm that whatsoever has been undertaken since is, directly or indirectly, attributable to influences which went forth from the character and deeds of this gifted and consecrated servant of Christ, whose endeavors for the Dark Continent were so herculean. He had written and spoken much to the churches of Great Britain to quicken their consciences and inflame their zeal. The earliest response was made in the organization of the Universities' Mission in 1859, and the sending later of a pioneer force, which finally located in Zanzibar in 1862 to make preparation for an advance upon the mainland, in the meantime training a company of released slave children, that they might form the nucleus of a Christian settlement. Here is the central seat of the mission. A church has been erected upon ground once occupied by a slave market, where thousands of slaves were once sold every year. About the same time most costly efforts were commenced to open work upon Lake Nyassa, as well as at some eligible points between the coast and that important body of water. It was not until 1882, and after various experiments, that a permanent location was finally secured upon the east shore, though a half-way station had been occupied to the north of the Rovuma River six years before. A steamer now traverses the lake, doing valuable service for the kingdom. This body of missionaries represents the high church section of the Church of England, but is second to none for devotion and readiness to risk all and suffer all with joy. Celibacy is an essential qualification, while clergymen, teachers, mechanics, etc., are held in equal honor, and none receives any remuneration beyond board, clothing, and money sufficient for correspondence. The entire force numbers 194, of whom 85 are Europeans and 109 are Africans, and 23 are women. The pupils in the schools number 2,106, the communicants 1,166, and the adult adherents 3,551.

The English Church Society, which, as we have seen, had entered East Africa in 1844, was stirred to new exertions and substantial enlargement in 1876 by the famous letter of Stanley relating to Uganda, and the subsequent special gifts, amounting in all to £24,000, and a party of eight was consecrated to the momentous task of planting Christianity far inland upon the northwestern coast of Victoria Nyanza, a region almost inaccessible. Alexander Mackay was among the number. A year after arriving at Zanzibar only one-half of the party were left alive to reach their destination, and two of them were soon murdered by the natives. The events which have since transpired are both inspiring and tragic in the extreme, but for lack of space must be left unmentioned in detail. Suffice it to say that to Hannington, slain by savage hands, Bishop Tucker has succeeded ; British authority is firmly established in Uganda, insuring for the future good order and safety to life and property ; a railroad to the coast is in fair prospect, and several intermediate mission stations have been occupied. The work of this society, including the coast district and the interior, may be summed up and set forth by these few figures. The stations number 12, the clergymen 25, laymen 14, and women 17; 8 ordained natives and 87 unordained; 1,170 in the schools; 756 communicants; and a body of nearly 5,000 adherents.

In 1875 the Scottish Free Church sent a missionary expedition up the Shiré in a little steamer provided for the purpose, which was transported on the backs of men past the obstructing cataracts, and finally launched upon the waters of Lake Nyassa. The location for a mission was fixed about half way up the western shore, to which others have since been added near the north end and also towards the interior to the west. Especial trouble has been experienced from the violence of the slave-stealers. A total of 135 Christian agents are employed, of whom the bulk are native teachers, but 6 are ordained, and as many are unordained Europeans. In the schools 3,900 were enrolled in 1892, and the churches contained 185 communicants.

Almost at the same time the Established Church of Scotland was looking towards the same region, so closely connected with the career of Livingstone, as a field for the planting of Christian institutions, and in 1874 commenced operations which now center in Blantyre, situated at some distance to the south of Lake Nyassa, and east of the Shiré in the vicinity of Lake Shirwa. In the earlier period serious trouble befell on account of the zeal displayed in harboring fugitive slaves, and because the missionaries hesitated not to execute "Scotch justice" upon the natives for their criminal misdeeds, but of late solid progress has been made.

Among other things, a beautiful church has been erected almost wholly by native hands.

As yet Tanganyika, the third of the large African lakes, remained unvisited by messengers of the Gospel. But in 1877 the London Society began an arduous attempt to reach and hold its shores for the Master. A party of six set forth westward from Zanzibar, later dividing into two parties, of which one reached Ujiji after some sixteen months of struggle and vexatious delays, while the other reached Urambo, a point lying between the lake and the coast, not until 1879. "The mission has passed through ten years of almost unprecedented trials, owing to the failure of health, and deaths, in the mission circle." Troubles are not yet ended, though it is hoped that the worst has been endured. A steamer is now in use which cost the toil of six years to construct.

In days yet more recent the Moravians and the Berlin Society have opened work to the north of Nyassa, between that and Tanganyika, and the East African Scottish Mission has been located some two hundred miles to the northwest of Mombasa, and about fifty miles to the north of Kilimanjaro, Africa's highest mountain. Kibwezi, which is chosen as the center, lies upon the caravan route to Uganda, and at an altitude of three thousand feet above the sea. And finally, to the south and west of the lake region, upon the upper Zambezi, among the Barotse, for several years has labored and suffered M. Coillard of the Paris Mission, with Arnot's Mission in Garenganze not very remote.

All these undertakings, second to none for difficulties and dangers attending their progress, and urged on with resolution and devotion nowhere surpassed, are yet in their feeble infancy, and the glad harvest season is in days to come. And there remaineth yet very much land to be possessed. The few toilers now in the field must be increased to a host, and over all this vast area, one-third the size of the United States less Alaska, must be heard the sweet story of the cross, and be planted the various institutions of Christianity. And all this shall surely come to pass.

North Africa.

There remains to be mentioned a division of the continent which extends from the Red Sea to the Atlantic, and from the Mediterranean to the southern boundary of Abyssinia and the desert of Sahara, or spreads over about fifty degrees of longitude, and twenty-five of latitude. According to the best estimates the population is at least 25,000,000. Almost everywhere Mohammedanism holds the seat of both religious and political power. The only exceptions are, Algeria under French sway, Abyssinia where an exceedingly corrupt form of Christianity wields the scepter, and among the Copts, an insignificant fraction of the inhabitants of Egypt. The northern and eastern portions, covered by six states, were the theater of some of the early and notable triumphs of the Gospel, for centuries were well covered with churches and monasteries, and the millions of those who professed to honor the Nazarene were second to none for zeal fiery and even furious. But with the fall of the Roman Empire came the irresistible barbarian hordes, the Vandals among the rest, and a few generations after the terrible Arab invaders bringing with them the Koran and the sword. Last of all the Turks attained sovereignty, holding at least nominal rule even to the Pillars of Hercules. Through all the early decades of this century the pirates of the Barbary States were the terror of Christendom, so destructive were they to commerce, and so eager to capture the "infidels" and hold them in slavery until ransomed. Better days for civilization began to dawn when in 1830 France began to take vengeance for damage and insults upon the dey of Algiers, and later when Mehemet Ali began to introduce reforms into the old time government of Egypt. These and other political revolutions prepared the way for the re-introduction of Christian offorts and the rebuilding of Christian institutions.

The work of evangelization began in the Nile valley, and in the highlands far to the south of the Cataracts, and in 1819 under the auspices of the English Church Society. In those primitive days the heart of Christendom went out with especial warmth of desire towards the corrupt Oriental churches, and hope was strong that if a pure Gospel was presented, they might be thoroughly reformed as organizations, in both creed and practice. To hasten this happy consummation, five missionaries were despatched to Egypt to recover the Coptic clergy and people from the error of their ways, but, after long and strenuous endeavor, with only complete failure as the result. However, while there a manuscript translation of the Scriptures in Amharic, the vernacular of Abyssinia, was discovered, and this led to the founding of a mission in that country in 1830. After eight years of toil, through the malign influence of two French priests, the entire company was expelled. Among them was Dr. Krapf, who by this repulse was led to transfer the scene of his apostolic labors to the East African region. For an entire decade Bishop

Gobat was closely identified with this enterprise as leader. It was not until 1860 that the Egyptian mission came to an end. And it was about this time that the late Miss Whately, daughter of the famed Archbishop of Dublin, commenced her devoted and most valuable school work in Cairo, designed especially for Mohammedan boys and girls, which was also continued, at great cost to herself, for nearly thirty years.

But 1854 is the true Christian era for modern Egypt, since it was in that year that the "American Mission" was founded by the United Presbyterian Church, by the entrance of two missionaries into Cairo, joined three years later by Dr. Lansing, who fixed himself in Alexandria, and three years later still by the Rev. John Hogg. As soon as possible public services were opened, and schools both for boys and girls, and tours were made for the sale of Bibles and other religious books. The Coptic Church was the special object held in mind, though no direct notice was taken of it, and the immediate result sought was the enlightenment of individual men and women, and the quickening of spiritual life. Persecutions have been by no means wanting, from both *quasi* Christians and Moslems, to try the endurance of missionaries and converts, and not a few remarkable tokens of favor from God and man have been vouchsafed. Thus, through Said Pasha and Ismail Pasha real estate was donated in the Coptic quarter of Cairo worth some $40,000. And a wealthy Hindu prince, Maharajah Dhuleep Singh, son of the redoubtable Runjeet Singh, monarch of the Punjab, having married one of the girls from the Cairo mission school, as a token of his grateful interest, sent an annual gift until the total reached $90,000, besides presenting to the mission his boat, the Ibis, for use in frequent evangelizing tours up and down the Nile. Among the happiest phases of the work is to be named the fact that other Protestant societies have not interfered by trespass and competition, so that the brethren engaged could bestow their undivided attention upon the common foe. With such advantages, and the smile of the Lord appearing in various seasons of revival, progress in every sphere of effort has been steady, and quite marked. In 1865 Mr. Hogg and others ascended the river two hundred miles to Assioot, to make that city of 30,000 a second center, and the year following a further advance was made of two hundred and fifteen miles by the occupation of Koos, in the vicinity of Thebes. Finally in 1887 a station was opened at Assouan (Syene), hard by the First Cataract and on the border of Nubia. At the end of about forty years the Gospel is preached at nearly one hundred and fifty points in the long, narrow valley of the Nile. A profound impression has been made upon the Coptic Church, and even upon the Mohammedan population, for from the latter nearly a thousand children are found in the mission schools. It is not often in the foreign field that the toilers in publishing their statistics can affirm : "Nearly all the items have more than doubled in every ten years, and some of them have doubled in every five years." The figures for the close of 1893 are as follows : Number of ordained missionaries 14, with 9 unmarried women, 17 native ministers, and 31 native licentiates. In the churches are 4,091 communicants, and in the schools are 7,613 pupils. For all church purposes the people contributed $10,888, and for all school purposes $13,538.

The work of the North African Mission (English) remains to be mentioned. This society was organized in

1881, to meet the spiritual needs of the Kabyles of Algeria, but its sphere has since been enlarged to include work among the people of Morocco, Tunis, Tripoli, and more recently the Delta of Egypt. The force in the field numbers 75, of whom a large proportion are women. Hospital and dispensary work is made quite prominent, and also visiting from house to house. The Moslems are found not altogether unapproachable, but spiritually so barren is the soil, that the utmost of faith and devotion are required in order not to be weary in well-doing, and, not strangely, the results which can be expressed in a few words, or in figures, are not many as yet. O for the day to return when the glorious Gospel of salvation shall possess the entire southern coast of the Mediterranean!

If all the missionary societies engaged in African evangelization were included—the great and the small, the general and the special, the regular and the irregular—they would number nearly one hundred. In Dean Vahl's "Statistical Review," which is unapproached for comprehensiveness, and painstaking research, fourteen organizations are named whose headquarters are fixed upon African soil. But nine-tenths of the results achieved belong to less than fifty societies, and the bulk to such as have been named in this chapter with a summary of their doings. So many and so various are the kinds of toil bestowed, that entire accuracy of statement is impossible, and the best figures obtainable are only approximate. But fortunately, error is likely to be on the side of under-statement. Nearly 1,800 European and American missionaries are struggling in prayer and exhausting their strength that the Dark Continent may be filled with the light of life. Of these more than 700 are ordained. Over 200 natives are ordained pastors, and there are at least 5,000 other natives engaged in teaching or as evangelists, etc. Some 76,000 pupils are under training in the various mission schools, the churches have about 140,000 members, and perhaps as many as 800,000 are in some fair measure under the influence of the means of grace.

Such for substance is a statement of what Christendom has accomplished and undertaken for Africa with its 165,000,000. The results are most considerable in the south where the messengers of salvation soonest began to make proclamation of the good news, and where various circumstances are peculiarly favorable. Upon the west coast along a line of some three thousand miles at various points the graves of missionaries are dreadfully numerous, proving how general and ardent has been holy desire, and how deadly is the climate, while the hundreds of churches and schools, and the thousands of converts are conclusive evidence that these heroic men and women did not die in vain. Surely, the harvest gathered is by no means inconsiderable, and some slight return has been made for the woe immeasurable resulting from the slave trade. As for the immense basin of the Congo, its hidden recesses were first entered so recently by civilized men that thus far only time has been afforded to break the surface here and there and deposit the good seed. Only the first shoots are visible, while the full corn in the ear belongs to the future. In like manner, and for the same cogent reason, the region of the great lakes and the coast of East Central Africa see simply the laying of foundations, and the hewing out of material for the building of the glorious temple certain to be reared therein in days to come. Ending our review with the northern section, in Egypt alone do we find the toilers in sufficient numbers, and their plans carried forward so far towards completion as to discover results which can be tabulated or expressed in few words. And, alas, even now, what vast regions have not yet been entered by Gospel heralds, what millions both of pagans and Mohammedans have never looked upon the face of a loving, earnest disciple of Jesus! Who will help to hasten the day when in the largest and most blessed meaning of the words, Princes shall come out of Egypt; Ethiopia shall soon stretch out her hands unto God!

Madagascar.

This island takes rank among the largest, being surpassed in size only by New Guinea and Borneo. Its length is about 1,000 miles, its breadth about 300, while the area is reckoned at 230,000 square miles. Africa is distant only 250 miles at the nearest point, the continental and the insular mass are often classed together, the historical connection between them is quite intimate, and in various particulars a striking physical resemblance may be traced. Except at the north, where a few bays break the coast line, almost the entire 2,000 miles of circumference are surprisingly destitute of harbors. Nor are there any navigable streams by which the interior is made easily accessible from the sea. And therefore, like the Dark Continent, Madagascar is closed against free communication with the great outlying world. The outer rim, which varies in width from a few miles to more than a hundred, is low-lying and level, and has a climate deadly to all foreigners. A plateau of considerable elevation overspreads the central portions of the island, and from it rise several ranges of quite lofty mountains. Between the plain and the plateau at wellnigh every point is found a stretch of dense forest some fifty miles across, within which the surface rises by successive terraces to the higher table land.

No census has ever been taken, and the estimates of the population vary from 2,500,000 to twice that number. The Malagasy are not African in origin and race as we might suppose, but Malayo-Polynesian instead, and are believed to have entered by incursions separated by long intervals of time. Several distinct tribes may be traced, with the Hovas, Sakalavas, and Betsileos, among the most important, but all alike speaking substantially the same language. The islanders dwelling in the interior were not savage when first visited by Europeans, but had attained to no inconsiderable degree of civilization. They were decently clothed though the climate is tropical, cultivated the soil, were by no means lacking in mechanical skill, dwelt in settled communities, while the government, though a pure despotism, would compare not unfavorably with that of other oriental countries. *Tangena* was one of the peculiar civil institutions, or the ordeal of swallowing poison as a judicial test of guilt. The dominant religion was scarcely above fetish worship. There were no temples, or priesthood, or public religious rites, though medicine men were held in honor, as well as idol-keepers, and belief in charms, divination, and witchcraft, was universal. In general the people are said to be courageous, loyal to their rulers, affectionate, firm in their friendships, courteous, kind to children, the aged and the infirm, and hospitable to strangers. Slavery prevailed extensively, and as sources of supply not only were captives taken in war, held in bondage and sold for gain, but multitudes of Africans imported by traders were purchased. Wheeled vehicles and beasts of burden are unknown in the island, and this because of the utter absence of roads. Narrow footpaths, runners, and the shoulders of men, furnish the only means of communication. Even Antananarivo the capital, a city of 100,000, though some two hundred and fifty miles from the sea, has no better connection with its port, Tamatave. And no improvement in this particular is undertaken, in great part because the existing difficulties of travel are such as to make it next to impossible for an invading army to climb through the rugged forest region to the elevated and populous spaces beyond.

For many centuries intercourse had been quite frequent and intimate between the Malagasy and the Arab merchants and slave traders, who had made a few settlements upon the northern and western coasts. The Portuguese were the first of Europeans to visit Madagascar, and they undertook at various times, during the fifteenth and sixteenth centuries, to establish themselves upon the island, but, time after time, all who thus intruded were either massacred or driven out. Later the Dutch followed and the French, but making themselves equally obnoxious by their vices and crimes, their attempts came to the same end. The advent of the English was delayed until early in this century, and constitutes a most impressive providence, both with respect to the strange way in which it was brought about, and the momentous results to which it led. No mission field can be named whose story is fuller of incidents more striking because out of the common order. And the Gospel message was first carried in the very nick of time, for an all-important preparation had just been made. From time immemorial the island had been divided among divers tribes, between which desolating wars were frequent, but now appeared a certain Hova chieftain of unusual ability for statesmanship, and an ambition to subdue his neighbors on every side that he might rise to supreme power. Dying in 1810 he bequeathed his policy to his son Radama I. This young ruler was sagacious and full of political enterprise, and knew enough of European civilization to understand that he could borrow much that would be greatly to his advantage. Now it had strangely "happened" that in that same year, under the chances attending the Napoleonic wars, Mauritius, an island lying some hundreds of miles to the east, was wrested from France by Great Britain, and Sir Robert Farquhar was appointed governor, a man thoroughly imbued with horror and hatred for the slave trade, of which Madagascar was the chief theater in that part of the world. Nor was he long in entering into negotiations with the aspiring Malagasy monarch, offering to supply him with arms, powder, and other objects of desire, on condition that Radama, on his part, would abolish the traffic in human flesh. By 1820 a treaty was concluded on this basis. In the meantime Sir Robert had suggested to British Christians the advisability of opening a mission in this needy and promising field. As far back as 1811 Vanderkemp, with the consent of the London Society, had planned to exchange Cape Colony for this island as the scene of his consecrated labors, but had died just as he was about to set forth. It was not till 1818 that two missionaries with families landed on the eastern coast, to make proclamation of the unsearchable riches of Christ. And lo, tarrying too long in the fever-stricken lowlands, within two months, out of six persons only one was left alive, and he was compelled to take his departure. Rev. David Jones, the survivor, returned two years later, to be followed presently by quite a company of preachers, teachers and artisans, ascended to the capital, and was most graciously received by the king. It soon became apparent that the royal desire was wholly for material benefits. While without regard or respect for the religion in vogue, neither did he care aught, either then or at any later time, for Christianity, and was even afraid of its encroachments. So he cautioned the missionaries not to advance too rapidly with their innovations, forbade baptisms and the religious instruction of the children. As for education however, they might push it to their heart's content, while carpenters, blacksmiths, and the like, could scarcely be found in excess. Of religious liberty he seems never to have gained the least idea.

Of course the vernacular must be mastered at the outset, and since the Malagasy forms of speech had never been reduced to writing, alphabet, grammar and lexicon were to be created, as well as translations of the Scriptures to be made. At an early period schools by the score had been opened to teach the common branches, and in 1826 a printing press was set up in Antananarivo, to the exceeding wonder and delight of Radama. As opportunity offered the Gospel story was told and the teachings of the New Testament were imparted, but at the end of the first decade no baptisms had been allowed, and no public professions of faith in Jesus had been made. And now of a sudden, when an impression, wide-spread, if not deep, had been made, but while the great work of transformation was still in feeble infancy, the king died, to be succeeded by one of his twelve wives, Ranavalona, a passionate, unscrupulous, blood·

thirsty and brutal creature, who feared and hated the Europeans and all their ways, while she was full of superstition and clung to her idols, with the wizards and sorcerers. Wars were almost constant during her long reign of three and thirty years, in one of which it is said that 25,000 of the natives were killed, and 50,000 were captured and sold into slavery. For a while her reactionary policy was not fully inaugurated. For a few months she even allowed public assemblies for Christian worship and baptisms, but then ordered them to cease. Later a great gathering of the people was called, accusations were brought against all Christians, and every one infected with the foreign faith was commanded to come forward within a given time and confess the fact. Thus far the schools were not interfered with, and the missionaries were treated with reasonable consideration, but in 1836 they were ordered to leave the island. This mandate was not to be trifled with, and with deepest sorrow and gravest apprehensions the poor converts were left to themselves, as sheep without shepherds but in the midst of ravening wolves; but fortunately not until the whole Bible had been translated, and a thousand copies had been printed and distributed to the most earnest and intelligent of the flock.

Days of darkness now befell, and were destined to last a full half-century. Not that there were no seasons of comparative freedom from savage persecution, for more than once the queen and her prime minister seemed to grow weary of shedding blood, or their attention was drawn to other occupations, but there were four periods of frenzy and pitiless infliction of suffering, which varied in length from two to seven years, and each one more terrible than any preceding. The saints were imprisoned by the wholesale with heavy chains upon their limbs, with confiscation of property, they were condemned to lifelong slavery, were burned at the stake or scalded to death, were buried alive, were speared, were flung over the edge of lofty precipices. And in the incidents and the outcome of those woful times of measureless suffering are to be found some of the shining marvels of Christian history. Seldom if ever elsewhere has it been so astonishingly true that the blood of the martyrs was the seed of the church. Remember that they who suffered for righteousness' sake were deprived of their trusted teachers and guides, all Bibles and other religious books were destroyed so far as they could be found, all assemblies were forbidden, spies were everywhere watching the suspected, they were scattered everywhere in the mountains, the caves, the jungles. And the phenomenon is two-fold. First, that during all those twenty-five dreadful years, so few who had been baptized fell away and turned back through fear of pain and death. From among all classes, from high-born and low-born, the aged and also the young, men and women alike, faced heroically and without flinching the severest penalties, and in all their agonies were calm and joyful. And, second, in spite of all, even by means of the tragical scenes enacted, the number of believers steadily increased, and so rapidly that the 2,000 at the beginning had become 40,000 at the end. The contagion of zeal and devotion infected the court and entered the very palace of the queen, so that her son, and a son of the prime minister, took rank with the abhorred Christians, and also many of the higher nobility.

It was not until 1861 and by the death of Ranavalona that effectual relief came. Then her son reigned in her stead, who, though not a true disciple, yet held Christianity in honor, and gave every encouragement to its adherents. The transformation was sudden and complete from the depths to the heights, from the horror of great darkness to brightest sunshine, from almost despair to hope and glad fruition. Back flocked the thousands from slavery, bonds and long imprisonment, and from various places of concealment. The maimed and half-starved came forth as from the grave. Within a single month eleven places of worship were opened in the capital alone, and many more in the region surrounding. Presently, too, the missionaries were back again and in larger numbers than before. Several memorial churches were built upon spots where martyr blood had most freely flowed. This reign was but brief, and the next ruler was a queen not Christian, but wholly favorable to those who were. Dying in 1869, she was followed by Ranavalona II., who with her prime minister, was baptized not long after and received into the church. The burning of the nation's idols followed in due season, and the proclamation of the fullest religious liberty. Christianity, from being hated and proscribed, had now become popular and fashionable, and multitudes of all classes and conditions flocked to the missionaries to be baptized. The only trouble was to sift the candidates, and repress those who were unfit to be received to fellowship. In 1868 there were 20,000 who professed to have forsaken their idols, the next year the number had risen to 163,000, and the year after to 231,000. In spite of the utmost of caution and care many were admitted to the churches who have since proved their utter lack of vital godliness, and even to this day the harm then done is felt far and wide among the churches.

In 1866 the Norwegian Lutherans entered Madagascar

and opened a mission, and the next year came also the English Friends, and both not to divide and proselyte, but to aid and co-operate in gathering in the abundant harvest. All these have richly shared the divine blessing which has been vouchsafed to this field. Schools have been planted in large numbers and are everywhere held in high esteem by the people. Schools for normal, medical and industrial training are sustained. Besides what the missionaries are doing, the government makes education compulsory for those of a certain age. From among the Hovas evangelizing efforts are spreading in every section to the more degraded tribes; and the churches are sending out a number to do home missionary work, meeting also the expense incurred. But, for all that so much has been accomplished, though the triumphs of the cross are already magnificent, much more still remains to be done. It is estimated that more than two-thirds of the population of Madagascar is yet pagan. Besides a large proportion of those who have honestly received the truth, and walk to the best of their ability in the light, have sorest need of further enlightenment. The government, though Christian in spirit and sympathy, is neutral as to its attitude towards different denominations and different religions. The Jesuits from first to last have been mischief-makers, seeking to rule in every sphere, and always acting as the spies and schemers for France; and for years the French Republic has been endeavoring in every possible way to reduce the Malagasy to the estate of vassalage, and finally succeeded a few years since, after several bloody wars, and with the consent of Great Britain, in establishing a protectorate of the African style over the island. And it is perhaps just at this point that the future of Madagascar is clouded with omens of evil.

CHAPTER XV.

THE ISLANDS OF THE SEA.

"THE Lord reigneth, let the earth rejoice; let the multitude of isles be glad thereof." "And the isles shall wait for his law." If we omit from the list such insular tracts as lie within the pale of Christendom, with New Zealand and its only forty thousand aborigines, and Tasmania whose native races have utterly disappeared; and further omit a half-dozen of the largest which remain; and besides reserve Japan for a separate treatment, the thirty thousand islands, more or less, scattered over the earth's surface, constitute but an insignificant fraction of the land area. Nor taken altogether, great and small, do they compare for size with the least of the continents. And again, if we leave out of the account a few which are most thickly inhabited, the aggregate population of those remaining is as nothing to the hordes and masses which crowd such countries as India and China. The number is not much greater than that found in the Turkish Empire, or in Italy, or Spain. This table will present these two facts impressively to the eye.

	AREA.	POPULATION.
New Guinea,	310,000	660,000
Borneo,	285,000	1,600,000
Madagascar,	230,000	3,500,000
Sumatra,	160,000	2,718,000
The Philippines (1400),	114,300	7,000,000
Celebes,	70,000	800,000
Java,	50,800	23,900,000
West Indies (1000),	92,270	5,500,000

	AREA.	POPULATION.
Cuba,	41,650	1,632,000
Haiti,	28,250	1,500,000
Ceylon,	25,364	3,008,460
New Caledonia,	7,750	63,000
Fiji Group (200),	7,740	125,400
Hawaiian Islands,	6,640	90,000
New Hebrides (30),	5,300	75,000
Porto Rico,	3,550	806,700
Trinidad,	1,750	200,000
Caroline Islands,	560	35,000
Society Islands,	375	23,000
Gilbert Islands,	170	36,800

And yet, the historic importance of the islands is exceeding great, is out of all proportion to their relative superficies, or to the number of their inhabitants. Take, for example, the scores which dot the surface of the Ægean, or Sicily, or Malta, or England. Islands have played from the very first a most prominent part in the spread of the Gospel. The fact is prophetic that the earliest missionary tour outside of Asia was directed to Cyprus. For long centuries Ireland was emphatically the "Isle of Saints," and with Iona, a mere speck of soil and rock off the Scottish coast, supplied a large part of the spiritual force which wrought the conversion of Europe. For centuries also Rhodes and Malta stood as impregnable bulwarks against the assaults of the Saracens. And no continent to-day can match Great Britain, as a civilizing and Christianizing power throughout the whole world. Moreover, the first Moravian missionary undertaking had the evangelization of the West Indies as its object, and of Greenland as the next. For years Carey planned to devote himself to the enlargement of the kingdom in the South Seas, a region selected a little later by the London Society for the beginning of its work. The American Board established its second mission in Ceylon, and soon after despatched a company to bear the message of salvation to the Sandwich Islands. Nor is it to be forgotten, that nowhere else have the conquests of the cross been so astonishing or so complete. The import of this suggestion is sufficiently set forth by a mere reference to the group just named, or to Fiji, or Tahiti, or Madagascar, or Japan that marvel among missions during the last two decades. And finally, if we are in search of great names intimately connected with the introduction of the Gospel into heathen lands, names which stand for eminent genius, energy and consecrated zeal, we can be easily content with such as Williams and Marsden, Selwyn and Patteson, and those who in Fiji and Hawaii bore the heat and burden of the day.

Of the multitude of the earth's islands by far the greater portion is found in the southern Pacific, the South Seas of a century since. And they lie on both sides of the equator, between twenty degrees north latitude and twenty south, and extend over one hundred and ten degrees of longitude, stretching from southeastern Asia far towards distant South America. The expanse covered is something like two thousand miles by eight thousand, and within these roomy limits, the greatest of oceans is a vast archipelago, a very "milky way of islets." A hundred years ago this immense island world had but just been revealed to the knowledge of civilized men. Captain Cook more than any other was the honored discoverer (1768-79), and a little later many eyes were turned thither by reading of Captain Bligh and the mutiny of the ship Bounty. It was a famous day, an occasion big with meaning for the world's redemption, when the *Duff*, in 1796, sent forth by the London Society which had come into existence only a few months before, with thirty missionaries on board set sail from the mouth of the Thames, bound for the Society Islands, then thought to be an earthly paradise inhabited by simple, docile, innocent and most lovable children of nature. The tide of enthusiasm ran high, and great things for the Gospel were expected soon and easily to be brought to pass. But bitter disappointment, and sorrow, and pain were in store, for the better part of two decades the two words, failure and waste, seemed to sum up the results, though as we now can plainly discern, the results of that undertaking, direct and indirect, near and more remote, were so various and so great, that the ship which bore the pioneers to their destination may fittingly be classed with the Mayflower, and even with the three caravels which some three hundred years before put forth westward from Palos. Of the thirty missionaries only four were clergymen, for men of that class who were both fit and willing to exchange Christian for pagan lands, were scarcely to be found, while six women and three children were added to the company. Unlearned artisans were in a large majority, blacksmiths, carpenters, shoemakers, weavers, butchers, etc. In seven months Tahiti was reached, eighteen were landed, while the rest were carried on to other groups. Like all the Polynesians, the natives were in demeanor gentle and genial, were social and hospitable; they received the white strangers with great demonstrations of joy and kind feeling, supplied them with food in abundance, and showered upon them favors of all sorts, while King Pomare made a liberal grant of land, and bestowed the gift of a large building. And so, what could be more delightful, or fuller of encouragement? But all these appearances proved most deceitful. With two shipwrecked Swedes found upon the island to help as interpreters, religious services were held almost at once, the study of the language was commenced and explorations were made in all directions, extending to other islands of the group. For some months all things went well, though signs quickly appeared that this was not Arcadia, and that these were none other than downright savages of the vilest and most villainous sort. Depravity in exceedingly revolting shapes thrust itself upon their notice, indecency was shocking for both amount and degree, some were cannibals, infanticide was common, and chastity was unknown. The property of the missionaries was coveted, especially their axes, knives, and other tools, and a plot was formed to rob them of all they possessed. Then a little later, perhaps in some considerable measure through their own unwisdom and lack of tact, three were assaulted and barely escaped being thrown into the sea. As a result, so much were they cast down, and so full of fear, that eleven took advantage of the presence of a vessel to depart from this land of horrors. Of the seven who remained, one presently joined himself to a native woman and not long after was found dead, while another fell into gross immorality and renounced Christianity. The little remnant, however, toiled faithfully on, with frequent wars to add to their woes. In 1801 a reinforcement of thirteen was made to the mission, and several who had abandoned the work returned. Schools were opened in various places, the language was reduced to writing and a translation of the Scriptures was pushed forward. Even yet, and in spite of their best endeavors, they often found themselves the objects of ridicule and evil treatment, thieving continued, and their lives were finally in such danger that the entire company turned their backs upon the island. The king, however, hearing of this, was sorry and sent an urgent message urging them to return, nor was it long before he began to display manifestations of a radical spiritual change in progress. He had learned to read and write, and now made many inquiries concerning God and the way of life, as well as declared plainly by his conduct that he held idols in contempt. Next, several of the principal chiefs became interested in things religious, and requests for baptism began to be made. Then one day a native was overheard in the forest pouring out his soul in prayer. Upon Eimeo and Huahine, as well as Tahiti, such tokens of good things at hand steadily increased. In 1813 upwards of fifty expressed a readiness to cast away their false gods, and then began a destruction of all emblems of idolatry. In 1817 a printing press was set up and produced a tremendous impression far and wide. In 1819 Pomare built a chapel 712 feet by 54, and soon after in the presence of a great multitude was baptized, the first of all the pagans in the South Seas. The number of converts rapidly rose to hundreds and thousands, idols were burned by the wholesale, nor was it long before almost the entire population was under careful religious instruction and had become Christian at least in name. But this day of joy dawned not until after two and twenty years of tearful seed-sowing and tilling of the soil. At the end of twelve years the field still appeared to be hopelessly barren and desert; when fifteen years had passed no fruit had been gathered, but now a great harvest was ripe and a blissful period of reaping ensued.

In 1835 a complete translation of the Scriptures was printed.

The full significance of the evangelization of the Society Islands does not appear until account is taken of the effects of this notable religious overturning which were felt throughout Polynesia. Starting in Tahiti, the tide of spiritual blessing and renovation spread in all directions, the divine impulse was imparted to other groups, and scores of islands were lifted into a new and heavenly life. Having had joyful experience of pardon and cleansing and peace with God through Jesus Christ, the happy converts were wisely taught at once to impart to others of the unspeakable gift. The Hervey Group was among the earliest recipients of the message of salvation, consisting of six islands, and lying some six hundred miles to the west. In this and various similar undertakings, John Williams, the future martyr of Erromanga, played a prominent part, was perhaps the chief personal force. He had been sent to the South Seas in 1816, had made his headquarters upon Raiatea, one of the largest islands in the Society Group, but ere long his faith, and desire, and endeavor, had become coextensive with the bounds of the Pacific, and he began to push out in all directions. In 1821 two Christian natives were ordained as teachers and set apart for service in the regions beyond. Mr. Williams sailed with these for Aitutaki, where they were kindly received with promise of protection. However, persecution befell at first, and great discouragement, though after a year had passed a general movement against the worship of idols set in. Hearing of this, the brethren in Tahiti determined to enlarge the force, and despatched two missionaries and six native teachers to occupy the other islands. Arriving at Aitutaki they found the Sabbath carefully kept, all the people attendants upon the public services, and family prayer generally instituted. But as yet Rarotonga remained undiscovered, and so Mr. Williams sailed in search of it. Success at length rewarding his attempt, two teachers were landed upon its shores to tell the story of a Saviour's love to the ignorant and vile. Within two years as much was accomplished as had required the labor of fifteen years in Tahiti. In later times this great leader and apostle of the Gospel declared concerning the Rarotongans: "When I found them in 1823 they were ignorant of the nature of Christian worship; and when I left them in 1834 I am not aware that there was a house in the island where family prayer was not observed every morning and evening." Here it was also that a training institution was established where teachers and pastors were fitted for lives of usefulness.

In the same year, 1821, Christianity was introduced into the Austral Islands, situated about the same distance to the south, and on this wise. A young chief had left home while a destructive pestilence was raging, and had finally drifted to Tahiti. Here he learned to his astonishment that idolatry had been everywhere overthrown, and the worship of the unseen God set up in its place. He sought out the missionaries and attended the services, was convinced of the truth, desired to take back to his friends the good things he saw and heard, and asked for teachers. Two native deacons volunteered to go, and with them some books were sent, including a few copies of the New Testament. Other Tahitan toilers were added later for the other islands of the group. A general stir resulted, attended with not a little debate and some opposition, but within less than half a decade, with only an occasional visit from the missionaries—that is, almost wholly by the efforts of those who themselves had but recently emerged from the follies, and sins, and abominations, of heathenism—the institutions of the Gospel were well planted, and multitudes were redeemed.

Samoa, or the Navigator's Group, was the next to be entered from the Society Islands by those who carried the bread and the water of life. And here too, John Williams was the chief instrument. In this case not less than two thousand miles of ocean space lying to the westward must be sailed over. In those days commerce and travel were but slight in the South Seas. In order to make the long passage it became necessary to construct a ship sufficiently large, and this in the well-nigh utter absence of all facilities for the performance of the task, with the added serious lack of all experience in such undertakings. But unappalled, he set resolutely about the task, and tugged away at the seemingly impossible, until finally the "Messenger of Peace," sixty feet in length, and of seventy-five tons burden, was launched and ready for use, as nondescript a craft as ever plowed the waves. It was in 1830 that this missionary ship-builder and navigator set sail for Samoa, with seven teachers, bent on errands of salvation. For two years the latter were left to themselves, to till the soil and plant the seed of the kingdom in the thirteen islands with some thirty-five thousand inhabitants. Their labors were richly blessed from on high, so that by the end of that period consciences had been quickened, and the foundations of idolatry had been shaken. In one locality fifty were ready to come out on the

Lord's side. In 1835 a company of missionaries with their wives made their advent to aid in evangelizing and instructing the willing-hearted, and at the close of a decade the outward symbols of paganism had disappeared, and Christianity was triumphant. Where before rapine and violence were universal, and as good as constant, with the accompaniment of murder, and cannibalism, and all manner of horrors, were now found many godly lives, happy homes, large congregations of devout worshippers, with public peace and the spirit of brotherly love.

All the wonders thus far recorded were wrought, by divine grace, through the instrumentality of the London Society, which was the first to enter this broad and desolate field. But this organization was not left alone for many years to struggle with the mighty powers of darkness, with none to sympathize and co-operate. For the English Wesleyan Church had begun to turn with burning desire and determined zeal towards the same perishing millions in the South Pacific. The Friendly Islands, called also from the principal island the Tonga Group, fifteen in number, and situated to the southwest of Samoa at a distance of three or four hundred miles, were selected as the place of beginning. The pioneer heralds of the cross were transported thither in 1822, that is, when after the long night of almost toil in Tahiti the morning had dawned, and just after the light had begun to break upon the Hervey, and the Austral groups. The *Duff*, after leaving a company of missionaries in the Society Islands, had taken ten others to Tongabatu. Though their reception was sufficiently pleasant, not many months elapsed before in a war which broke out among the savage tribes they were robbed of everything they possessed, three were murdered, and the survivors were reduced to utter destitution. After three years of suffering, with no hope of relief from England, they abandoned the mission. The first Wesleyan who landed on the same island fared no better, and was treated with such rudeness that he, too, took his departure. In 1826 two more were sent to this desert field, with others to follow later, and in spite of provoking and disheartening opposition, and seemingly with only their labor for their pains, set about the construction of buildings and the study of the language, meanwhile watching for opportunities to find access to darkened minds and obdurate hearts. Besides, certain teachers from Tahiti had been at work with better results, having even gathered quite a number of disciples. By 1830, in not a few, faith in idols had been shaken. In one of the islands a prominent chief hung up by the neck five famous gods of wood and stone that the people might see that they were dead, while in another eighteen temples were burned with all their images. After this turning to the Lord, churches were organized, schools were opened, and in all the islands hereabouts the sway of the Gospel was inaugurated. In 1833 king George of Tonga became supreme ruler throughout the group, while the year following a remarkable visitation of the Spirit was vouchsafed resulting in thousands of genuine conversions, the king being among the number. This truly eminent chieftain has only recently died, and, for the most part, through a long career proved himself a humble and faithful servant of Christ, and a tower of strength to truth and righteousness.

And it was from Tonga, and by the Wesleyans, that the name and spirit of the Prince of Peace were carried to Fiji, then a spot as vile, and as full of demoniac horrors, as the earth's surface contained. For years the name had been a synonym for the extreme of the beastly and the ferocious. Lust ran riot unchecked, and every vilest passion, the sick and aged were killed without pity, widows must needs die with their husbands, and slaves were slain to accompany their masters to the world of shades. But more than all, cannibalism was in the forefront among barbarous practices. It had become a part of religion, the matter of every day, to kill, and roast in ovens, and devour captives taken in war, the shipwrecked, etc., and for wanton destruction of human life on slightest occasion the demands were numberless. Scores at a time would be slain, far more than it was possible to eat, so that only the arms and legs of the victims were cooked, while the trunks were thrown away. And it was to this veritable pandemonium, to such hell-hounds as these, and knowing full well the import of the undertaking, that in the year of grace 1835, inspired by the great revival in Tonga, Cross and Cargill, with their wives and a few native Christians, stepped courageously on shore in Lakemba after a voyage of about two hundred miles to the westward. Of the nearly two hundred islands something like eighty are inhabited. A volume would be required to tell what was endured by these and others equally heroic who were added to their number. Seldom if ever has it fallen to the lot of the servants of the Most High to be placed in the midst of surroundings at once so full of peril, and so loathsome. But they held calmly on without flinching, teaching, preaching, playing the part of peace-makers, in their own lives showing the more excellent way. Schools, a printing press, and various appliances of civilization, were called to their aid. After about ten years of prayers and tears and toils, sowing beside all waters, the Spirit of God with wonderful renewing power was poured out upon this scene of darkness and depravity. The phenomena attending the revival were in keeping with the savage natures wrought upon, there was sore wrestling, and groaning, and crying out, but the devil of beastliness was effectually expelled. Not that all, or many, were lifted at once to the heights of saintliness, but that an extensive, an almost general beginning ensued of turning away in all sincerity from a multitude of evil things, and towards things which are pure, and honest, and lovely, and of good report. From that day to this, perhaps nowhere else in Christendom can communities be found in which so large a proportion are able to read, are found regularly in attendance upon public worship, and faithful in maintaining family prayer, and according to their knowledge and ability bringing forth fruits meet for repentance. Darwin's emphatic words find nowhere better proof and commentary than in Fiji : " The march of improvement consequent upon the introduction of Christianity throughout the South Seas probably stands by itself in the records of history. Within twenty years, human sacrifices, the power of an idolatrous priesthood, profligacy unparalleled in any other part of the world, infanticide and bloody wars not sparing women and children, all these have been abolished, and dishonesty, intemperance and licentiousness have been greatly reduced."

The scene changes once more, and this time to the north Pacific, as well as to the operations of a third society, whose work for the welfare of the islands of the sea began early, was carried on with vigor and sound discretion, and was crowned with distinguished success. Of course the reference is to the American Board, and its mission to the Hawaiian Islands. This group, containing ten islands, is situated about twenty degrees north of the equator, twenty-four hundred miles north of Tahiti, twenty-one hundred miles southwest of San Francisco, thirty-four hundred and forty miles from Yokohama, and forty-nine hundred from Hong Kong. To Captain Cook belongs the honor of discovery, and in Kealakakua he met his tragic fate in 1779. The story has been told many times of Obookiah, found one day in 1809 sitting upon the steps of one of the buildings of Yale College, and weeping because he longed to gain an education and knew not how it could be secured. And how he said later: "The people of Hawaii are very bad; they pray to gods made of wood. I want to learn to read the Bible, and go back there and tell them to pray to God up in heaven." This youth was befriended by Samuel J. Mills; next a mission school was opened at Cornwall, Conn., in which he and certain others could be fitted to labor for the evangelization of their countrymen, and at length, in 1819, the brig *Thaddeus* with nineteen missionaries was ready to sail. And stranger still was the varied providential preparation made for this eventful undertaking. First, after a period of bloody wars, the islands had all been brought under one government by King Kamehameha. Next, this same able ruler had become restive under the tyranny of the priesthood and the bondage of the *tabu*. In 1793 he had asked Vancouver to see that religious teachers were sent to him from England. And finally, the news had reached Hawaii of the complete overthrow of idolatry in the Society Islands, as well as various letters from Obookiah and others in America telling of the Christian faith. So that when Kamehameha died, while the messengers of peace were on their way, an open revolt against idolatry ensued. After a voyage of five months, when the brig cast anchor the astounding intelligence was imparted that no small portion of the work they had come to perform was already accomplished, for they were to labor among a people without a religion. After a little hesitation, Thurston, Bingham and the rest were received with kindness, and were soon at work. The chief opposition originated with sailors and other foreigners, to whom the presence of earnest Christian men and women was not in the least agreeable. The good seed sown began almost at once to spring up. The king and queen, and divers influential chiefs, were usually in attendance at public worship, with large numbers of their followers. At the end of eight years twelve thousand hearers of the word could be counted, and twenty-seven thousand pupils in the schools. The New Testament was presently in circulation in the vernacular, and was read with eagerness, and among high and low deep conviction of sin began to appear, with hundreds of sound conversions to righteousness. In 1836 a large reinforcement of laborers was received and distributed among the islands, and two years later the heavens were opened for the outpouring of such a spiritual blessing as has seldom been bestowed upon any people. For six years together the power of the Spirit was displayed, with Hilo, and the ministry of Titus Coan, as the most notable scene of the wonders wrought. Among the results twenty-seven thousand were added to the churches, a radical and general change came to social customs, and the government became Christian to an extent seldom elsewhere seen. By 1863 the American Board deemed the work of founding and building for the kingdom so thoroughly accomplished as to justify its withdrawal from the management of religious affairs, and to demand that upon the native churches should be put the entire burden of maintaining and pushing forward the King's business.

And furthermore, Hawaii, like Tahiti and Tonga, was called to impart of what it had received, and to bear the Gospel to other groups of Pacific islands. In 1850 a missionary society was formed looking to the evangelization of Micronesia, with its thousands of islands, and lying far to the south and west. In 1852 the Board despatched several missionaries to open work in the Caroline and the Gilbert groups. Calling at Honolulu, seven native Christians were found ready to accompany them, though only two with their wives went at that time. This was only thirty-three years from the date of the sailing of the brig *Thaddeus* from Boston harbor, and behold, a nation which then had never heard the Gospel, is now ready and eager to proclaim to the perishing in the desolate regions beyond the unsearchable riches of Christ. Kusaie and Ponape were chosen as centers of influence, though various other islands were occupied then or later, and in 1857 a beginning was made in the Marshall Group also. Here, too, Americans and Hawaiians were associated in effecting the overthrow of idolatry, the banishing of gross superstitions by the diffusion of the truth, and the kindling of holy desires. But the same year a mission, purely Hawaiian in its management and members, was founded in the remote Marquesas Islands. An urgent request for teachers had been brought in person by one of the prominent chiefs who had heard of the Gospel and its blessings from the lips of a young Kanaka trained in one of the mission schools, then left sick in the Marquesas, and finally marrying a daughter of the chief. In response to this Macedonian cry two native pastors were sent out and an English mechanic. These four missions have passed through their full share of vicissitudes, have suffered discouragement and serious disaster, not from outbreaks of savagery, or from the hardness of the heathen heart, but from the officious intermeddling of European governments and the machinations of Roman Catholic priests. But in spite of all, the institutions of the Gospel have been reared, and thousands have been redeemed from sin and raised to a new life.

The story of how Christ was preached to the perishing in New Zealand is next in order. Two islands, the North and South, are included under this name, and they lie some two thousand miles to the southeast of Australia. An area of 100,000 square miles is divided nearly equally between them. This is a land of fountains and streams and charming lakes; manifold attractions abound, and the climate is delightful. The inhabitants when first visited were found intelligent, brave, and not without various other attractive traits, but taken all in all, were wellnigh a match for the Fijians in the diabolical outbreaks of ferocity to which they were addicted. Thieving among them was a virtue, war was a passion, and they ate their enemies out of the impulse of pure revenge. Samuel Marsden, the apostle of New Zealand, while a convict chaplain in New South Wales, had met some of these fiends incarnate, his soul was strangely drawn out in sympathy for them, and in 1807, while on a visit to England, he urged the Church Society to undertake the task of preaching Christ in these dark abodes of cruelty.

Since no clergymen were to be had in those primitive days, three artisans were selected to lead in making the perilous attempt. On board the ship which bore them to their destination there "chanced" to be a poor Maori, who had been beguiled into working his passage to England, and then had been robbed of his wages, and left at the point of starvation. Marsden befriended poor Tuatara, both on shipboard and afterwards while waiting in Australia, and sent him forward to his home and friends to prepare the way for the advent of the evangelists. Not until 1814 was the master-missionary able to lead a company to the islands, composed of mechanics, settlers, and some chiefs who were returning, transporting also horses, cattle, sheep and poultry, which were altogether unknown to the natives. Casting anchor in the Bay of Islands, with Tuatara on hand to welcome and introduce him, he was received with *eclat*, and kept Christmas on shore with a religious service, and a sermon from the text, " Behold I bring you good tidings of great joy." Afterwards, to testify their great delight, a troop of three hundred cannibals, scantily attired and thoroughly tattooed, surrounded the missionary, dancing, shouting and yelling in fashion most blood-curdling. Other helpers came in due season, a few clergymen at length, and attempts were made to teach and preach; but little heed was paid to the heavenly message, and all hearts were found stony, and sordid, and altogether earthy. Besides, in the frequent wars, their lives were often in greatest peril. After eleven dreadful years, in 1825, a single native seemed to be penitent and was baptized, and then ensued five more years without any semblance of fruit. The saintly and apostolic Bishop Selwyn came to his forbidding diocese in 1842, bringing also a large reinforcement. Nor was it long before a most abundant and wide-spread harvest of souls was gathered in.

But while the English Church was toiling, watching and waiting, the Wesleyans also had entered to co-operate, coming in 1818 at the suggestion of Mr. Marsden, though the appearance in London of two Maori chiefs gave a great impulse in the same direction. Choosing Warangoa in the northern island as the site for a mission, the foundations were scarcely laid when a furious war broke out, and the missionaries barely escaped with their lives. A second start was made the next year, and after the utmost of endeavor, as late as 1830 no encouraging token appeared, so that abandonment of the work was in contemplation. But a few months later saw several scores of savages under instruction, and a class with five members was formed. On a single Sunday in 1834, eighty-four converts were baptized, and fourteen couples were married, and by 1838 sixteen chapels had been built, at one of which a thousand worshippers were wont to gather.

So many and so zealous had been the heralds of the Gospel, so copious had been the outpourings of the Spirit, and so mighty to convince and convict had been the word, that at the end of thirty years from the landing of the devoted convict chaplain, New Zealand could be regarded as at least evangelized, if not also Christianized. But, unfortunately, as it seems to human gaze, Great Britain was led, for reasons which cannot here be given, to set up a protectorate over the islands. This led to the entrance of settlers, and to furious and protracted land disputes, and finally to years of armed strife, among whose most lamentable results were these two; multitudes of the Maories were slain in battle, and for multitudes more the strain to faith, and patience, and endurance, was too great, and they fell away into their old superstitions. This calamity befell in the sixties, and its evil effects are still widely felt. Out of some two hundred thousands of natives only about forty thousand remain, and these are gathered upon a reservation in the northern island.

The New Hebrides easily take rank with Fiji and New Zealand for the unspeakable and measureless atrocities to which their population was prone, and fairly excel either or both in respect to the loss of life by violence which their redemption has cost the Christian Church. This group is situated about a thousand miles to the north of New Zealand, and about six hundred miles to the west of Fiji. The islands number about thirty, and nearly twenty languages are spoken upon them, sometimes two or three in different parts of a single one. However unlike the inhabitants may chance to be, they are all alike passionate, treacherous, and hold strangers responsible for storms, death, disease or any other visitations of evil. In justice however it should be added, that they are inhospitable and blood-thirsty in no inconsiderable degree because of the cruel wrongs which they have long suffered at the hands of sailors, traders, and labor agents if possible more unscrupulous and abandoned to wickedness than themselves. This annex to the pit of woe was first visited in 1839 by those who pitied the people and would endeavor to melt their hearts by telling the story of redeeming love. John Williams for almost a quarter of a century had been sailing hither and thither over the South Pacific founding missions and distributing preachers and teachers, and now came hither on the same errand. He had brought a number of Polynesian disciples who were ready to jeopardize their lives that they might win souls, and had put them on shore at various points which seemed most eligible. Reaching fateful Erromanga he landed with a companion, and in a few minutes both were murdered to furnish a cannibal feast. Not long after this dreadful tragedy the London Society sent two missionaries to Tanna, but after a sojourn of a few months they were compelled to flee for their lives. Then native teachers were again and again located upon various islands, with the only result that most either died from the effects of the climate, or were killed and eaten by the savages. It was not until 1848 that a permanent mission was established, and on Aneityum, by John Geddie, sent out by the Presbyterian Church of Nova Scotia. With only his wife for counsel and comfort, he endured untold trials for four years, including frequent thefts of property, and threats to burn their buildings and take their lives. Then Mr. Inglis came from Scotland, as an associate in labor and suffering. In particular, the remarkable genius possessed by Mr. Geddie for doing many things, whether in sailing or journeying on foot, in carpentry, translating, printing, teaching, preaching, administering medicine, and all with unmistakable and every day tokens of his ardent love for the very worst, excited admiration and finally conquered confidence and even affection. Within two years he could gather a congregation on the Sabbath to listen to the Gospel story and join in worship. In 1852 thirteen were baptized and a church was formed, and by 1854 the whole population had abandoned heathenism, while by the end of another decade the island could fairly be called Christian. As substantial evidence that the conversions were genuine, it is enough to state that by the time the entire Bible was translated and ready to be printed, by cultivating and manufacturing arrowroot the poor people had $6,000 in hand to meet the expense, and that they have sent out one hundred and fifty of their best men and women to adjoining islands as teachers.

Fotuna was entered by teachers from Samoa in 1841, but by the end of two years all had been killed and eaten, or thrown into the sea. Their place was taken later and held by Christians from Aneityum, and another from Rarotonga, for twelve years, or until a missionary came with his wife in 1866. It was at this date that the Rev. J. G. Paton began his notable career in the New Hebrides, locating upon Aniwa, where native teachers had long been bearing the brunt of the fierce warfare against the kingdom of darkness, a mission house was erected on a spot frequently used for cannibal feasts, and eight years more sufficed to establish the kingdom of light. But Tanna was the principal scene of the almost unmatched experiences and achievements of this prince among heralds of the cross in pagan lands. Thrice over Samoan teachers and others had made the attempt to introduce the Gospel, but had been compelled to save their lives by flight. In 1854 however, some of the natives on a visit to Aneityum, were so deeply impressed by what they saw of the results of Christian civilization that they asked for teachers, and these were able to remain. Mr. Paton and others ventured into the den of lions in 1858 and years following, though with harrowing scenes, deadly perils and fleeing for life to endure for a decade. And Erromanga also, worst of all, was evangelized, but only after much shedding of precious blood. After the murder of Williams, Samoan teachers played the part of pioneers in spite of frequent persecution, and occasional expulsion by violence, several of the islanders were sent to Samoa and Auckland to be trained and Christianized, and were then returned to labor among their countrymen, and Aneityum disciples added their efforts. In 1857 the Rev. G. N. Gordon was sent from Nova Scotia, filled four years with labors of love, and then, their fury excited by the destruction wrought by a hurricane, and a plague of measles introduced by a trading vessel, both he and his wife were killed. After three years a brother of the martyr, the Rev. J. S. Gordon, offered himself to fill the vacant place, devoted his strength without stint to the material and spiritual well-being of all about him, and in 1872 met his death at the hands of a treacherous native. But by this time the powers of evil had spent their violence, other fervid and fearless souls took up the Christlike task, converts soon began to multiply, and now the forces are uppermost which make for righteousness, and peace, and joy. About twenty of the islands may be called Christian, and some fourteen thousand have been gathered into churches. Eight branches of the Presbyterian Church are happily joined in the New Hebrides mission. Mention must not be omitted of Bishop Patteson and his distinguished services in Melanesia, a man whose gifts and graces, whose godly ambitions and achievements in a broad and desolate field belong in the same list with those of Williams and Selwyn. He also attained to the crown of martyrdom in 1871 in Nackapu, one of the northern islands of the group, being slain by the savage natives, and because his vessel was mistaken for the craft in which a party of kidnappers had paid a visit not long before in the pursuit of their nefarious business, and which they had painted to resemble the one in which his frequent voyages were made.

A few words must suffice for New Guinea, the largest of islands, but sparsely populated, little known in the interior, and besides so recently visited with the Gospel that not much of progress can be narrated. The Dutch, the Germans and the British have divided the area beween them, the latter taking the portion lying to the southeast and nearest to Australia, from which it is separated by Torres Strait. The Utrecht Society began work as far back as 1863, and the London Society followed in 1871, securing the bulk of its teachers in the South Seas. Upwards of fifty stations have been opened along the southeast coast, while the churches have about five hundred members, and the schools about two thousand pupils. The Wesleyans also have a mission in which similar results can be reckoned, and the Rhenish Society is engaged in breaking ground in Kaiser Wilhelm's Land at the north. In all some seventy churches have been formed, and nearly thirty native preachers are in the field.

The East Indies.

Other terms applied to this vast and wonderful island region are, the Spice Islands, the Moluccas, Malaysia, the Indian Archipelago and the Malay Archipelago. And the numerous bodies of land are included which stretch over such a long line from the southeastern corner of Asia almost to Australia. Since the seventeenth century, the Dutch have been in possession at most points. The Philippines are Spanish dependencies, and being also intensely, and exclusively, and intolerantly Roman

Catholic, may be omitted from this review. The mingling of races, and tribes, and religions, in these parts is something amazing. In Singapore alone a hundred tongues are said to be spoken, and the Bible is distributed in no less than forty-five. With Malays in a vast majority, are jumbled Arabs, Chinamen, Siamese, Battas in Sumatra and Dyaks in Borneo, etc., etc. The total population of the East Indies is about 40,000,000, of whom most are Moslems, and more than half are found in Java. From the beginning Christian missions have been very generally in the hands of Netherlanders, though the Rhenish Society has toiled faithfully and with most encouraging success, and the English Propagation Society in certain sections has made an impression both deep and broad.

Though Java is but the fourth island for size, in almost every other respect it is of more importance than any of its neighbors. The density of the population is nearly equal to that of many portions of Europe, while the soil yields a store of valuable productions such as few territories of equal extent can match. With the Dutch East India Company in political control, a corporation whose narrow and non-Christian policy much resembled its British counterpart, we are not surprised to learn that not much of value was undertaken for the spiritual elevation of the natives. Though chaplains and others did some evangelizing work, and several truly devout and earnest men made proclamation of the Gospel, yet on the whole the state so seriously defiled the church that the conversions were but superficial and scarcely more than in name. And hence it signifies little when we read that in 1712 there were in Java 100,000 "Christians." But during this century missions have been on a vastly better basis, and the Netherlands Society reports 12,000 converts who have been secured in the main from the ranks of the Mohammedans. A seminary has been opened in Depok for the training of evangelists, from which seventy-one have already graduated, coming from Borneo, Sumatra, Sangir, Almaheira and Dutch New Guinea. And this further should be said, to the praise of the Dutch East India Company, now happily extinct. The New Testament was translated into Malay as far back as 1688, and the Old Testament in 1733, and both were printed at the expense of this body of merchants.

The English Baptists sent missionaries to the Battas, the aboriginal tribes of Sumatra, and dwelling in the interior, in 1820, but for some reason their presence excited the jealousy and suspicion of the Dutch rulers, who put so many hindrances in their way as to make it seem expedient to abandon the field. Between 1827 and 1836 several missionaries from Holland entered the island, to bestow their main attention upon the Chinese immigrants, and yet making also not a few converts among the Malays, and whether heathen or Moslem. In 1834 the American Board designated Munson and Lyman to carry the Gospel to the Battas, but while they were exploring to fix upon the best location for work, a war broke out among the savages, and both were murdered. It is the Rhenish Society of Germany which has wielded the chief evangelizing force in Sumatra. Beginning in 1860, two quite extensive fields have been tilled, with Toba Lake yielding the richest harvest of souls brought to a knowledge of Jesus. And not only are the heathen casting away their idols, but more and more the followers of the false Prophet are turning from him to the Saviour of the world. In the neighboring island of

Nias many converts have also been made. The entire number of adherents exceeds twenty-five thousand, the communicants are about six thousand, and forty-two hundred were baptized in 1892. It is in Sumatra that this society finds its strongest mission.

Borneo is the largest island in the East Indies, but is thinly inhabited. The aboriginal Dyaks of the interior deserve a place among the strangest of people, whose houses are commonly built on piles, and numerous families are found dwelling in a single structure several hundred feet in length. Until Christianity and civilization had done their work, war was their chief end, with head-taking as the special concomitant. Beheading was performed by the wholesale, on the slightest occasion and without ceremony, and with very much the same idea as scalps were removed by our Indians. A young man was not allowed to marry until he was possessed of a number of these hideous tokens of his skill and prowess, while a large assortment constituted the glory of the family. The graves of chiefs were fenced about with a line of heads, and there was no more efficacious safeguard against evil spirits than that secured by a pious offering of sculls. In 1839 the American Board sent a company of missionaries to this island, to enter upon what proved to be a ten years' struggle with the Dutch authorities, whose settled policy was to exclude all foreigners from the interior, and finally, after some had died, the survivors were instructed to retire from the field. Beginning in 1834, within twenty years a score of ambassadors for Christ were located among the Dyaks in South Borneo by the Rhenish Society. With slight encouragement at first, at length a marked change began to be visible in the barbarous head-takers. But of a sudden, in 1859, stirred up by the fanatical Mohammedans, the heathen party rose in murderous fury and killed four, with three of their wives and several children, pillaged the mission and pulled down the buildings. And so in an hour the work of a quarter of a century was practically annihilated. To crown their sorrows, the missionaries were held responsible for the outbreak by the Dutch rulers, and were treated with worse than coldness and neglect. But with the utmost of Christian heroism they held on, and in 1866 better days began to dawn. Upwards of thirty native helpers have been raised up, and a training school is maintained to fit evangelists to labor for the redemption of their Dyak countrymen. Some seven hundred are found in the churches and the adherents are numbered by the thousand. The Propagation Society (S. P. G.) came to North Borneo in 1847, and through the presence there of the famous Englishman, Rajah Brooke of Sarawak, and from that day to this a body of godly and self-denying men have devoted themselves to the welfare of certain tribes notorious and dreaded far and wide for frequent acts of piracy, as well of others further inland; nor have their arduous labors been in vain. The beneficent institutions of the Gospel have been planted and are steadily growing, and many souls have been redeemed from sin.

Nowhere in the Indian Archipelago do the effects of Dutch rule and evangelistic effort appear to better advantage than in Celebes, and especially in Minahassa, the northeast portion. Many heathen were instructed and baptized during the last century, and in 1822 the Netherlands Society sent its representatives to begin special and systematic work. Other organizations have followed to assist in sowing and reaping, and with such success that now in a total population of 145,000 about 125,000 Protestant Christians are to be found. In Sangir also, an island lying not far to the east of Minahassa, and so recently desolated by a terrible catastrophe, where the inhabitants number 80,000, more than a third have forsaken their heathenism. And Amboyna has scarcely any non-Christians left, whether pagan or Mohammedan.

In all the Dutch East Indies, according to Dean Vahl, there are 60 European missionaries engaged in efforts to Christianize the natives, representing 10 societies, with 31 native ministers and 253 other native helpers, and 49,882 communicants among the fruits of toil. The Netherlands Society alone has some 90,000 adherents. At the end of 1892 the Rhenish Society was maintaining a staff of 46 Europeans, and 144 paid with 419 unpaid native helpers. In the schools were 4,779 pupils, and in the churches 6,809 communicants, while the adherents aggregated almost 27,000, of whom 4,550 were added last year. According to the census of 1890 there was a total of 277,450 Christians.

The West Indies.

This is a name bestowed by the immortal discoverer under the impulse of a mistaken conviction, and it stands for what a world of tragedy, of depravity, and of shame! " From the second visit of Columbus until the present century, these islands have been the scene of sorrow and oppression. Their waters have been dyed with human blood. . . . Piracy was rife, and the commerce of Europe suffered from the marauding buccaneers who smarted from the wrongs they suffered, and retaliated on the innocent as well as the guilty. The slave trade had its origin here, and the hardly less cruel importation of coolies has left its curse. For years these islands were England's penal colonies. Into this moral sewer was swept the refuse of Europe. Is it strange, then, that these lands should have been sunk in the lowest depths of sin and degradation? Various European nations have parcelled out among themselves the islands which number nearly a thousand, and only Haiti is left independent. Spain holds Cuba, whose area almost equals that of all the other members of the group combined, and Porto Rico; Great Britain claims ownership in the Bahamas, Jamaica, Barbados, etc.; France is master of Guadaloupe, Martinique, etc.; Denmark of St. Thomas, Santa Cruz, etc.; and the Netherlands of four small islands. The original inhabitants have entirely disappeared. For years they were enslaved, worked to death in the mines, or shipped over seas by their Spanish masters, and then with the energy of despair rising against their inhuman oppressors were annihilated. In Haiti alone two millions of aborigines were found, but in *thirty years* scarcely one was left alive. Then Negro slaves began to be imported, the Portuguese setting the iniquitous example, and later every nation possessing colonies in this region shared in the infamy to the full. It is estimated that to Jamaica alone, between 1700 and 1786, not less than 600,000 were brought from African shores. Almost everywhere the Negroes far outnumber the whites. Hindus and Chinese, who are held in at least semi-slavery, also constitute no inconsiderable part of the population.

The Moravians were the first to hear and heed the cry of woe which ascended to heaven from these dreadful depths, and away back in 1734, when the whole Christian world was dead to such sympathy and longing, and sent two men to carry the light to those who sat in the shadow of death. The scene of their earliest labors and sufferings was in the Danish possessions. The degraded and most wretched creatures, who had never heard of joy and peace and salvation, at first wondered and were incredulous concerning the message which offered the riches of Divine love to such as they, but were soon eager to listen and glad to accept. Aside from the dense ignorance and superstition of the slaves, the principal obstacles were placed in the way of the missionaries by the Europeans, through their ungodliness, sectarian prejudice, and the interference of the civil authorities. In addition, the climate was so deadly that at the close of eleven years thirty-five had found graves in West Indian soil. But there was no lack of volunteers to fill the places of those who were glad to die if need be. For almost one hundred and sixty years these humble, patient, much-enduring bringers of good things to the lowest of the low have held on, occupying in later times Jamaica, Antigua, Barbados, Tobago and Trinidad. And their reward also has been commensurate with their toil, in souls enlightened and sanctified and raised to heaven. According to the latest report 46 principal stations are occupied by 58 European missionaries of both sexes, the pupils in the schools number 16,588, the communicants 17,336 and the native Christians upwards of 40,000.

The English Wesleyans were the next to offer to the bondmen the freedom of the Gospel. In 1758 an English planter of Antigua while on a visit to his native land had heard Wesley preach, was deeply wrought upon, turned Methodist, and two of his slaves were baptized by the great evangelist. Returning, he carried the truth as it is in Jesus, and proclaimed it to both black and white until his death. His place was filled by two slaves for a season, but at length one Baxter, a shipwright and local preacher, came to lead, and the congregation steadily grew until large numbers were wont to assemble for worship. Then in 1786 came a reinforcement, and through one of the strangest of providences. Dr. Coke had sailed for Nova Scotia with several missionaries, but in a long and furious tempest had been driven far to the south. On Christmas Day the party, all weather-beaten and covered with brine, landed in Antigua, and met Baxter just on his way to hold a service. A thousand Negroes were in attendance, to whom Coke preached, and was so deeply impressed with their need and their eagerness to receive, that he left the helpers he had with him in this and the neighboring islands, and sent others in addition. One after another, twenty islands received the Gospel by this "accident," and among them were the Bahamas, Barbados, Trinidad and Jamaica. Several attempts were made to enter Haiti, but on account of the trying climate, frequent revolutions and Roman Catholic intolerance, not much has been accomplished. In Jamaica and elsewhere for many years constant opposition was experienced, at first because of intense prejudice against Methodists, and later because in all the bitter struggle with slavery these missionaries gave their hearty sympathy to those in bondage. But in spite of all a great work has been accomplished, so that the converts now number upwards of 40,000 and the attendants upon public worship are more than 125,000.

The English Church Society and the Propagation Society have labored long and faithfully in the West Indies, not only for the blacks, but for the white colonists also. In 1813 the Baptists of Great Britain undertook missions in behalf of the enslaved, and by 1831, 31 churches had been formed in Jamaica with 10,838 members. But in that year occurred an uprising of the Negroes, which the missionaries were falsely accused of countenancing, if not even instigating. William Knibb and others were arrested, charged with rebellion, and threatened with lynching by the planters, and several chapels were burned. Other trials of a different kind followed emancipation in 1834, but such was the growth of the good work that in 1842 it became self-supporting. The Jamaica Baptist Union now includes 173 churches with 39,065 members, and there are 21,709 pupils in the schools. Elsewhere among the islands considerable work is done.

At its formation in 1847, the United Presbyterian Church of Scotland entered into the labors of two societies, which had been engaged in the field for years, but was called almost at once to pass through a most remarkable and trying series of calamities, caused by climate, by cholera, by tempest, and by the burning of a vessel at sea, among the rest, to the loss of the lives of half a dozen missionaries; but enduring to the end, are able to point, both in Jamaica and Trinidad, to not a little of substantial results for the furtherance of the kingdom of righteousness. Thus the mission churches contain 11,647 members. The Presbyterian Church of Canada is in joint occupation of Trinidad, entering in 1869, but makes a specialty of caring for the bodies, and minds, and souls, of East Indian coolies, who in that island and the neighboring regions number more than 300,000. While many are continually coming and going, many others become permanent settlers. To these heathen whose case is so forlorn, who under contract-labor upon the sugar plantations are in a condition of semi-slavery, the glad tidings were carried, that, even for them the Son of God offered his life in loving sacrifice, and so freedom, and full manhood, and holiness, and joy eternal, are possible. Six ordained missionaries are now cultivating this field, and four unmarried women give themselves to teaching. Two ordained Hindus are associated with them and, also 39 more are under training for the ministry. In 52 schools are 4,324 pupils. The communicants number 573, and the native contributions reached $2,785 in 1892. A college has recently been established.

Perhaps in no other mission field is it so difficult to set forth in a brief summary an adequate statement of the work of the Gospel. The totals for the organizations named, and for a few others which are bearing a part in illumining the darkness, are these, approximately: The European missionaries number 130, with nearly 90 ordained natives is efficient co-operation. There are some 50,000 pupils in the mission schools, and 113,000 members in the churches. For the adherents 300,000, is a conservative figure. But to these sums is to be added a very large increment, resulting from what is accomplished by various organizations representing the English Church, and whose toil is bestowed upon Europeans and Negroes together. Ten years ago it could be affirmed: " In all of the British West Indies, with over 1,000,000 inhabitants, 248,000 are regular attendants at the house of God; about 85,000 are communicants in the various mission churches, and 78,600 children are being instructed in 1,123 day schools (about 45,000 of these in Jamaica.")

CHAPTER XVI.

MISSIONS IN THE TURKISH EMPIRE.

OR perhaps the phrase "Missions to the Oriental Churches" would be more fitting, since the Nestorians are included; or "to Western Asia," for though Egypt is omitted, a portion of Persia is to pass under view; or with certain limitations, "to Mohammedan countries." This undertaking of the modern church is second to none, either for interest or importance. For it relates almost wholly to Bible lands, Palestine, Babylon, Assyria and the rest, and is intimately connected with Jerusalem, Antioch, Damascus, the Seven Churches of Asia Minor, and scores of other names, which call forcibly to mind the godly lives and inspiring deeds of patriarchs, prophets and apostles, as well as the heavenly ministry of the Man of Nazareth. Classical history is also constantly reproduced by the story of missionary toil, for it relates to Tyre and Troy, Byzantium and Athens, Cyprus and the Bosphorus, cities which live in the literature of Greece and Rome, and regions in which Alexander and the Cæsars wrought, at least in part, the wonders that gave them undying fame. Then, too, this was the theater in which the Gospel achieved its earliest victories, from which later it was well-nigh altogether expelled, and where ever since the prophet of Arabia has been held in highest honor, while to be a disciple of Jesus was to be in subjection, most cruel and degrading servitude, and to court continual insult and scorn. Therefore, in a peculiar sense, to carry Protestant Christianity to Western Asia was to avenge a shameful robbery, was to restore to Christ his own. As no other mission, this one partakes of the nature of a crusade.

It is also worthy of notice that a peculiar and remarkable providence is discernible at many points in the narrative of the re-introduction of the Gospel into lands long possessed by the Moslem. And beginning as far back as the day when the fearful catastrophe befell the church. How strange, but how fortunate beyond expression, that when the fanatical Arabs made their conquests with a fury which nothing could resist, and also afterwards when the Turks entered into supreme power, the Christians were not all put to the sword, were not even compelled to accept the Koran, but the only demand was for submission to political rule. Within certain limits each sect was left autonomous, possessed a separate existence inside the state, its ecclesiastical officers and religious customs were recognized and protected by law. And so for twelve centuries a half-dozen or more of churches, having indeed a faith and practice at many points exceedingly corrupt, but also retaining not a few germs of truth and Christian virtue, had lived on and on, in spite of unspeakable trials and hindrances of all sorts, and as if preserved of God in waiting to perform an essential service, when a brighter day should dawn. If the fact had been otherwise, if the Crescent in every particular had triumphed over the Cross, if the Oriental Churches had been destroyed in form and in substance, it is impossible to see how the truth as it is in Jesus could ever again have gained a foothold in the land of its origin. But not so now. For millions are found scattered through every province and almost every community of the Turkish Empire, who love the Bible, hold in reverence the name of Christ, and are not without appreciation for better spiritual things, and longings to possess them. And only let these Christians, or even a large proportion of them, be turned from their serious errors and their lamentable shortcomings, let the pure light which once shone be rekindled, and the ancient flame of love and zeal and devotion, and then the day of redemption for their Mohammedan masters will be at hand. Why should the Turks accept such scandalous perversions and caricatures of Christianity as have been from the beginning presented to their gaze? Why should they not despise and abhor the superstition, and idolatry, and moral corruption, which have universally been identified with those who claimed to be representatives of New Testament piety? And we cannot but believe, the signs of the times unite to inspire the blessed expectation, that it is the glorious mission of the Oriental Churches, reformed, renewed, refilled with life divine, to play for the Turkish Empire the part performed on a scale so vast by the Jews in the early spread of the Gospel.

And further, we must not fail to take note how curiously it has come to pass that while the movement to re-evangelize the Orient was in the days of feeble infancy, and the corrupt hierarchy rose up in opposition and determination to crush it out by violence, countenance and protection were frequently vouchsafed by Moslem authority, the hand of persecution was stayed, and the right to live unmolested and to grow was established on firm foundations. It almost provokes a smile to recall how when the ecclesiastical authorities resented and resisted the attempts of American disciples to substitute a pure religion for a corrupt one, they were compelled by the Sultan, universal head of Islam that he is, to refrain from the use of all carnal weapons and to suffer truth and righteousness to work their revolutions. And how surprisingly near to the irony of fate will the outcome approach when, after the irresistible forces resident in New Testament ideas and convictions and longings have thus been developed and massed and marshaled, these same forces shall work mightily and most effectually for the utter overthrow of the political and religious system without whose aid, at least so far as human eye can see, energy and momentum sufficient for so great a task could never have been gained. But we need not wonder at this, for ours is a God who is easily able to make the wrath of man to praise him and the remainder of wrath to restrain.

For some reason it has happened, and very fortunately, that among important missionary fields this one has been left largely, and for the first fifty years almost wholly, under the care of a single society, the American Board. But not, however, to be supported and managed by the Congregationalists alone, for no less than five denominations were then united under one organization, including the Presbyterians, Dutch Reformed, German Reformed and Associate Reformed. Moreover, the Turkish mission is one of the largest anywhere to be found, whether for the cost of maintenance, the force of laborers engaged, or the number of members gathered into the churches; and upon it are expended just about one-third of the income of one of the foremost of all the societies, as well as one-third of the energies of all the men and women employed; while, curiously, within its limits are found also one-third of all the communicants, of the native Christians, and of the children under instruction in the schools. Only two missions of the American Board are older than this one, those in Bombay and Ceylon, though a party of pioneers for the Gospel was despatched to the Sandwich Islands almost simultaneously with another to Western Asia. When Fisk and Parsons were set apart to their work in 1818, though Palestine was named as their destination, and the Jews were thought of as the objects of their toil, the future was entirely hidden from their gaze. And when a year later they set forth, they went out not knowing whither. The official instructions suggest: " From the heights of the Holy Land you will take an extended view of the wide-spread desolations and variegated scenes presenting themselves on every side to Christian sensibility; and will survey with earnest attention the various tribes and classes who dwell in that land and in the surrounding countries." And they were bidden to search with all diligence to ascertain what good could be done, and by what means, for Jews, for pagans, for Mohammedans, for Christians, for people in Palestine, in Egypt, Syria, Persia, Armenia, and in other countries to which their inquiries may be extended. For those were primeval days, the world was largely unknown and inaccessible, and open fields were few and hard to find. After a halt at Malta, Smyrna became their headquarters while endeavoring to master several Oriental languages, and tours were made through the Ægean, and to the sites of the Seven Churches of Asia Minor. In 1821 Parsons entered Jerusalem, but was not able to make it his abode, and a few months later his health failing, with his companion voyaged to Egypt where he died. By this time Beirut had been found to be a most convenient place for a central station, and Fisk, with Jonas King for associate, resorted thither, journeying also here and there, among the rest over the Lebanon range, and to Jerusalem, if haply they might remain. But in 1825 the former fell a victim to the climate. The work was taken up and carried on by Bird and Goodell and Eli Smith, who fixed themselves in Beirut and at once began to distribute in several languages the Word of God and other Christian literature, to open schools, and in every possible way to do the work of evangelists. Their hearts were also cheered by the visits of various inquirers, and by being able to lead a few to embrace the truth. The Greek Revolution was now in the midst of its course, and the excitements attending the struggle led to so many embarrassments and to such perils that in 1828 it was deemed prudent to retire to Malta, and for two years the mission was suspended. Six years before a printing press had been set up in this island by the Board, and had been kept busy sending forth a variety of books and tracts in seven languages of the Orient.

During these trying days of watching and waiting for the pillar of cloud to rise and move forward, it had already come to pass that in several ways the indication had been given that the Armenian Christians, numbering two or three millions, and scattered everywhere throughout the Turkish Empire, were easily accessible and would welcome the presentation of a pure Gospel. The capital alone contained some one hundred and fifty thousand, and as many Greek Christians, the two together constituting a third of the entire population. And at a conference held in Malta it was determined to divide the mission, and while reoccupying Beirut, to send Mr. Goodell to begin work in Constantinople. Though it seemed at the time so insignificant, it was really one of the great events which occurred when in 1831 this solitary stranger from America took up his residence in the famed metropolis of the Ottoman realm. While he was looking about, laying his plans and setting in operation various intellectual and spiritual forces, two men, Smith and Dwight, had started upon a memorable exploring tour through Asia Minor, as far as to the Nestorians in northwestern Persia. Nearly a year and a half was consumed, and some twenty-five hundred laborious miles were gone over, but the undertaking was destined to bring back a rich return.

Leaving for the moment the further notice of this movement, which soon proved to be the supreme task on hand for the society in these parts, let us glance at two or three other attempts already begun, and for quite a period pushed forward with vigor and great expectation, but ending in discouragement and practical failure. And first, with regard to the Jews. Concerning the proposed Palestine mission the Prudential Committee wrote: "We owe the Jews a great debt, and they are to obtain mercy. A disposition manifested lately and extensively, and recent successes among them, are indications not to be disregarded. Our minds and hearts have long been drawn to Palestine in particular." And, as one suggests in explanation: "The vision arose of a reconquered Holy City and a regathering of the chosen people. They were to go to Zion, behold her battlements, and from her towers get views of the land soon to be possessed for the Son!" Again and again the missionaries entered Jerusalem purposing to remain, but were compelled to withdraw, and similar efforts were to continue for yet a decade, when the inevitable was accepted, and the field was abandoned. In 1831 Mr. Schauffler was appointed to the Jewish mission, with headquarters at Constantinople where some seventy-five thousand Spanish Jews were dwelling, descendants of the hapless wretches who, expelled from Spain by Isabella the Pious, and refused a refuge by every Christian country, accepted the Sultan's invitation to partake of Moslem hospitality. The Hebrews were found stiffnecked and uncircumcised in heart and ears, but nevertheless much important work was done until 1846, especially in the way of translating and printing, when the Scottish Free Church entered the field with great zeal and vigor, and the Board determined to retire. Other attempts of a like character were made at Smyrna and Salonica, the last one ending not till 1856.

And also, while in search for the full import of their high calling, the attention of the society was directed towards the Greek Church as an encouraging field for sowing the good seed of the kingdom. The early missionaries at Malta, and in the Ægean, came across certain bright and promising youths, who were sent to the United States to be educated mainly at the expense of the Board, and took a course of study at Cornwall, Amherst and Yale. The Smyrna station was opened in 1826, because this branch of the Oriental Church was largely represented in that city. Soon after Grecian independence was established Jonas King was located at Athens, to open a school and to hold such religious services as seemed to be prudent. Several other men soon followed and began work in Argos, Cyprus, Scio, etc. But presently, both church and state showed themselves to be so rigidly intolerant, and put so many hindrances in the way of preaching and teaching, that by 1844 all the missionaries had been transferred to regions more favorable, except Mr. King, who remained until his death in 1869. Thus ended all special effort in behalf of the Greeks. While in the midst of their struggle for liberty, much enthusiasm had been excited in their behalf throughout the civilized world, they had eagerly sought sympathy and assistance from near and from far, and both had been lavishly bestowed, but when the hated Turk had been effectually expelled, their friends were forgotten, and they desired to be left wholly to themselves.

We return now to Mr. Goodell and his work among the Armenians. He was not left long to toil alone. Dwight was already in the field, others were added soon, Hamlin came in 1839, and ere long a noble company of saints and heroes were engaged heart and soul. With regard to the body of Christians for whose spiritual regeneration they were from henceforth to devote themselves, it must suffice to suggest, that like the other corrupt churches of Western Asia, it is of ancient date, its creed and forms of worship were fixed in days of theological and ecclesiastical corruption, and through all the revolutions and catastrophes which have since befallen, have passed unchanged, only lapsing farther and farther into formalism and moral stupor. They resemble Catholicism in most essential points, though while some of the branches are in a somewhat better religious case, others have departed even more seriously from the New Testament standard. Two facts in particular were of great value in helping on the introduction of Protestant Christianity among the Armenians. This people, wherever found, is possessed of unusual intelligence and intellectual vigor, and though the Scriptures were shut up from the use of the multitude in a language which only the ecclesiastics could read or understand, their use had never been forbidden, and the teachings of prophets, apostles, and the Son of God, were held in highest reverence. For some years the work of Bible distribution had been carried on quite extensively, and presently a translation was made in Armeno-Turkish which many could read. It was not long before a remarkable spirit of inquiry appeared, first in Constantinople, and later in neighboring cities and towns. Sin and salvation, repentance, faith, and the Gospel rule of life, were themes which interested scores and hundreds, and they began to call upon the missionaries, and to send inviting them to come and teach the new and better way. There was no disposition to attack the old church, or to denounce its errors and sins, nor was there any thought as yet of organizing another body of disciples. It was hoped that the priesthood would be found open to conviction and would lead in the work of thorough reform. By 1834 Brusa, sixty miles out in Bythynia, was occupied as a station, and the same year Mr. Johnston ventured off as far as Trebizond to plant for the kingdom of heaven. Public services were opened wherever possible, and schools were started at various points, in most cases with an attendance remarkably large and earnest. So deep and general became the religious stir, that not strangely the church authorities began to take alarm. The people in large numbers ceased to worship pictures and to pray to the saints, declined to come to confession, and even hesitated not to take their superiors to task for departures from the teachings of Holy Writ. The Catholic priesthood also, and that of the Greek Church as well, were moved with a great fear. By 1839 a furious crusade was launched against these obnoxious new practices, and these heresies so pestiferous.

It is a peculiar feature of Turkish rule that it bestows a large amount of civil authority upon the leading official of each recognized Christian sect. Within certain limits and under certain regulations, he is permitted to inflict upon offending members of his church the pains and penalties of the law. After months of distant ominous mutterings, in 1839 the thunder of denunciation and threatening began to sound and to wax louder. Through gross misrepresentations, and continued appeals, the Turkish authorities were prevailed upon to join in a vigorous attempt to crush out the evangelical movement with violence, and even to drive the troublesome missionaries out of the country. The first onset towards a sharp persecution had already been made, when suddenly the army of the rebellious pasha of Egypt began its march northward, another large force was gathered in the capital and sent forward to meet the foe, a battle ensued which ended in overwhelming disaster to the Turks, before the calamitous news arrived the Sultan was a corpse, and behold, in the excitement and panic, such trifles as religious affairs were forgotten, at least for a season. And as so often happens, instead of harm, great good came to the cause of reform from the sufferings and perils endured. In spite of all, the work rapidly spread and the number of desciples increased, so that missionaries were located in Nicomedia, in Adabazar, and in Erzroom. To the amazement of all, in 1840 the new Sultan pledged himself to secure religious liberty to all his subjects. It was an evil hour for despotism when that utterance was made, though in all probability it was designed to mean little or nothing. After a few years of quiet, it came to pass that once more the Armenian ecclesiastics were filled with alarm over the outlook, and set themselves with all diligence and fervor to the task of putting an end forever to the appalling heresy and backsliding. First came solemn warning and threatening, and afterwards terrible bulls of anathema and excommunication. In every community lists of suspected ones were prepared, the bastinado was applied, fines, and imprisonment, and banishment were inflicted, business was destroyed, all means of securing a living were cut off, and to the dead burial was refused. And to crown all, it was so in those days that whoso claimed to be a Christian, and did not belong to some one of the various churches recognized by the government, was an outlaw, possessed no civil rights whatsoever, might be robbed and wronged to any extent, and without legal remedy. And such was the very serious case in which those found themselves who would live godly in Christ Jesus, and upon whom fell the blighting curse of the patriarch. In the presence of these terrors, some paused appalled and turned back to make their peace with the priesthood, but a much larger number stood firm and could not be shaken. In 1846 the first Protestant church was organized in Constantinople, twenty-eight years after Fisk and Parsons were set apart to the Palestine mission, and five more were formed in months succeeding. And meantime the Sultan was petitioned for recognition and protection. By a good providence, a most timely and efficient instrumentality was in readiness to further this indispensable action. For years Great Britain was represented at the Porte by Sir Stratford Canning, a diplomat of remarkable energy and skill, and withal a devout and ardent Christian. He had already secured, in spite of long hesitation and the profoundest unwillingness, the abolition of the death penalty for apostasy from the Moslem faith—an achievement thought to approach to the miraculous—and presently, under his persistent urgency, a firman was issued setting up in the empire a new and full-fledged religious body, endowed with legal rights equal to those of any other. The famous Hatti Humaioun, Magna Charta of religious liberty for Turkey, was only the logical conclusion for the several steps which had preceded, and from first to last only the severest political pressure would have availed to secure such radical yielding to Occidental ideas and convictions.

Being now delivered from all entangling alliances with the old church, the way was fairly open for rapid and solid progress. By 1850 it was found that about a thousand Christians had separated themselves from their former ecclesiastical associations, and some three times as many had really adopted Protestant sentiments. In order to improve to the full the great opportunity, a large increase was speedily made to the missionary force, for a a hundred towns were reported as affected by the reformation, and open for evangelizing efforts. Indeed a wonderful revival now burst forth, and continued for more than a decade, extending from the Bosphorus to the Persian frontier, whose equal for length, breadth and depth has seldom if ever been seen in mission fields. Within the space of nine years twenty-three churches were organized in centers of population as important and as far apart as Aintab, Mosul, Diarbekir, Marsovan, Arabkir, Tocat, Cesarea, Aleppo, Marash, Sivas, Harpoot; with Bitlis, Adrianople, Adana and Van following not long after. Persecution was a thing largely of the past, though at the beginning of work in a new community mobs, with insults, stoning and other similar accompaniments, were seldom absent. Of course the work of translation and printing was pushed forward side by side with preaching tours and holding of all manner of public services, and schools of various grades were certain to follow close upon the heels of the evangelist. In particular the education of girls was provided for in boarding schools and later in colleges—a shocking innovation at first to the Oriental mind, but presently accepted with resignation, and now by Turks, Armenians and all the rest quite generally adopted. Bebek Seminary, which in a sense led to Robert College, was founded by Mr. Hamlin in 1840, and since four other colleges have been established at as many strategic points. Three theological seminaries are training a native ministry, whose graduates already approximate to four hundred. Nor is this all. Almost from the beginning a resolute effort has been maintained looking towards self-support and self-management on the part of the churches, and at the earliest possible day. The people were in desperate poverty, and were thoroughly accustomed to being held in leading-strings or far worse; but notwithstanding, they must be trained to independence and self-reliance, to build their churches and school houses, to support their pastors, to manage all matters of organization, discipline, and other ecclesiastical business, and especially to bear the heavy burdens of spreading the Gospel throughout the community and the regions adjacent. By 1860 the work had become so mature, and withal so extensive, that for the sake of convenience and economy, as well as to increase the feeling of responsibility, the vast field began to be divided, so that the one Turkish Mission has become four, called the Eastern, including the valleys of the Tigris and Euphrates; the Central, lying about the northeastern corner of the Mediterranean; the Western, covering the remainder of Asia Minor; and the European, or Bulgarian, stretching upward towards the Danube. Within each mission is an Evangelical Union, a body which plans and agitates in behalf of aggressive work both home and foreign, organizes churches, ordains and dismisses pastors, etc.

The Syrian Mission.

We have already seen that, in looking towards Western Asia as a possible theater for missionary endeavor, the thoughts and desires of American Christians were especially fastened upon the Holy Land, and upon the Jews, whose redemption and return appeared to be at hand. And that, disappointed in holding Jerusalem as the central station, as early as 1823 Beirut had been accepted as a temporary substitute, though a firm footing was not gained there until after 1830. The languages required were mastered in due season, the Arabic portion of the Malta printing establishment was removed in 1834 to this rising city upon the eastern Mediterranean coast, schools were opened for boys, and later for girls also, while to the northward and southward, as well as in various villages scattered here and there upon the flanks of the great Lebanon range, the invitations and warnings of the Gospel began to be heard. Together with numerous Armenians, the population includes such nominally Christian sects as the Greeks, Jacobites and Maronites, and also such strange religionists as the Druses and the Nusairiyeh, who though Moslem in name, are at least semi-pagan in fact. Turkish is the official language, but Arabic is widely spoken, and Syriac also. No sooner had the leaven of truth and righteousness begun to spread, than the ecclesiastics proceeded to institute the usual vigorous and violent measures to repress the mischief threatened to the old and established way. While scores and hundreds for conscience's sake suffered in person and estate, at least one, Asaad Shidiak, a young educated Maronite, and teacher of science and theology, was arrested and imprisoned, and is believed to have been walled up in a convent and left to starve. Here as in the Armenian mission, there was no desire to destroy or injure the existing organizations, but rather to co-operate and aid in their work, only agitating for needed religious reform. But this could not be. On account of the dominant bigotry and unwillingness to accept any changes, fellowship was out of the question, and after more than two decades of steadfast endeavor and patient waiting, separation was forced upon the Protestants, and in 1848 the first native church was formed in Beirut with twenty-six members, of whom ten were Greeks, four were Greek Catholics, five were Armenians, four were Maronites, three were Druses, one a Jacobite Syrian. The mission suffered much from the Egypto-Turkish war, and from various armed strifes between the several tribes and sects of the region, in particular during the terrible Druse massacres in 1860, but the Gospel proved itself invincible and clothed with conquering might. One after another, companies of disciples were gathered and joined in Christian fellowship and toil, in Hasbeiya, Abeih, Sidon, Tripoli, Zahleh, Hums, etc., etc.

Without doubt, the one greatest achievement made by the Syrian mission is to be found in the production of the Arabic Bible, upon which Eli Smith expended eight toilsome years, and Dr. Van Dyck as many more. When this noble task was completed in 1864, the volume was printed by the co-operation of the American, and the British and Foreign Bible Society, and ever since has been scattered almost literally throughout the world. It is now selling at the rate of about sixty thousand copies a year. And how extensive is the possible circulation may be seen by the statement that, of the earth's inhabitants not far from seventy millions speak Arabic, and that this is also the language of the Koran, the sacred book of nearly two hundred millions. Who can begin to estimate the moral and spiritual value of this product of combined scholarship and mechanical skill in the centuries to come, when the Church of Christ, clothed with divine might, and with fitting zeal, enthusiasm and vigor, shall undertake to vanquish Islam with the sword of the Spirit which is the Word of God, everywhere throughout Africa, and Eastern Europe, and Southern Asia from Arabia to China and Malaysia! And next after the Arabic Bible must be put the city of Beirut, with its manifold institutions and establishments, as a center and source of power destined marvelously to mould the entire Orient. "Within a radius of two miles are four Christian colleges, seven female seminaries, sixty boys' day schools, thirty-one girls' schools, seventeen printing presses, and four large hospitals. The boys' and girls' schools belong to the Protestants, Catholics, Greeks, Moslems and Jews, and sixteen thousand children are under instruction. From the mission presses alone nearly seven hundred different books have been issued, and a total of almost five hundred million pages. The Syrian Protestant College, combining literary, medical and theological departments, ranks among the very best to be found on missionary soil, and gathers its hundreds of students from many nationalities, and over a vast region.

Though the Syrian mission was planted and long cared for by the American Board, in 1870 it was transferred to Presbyterian hands, and without any important change in the spirit or methods of management, has ever since been vigorously sustained with money and men, and has gone steadily on from strength to strength. After seventy years from the beginning, 96 stations and out-stations are occupied by 40 missionaries, wives and unmarried women included, and 227 native helpers of all grades; the 26 churches have a membership of 1,958, together with about 6,000 adherents; and in the 152 schools of all grades are found 7,929 pupils, and in the college 237 more.

A large number of societies have entered Palestine in later years, and in the aggregate with preaching, house-to-house visiting, schools, hospitals, etc., have accomplished much towards the religious transformation of this, perhaps, most difficult and discouraging of mission fields. In every town of any considerable size are found representatives of Protestant Christianity. The English Church Society is most active, and is able to tabulate the largest results. Entering in 1843, work has been undertaken in Jerusalem, Nazareth, Nablous, Ramleh, Jaffa, Gaza, etc. The English Friends also bear a portion of the burden, as well as the Irish Presbyterians, the Established Church of Scotland, the Free Church and several special, or individual organizations. And besides, characteristically, the Moravians maintain a Leper Hospital in the Holy City.

The northern portion of Syria is left almost altogether to the American Reformed Presbyterians (Covenanters), with Latakia as the central station, a seacoast city of about 15,000, and with work carried on also at Antioch and Mersine in Asia Minor. Since 1856 faith and love, solicitude and untiring effort have been lavished mainly upon the mysterious Nusairiyeh, with religious beliefs and ceremonies kept carefully concealed from the uninitiated, who pass for Mohammedans, but rank as well with pagans. In addition to all the ignorance, superstition, bigotry and fanaticism of the people, through several years a succession of most trying fatalities befell from disease, shipwreck and the like. Nevertheless these men and women of heroic mould held on without flinching in the darkness and tempest. A missionary force of 20 is engaged, with 56 native helpers. Work is carried on at 15 points, the number of churches is 3, of communicants 241, of schools 20, and of scholars 618.

The Nestorian Mission.

This interesting field is located a thousand miles east of Constantinople, in the northwestern corner of Persia, or if the mountain Nestorians be included, extends also into Turkey. The people from whom the mission is named are gathered largely about Lake Oroomiah (Urmia), number some one hundred and fifty thousand, and are the feeble remnant of a famous Christian church, which for centuries was unsurpassed for evangelizing zeal, and carried the Gospel not only through all Central Asia, but even to far off India, and China. Under Mohammedan rule but little persecution was suffered, from some of the caliphs substantial benefits were received, but such was the ruthless rigor of the rule of

Timour that, by butchery and enslavement, the organization was brought so near to annihilation as never to recover. In their researches in 1831–2 Messrs. Dwight and Smith visited this region, and three years later, sent by the American Board, Justin Perkins and wife made their way across the plains and over the mountains, with Dr. Grant to follow in a few months. A hearty welcome was accorded to the strangers by both people and priests, and no very serious opposition was ever excited. Schools were made the entering wedge to enlightenment and reform, and met with such favor that by the end of a decade the number had risen to seventy. A printing press was received in 1840. In 1843, with many others like Coan, Lobdell, Shedd and others, came Fidelia Fiske to push with such fervor and efficiency the work among women. So desperate was the general poverty that at first it was deemed necessary to pay the children from twelve to twenty-five cents a week for board, to enable them to attend school, and the entire expense of the mission in all its departments fell upon the society. Later however, a more excellent way was discovered, and a constant drill was instituted looking to self-support. Ten years passed away before any notable signs of spiritual good appeared, but then began a cheering succession of blessed seasons of refreshing from on high. Beginning in the schools, the work spread to various communities, and by the score and hundred young and old together were brought to genuine repentance and a living faith in Jesus. The hope was long cherished that the dead Nestorian Church might be quickened again with heavenly life, but though the Patriarch and the inferior clergy seldom displayed open hostility to the missionaries and their endeavors, allowed the use of the church buildings for public services, and in various other ways displayed a spirit of fraternity, at the end of a generation the old body was as lifeless as at the beginning. No disruption occurred, but the two radically distinct parties gradually drew apart and went each its own way. Perhaps more trouble resulted from impertinent Roman Catholic meddlesomeness than from any other cause.

The press was kept busy turning out useful books of various kinds, and not only such as were religious, but those for use in the schools, etc. In 1852 was completed by Mr. Perkins a translation of the Bible into Syriac. This worthy founder was spared to continue in the work for thirty-six years, or until 1869, and remained until the light had been kindled in nearly ninety localities, and until a hundred native helpers had been trained and set to work, and upwards of nine hundred had been helped to enter upon a course of godly living. In 1870 this mission, like the one in Syria, was transferred to the fostering care of the Presbyterian church. Up to that date $580,000 had been expended upon it, or at the average annual rate of $15,470. Since then the progress, and the territorial enlargement, have been marked. Such important cities as Teheran, Ispahan, Tabriz and Salmas have been occupied in the Master's name, and the Armenians are joined to the Nestorians as objects of evangelizing effort, with a sharp lookout besides for effectual means of access to the Moslem population. The missionary force numbers 372 in all, including 16 ordained and 45 unordained Americans; with 37 ordained, 57 licentiate, and 215 other natives. The churches are 37, with 2,693 members; and the schools are 108, with 3,504 scholars.

For some twenty-five years representatives of the English Church Missionary Society have been pioneering in Persia. Henry Martyn may be termed the first evangelist, who during his stay in this country in 1811 made a translation of the New Testament. But it was not until 1869 that Dr. Bruce began to lay foundations for the Gospel by locating himself in Julfa, the Armenian suburb of Ispahan. Bagdad has since been occupied. Preaching to Moslems is scarcely possible as yet, and the main reliance is upon medical and school work, and the sale of Bibles. A force of six men and four women is toiling heroically and waiting for the dawn of a better day. The few converts gathered are almost wholly from the Oriental churches. Some two years since Bishop Stuart resigned his diocese in New Zealand to devote the residue of his days to toil in this hitherto barren field.

European Turkey Mission.

Or the mission to the Bulgarians, for such it is in the main. This people, though possessed of an independent ecclesiastical existence, yet really constitutes a portion of the Greek Church, and like all its sister bodies is filled with serious errors inherited from days of darkness. The region under view extends from Macedonia to the Danube, the population is Slavic for the most part, numbers some five millions, and for centuries groaned under Turkish tyranny. The Methodist Episcopal Church was first in the field, having voted an appropriation for Bulgarian work as early as 1852, and dispatched two representatives in 1857. The object was not to antagonize and proselyte, but to vitalize and reform the existing organization. But the hierarchy was joined to its idols, and was not long in manifesting a decided disposition to resent and resist with vigor any attempt to improve upon the good old ways. From various causes troublous times were in store. The effect of the Russo-Turkish war was disastrous in the extreme. And the vicissitudes of two decades are impressively set forth by this quotation from official sources: "In 1864 left without a resident missionary; in 1871 abandoned; in 1873 reoccupied; broken up in 1877; resumed in 1879; and made a missionary conference in 1892." The work is now carried on by 4 ordained missionaries and 6 assistants, 14 ordained natives and 22 other native helpers, the pupils number 123, and the church members 135.

In 1858 the American Board began to organize aggressive work among the Bulgarians, and chose as stations Sophia, Eski Zagra, Philippopolis, Samokov, Monastir, etc. Some fifteen years were required to lay foundations by learning the language, opening schools, preparing a literature, and gaining a knowledge of the people. During 1875-8 war, and consequent civil commotion, made progress impossible, but since peace has returned the seed sown has steadily grown, and the beginnings of harvest already appear. Robert College on the Bosphorus has proved a most potent factor in the regeneration of the country. A theological school has been established for the training of a native ministry, a girls' boarding school also, and in 1871 was completed the translation of the Bible into the vernacular.

In brief statement, such as these are the incidents and results of missionary effort in Western Asia containing a population of about thirty millions, of which three-fourths are Mohammedans, and the remainder represent various Christian sects, already sufficiently corrupt, but still further demoralized by the sufferings endured during twelve centuries of Moslem tyranny and hate. The stupendous task undertaken seventy-five years ago is not yet by any means accomplished, is only just well begun. Hitherto toil has been bestowed almost exclusively upon nominal Christians, and so upon the minority, while the even more spiritually needy majority has been passed by and let alone. The campaign thus far carried on is to be regarded as simply preliminary, a time of forging the instrumentalities required, of enlisting and drilling the forces, in preparation for the divine signal to march, and to fight the decisive battle which shall effectually humble the Crescent and exalt the Cross, and bring all the lands of the Bible once more under willing and blessed subjection to the Son. And with this conception of things, the outcome at this stage of the work is most remarkable, and not many pages of missionary history can be found more cheering and fuller of inspiration. It is not in vain, but rather to sublimest purpose, that millions have been expended, and hundreds of consecrated and precious lives. As standing for results of the more palpable kind, it will be well to scan these figures. The ordained missionaries sent out from Europe and America and now in the field number 120, and the unordained 230; while side by side with these is an even more important company of 162 ordained, and about 1,400 unordained natives; making a total force of 1,912. Then between the Danube and the Caspian are scattered 195 Protestant churches with a membership of 18,500. In addition, 1,000 schools are in operation, containing 46,500 pupils of every grade, of whom 21,057 are girls. In 20 of the 31 colleges, seminaries and boarding schools for girls, cultured and Christian American women are teaching, and in 11 the same type of womanhood sent from British homes. And finally, in spite of the limitless extortions of the Turks, and the consequent almost universal poverty, the native contributions reach annually the goodly sum of $61,000, though the entire Protestant population does not exceed 60,000.

But statistics set forth not the greatest and the best of what has been achieved. These general and quite indefinite statements, which relate to the silent, unseen, but irresistible sweep of spiritual forces, contain boundless significance with reference to years to come. In every seaport from Trebizond to Jaffa, and in every considerable city of the empire, Christian institutions have been planted to operate unceasingly as the leaven or the light. In particular, two mighty centers of intellectual and religious energy have been created, at Beirut with its population of almost one hundred thousand, and at Constantinople, the "eye of the East," the metropolis of the Mohammedan world, hard by the palace of the successor of the Prophet, whose word is sacred law to two hundred millions! In each of these the two chief Bible societies of Christendom have established their headquarters, and their presses, from which in all directions, in eleven languages, and as freely as the Koran, are shipped copies of the Sacred Scriptures by the ton. Yes, and with the imperial permit stamped upon every title page. Furthermore, about fifteen hundred different works, religious, educational, scientific, etc., have been published and circulated far and wide throughout the Orient.

And it may be that the indirect and incidental results of all this multitudinous preaching, and teaching, and praying, and printing through three-quarters of a century outmeasure and outweigh all the rest. It is beyond dispute that the Turkey of to-day is vastly different from the Turkey of three generations since. In such matters even as architecture, and modes of travel, and transportation. The railroad, the telegraph and newspaper have at least begun their revolutionary work. The laws are more liberal and humane, and the administration of justice is more respectable. Liberty, and whether applied to thought, conviction, or action, is steadily coming to have a larger and more definite meaning. The old churches are reforming themselves at various points, by spiritualizing the services, by mending the morals and increasing the intelligence of the clergy; changing thus not willingly, but because compelled in order to maintain their place, and on account of the new and higher standards set up by the Protestants. The government too, and from the same sort of compulsion, as far back as 1869 instituted a system of graded schools, whose number now approximates to twenty thousand. So the Ottoman Empire from top to bottom, from center to circumference, has been tremendously wrought upon of late, and chiefly by the glorious company of missionaries who have toiled and suffered for the kingdom of heaven's sake, emulating the example of the wisest and holiest, who in ancient days, in the same region, devoted themselves to the same sacred task of redeeming the world to righteousness.

CHAPTER XVII.

THE CHINESE EMPIRE ; KOREA.

"BEHOLD, these shall come from far; and, lo, these from the north and from the west; and these from the land of Sinim." The last clause of this verse is considered by most scholars to refer to the Flowery Kingdom of eastern Asia, that oldest of existing nations, whose history begins some twenty-two hundred years B. C., fifteen hundred years before the founding of Rome, seven hundred years before the date of the Exodus, and three hundred years before the call of Abraham. Only two empires, the British and the Russian, surpass in extent of territory the dominions of the "Son of Heaven," whose scepter bears sway over about one-tenth of the habitable surface of the globe. India is the only country at all approaching China in point of population. Though the number of inhabitants is by no means certain, 300,000,-000 appears to be a minimum estimate, some of the best authorities add one-third to this, and others deem 500,-000,000 to be a figure not too high. It is necessary to distinguish between the Chinese Empire, which includes Thibet, Mongolia, Manchuria, etc., covering in all 5,000,000 square miles, and China Proper, or the Eighteen Provinces, whose area is but about 1,500,000. Each province answers somewhat to one of our states, their average size is over 80,000 square miles, like our Kansas or Minnesota, or twice the size of Ohio, or Virginia. The average population is more than 16,000,000, and several contain each upwards of 35,000,000 inhabitants. The Great Plain, situated in the eastern portion of the empire, through which in their lower courses flow the two mighty streams, the Yellow and the Yang-tse', is 210,000 miles in extent, contains some 175,000,000 of human beings, or far more than can elsewhere be found dwelling upon an area of similar size.

India is the only other mission field at all comparable with China for either magnitude, or importance, or difficulty. Almost every feature pertaining to the land or the people is immense, ponderous, overwhelming, while much is also strange, unique, and without analogy elsewhere. Thus there is the Grand Canal six hundred miles in length, and the Great Wall stretching over mountain and plain for fifteen hundred miles, and estimated to contain material sufficient to girdle the earth along the equator with a wall twelve feet high and four feet thick. Then everywhere, upon water as well as land, are met such swarms, and hordes, and myriads of the queer creatures, our antipodes in almost all their ideas and customs. The language is the most difficult to master, and appears to have been fashioned for the express purpose of effectually preventing communication between this and other nations. Instead of an alphabet we find twenty-five thousand hieroglyphic, or ideographic characters, each constituting a word. In fact, one needs to master three languages. Thus there is the Wen-li for exclusive literary use, to be seen and not heard, not to be spoken but only to be read; and the easy Wen-li, similar to the other, only simpler, less stilted; and the mandarin, or court language, and spoken extensively in the northern and central provinces. Although ability to read, that is to pronounce the words, is a very common attainment in China, it is yet asserted by competent authority that the number of those who can understand what they read is not more than ten per cent. of the men, and one per cent. of the women. Still further, in the empire of the Celestials three religions dwell harmoniously side by side, and not seldom in the same mind and heart. The writings of Confucius are the source of supply for the rulers and the literati, with his five relations leading to the five supreme duties. Taouism is the second form of religious faith and practice, originating with Lao-tse about the same time as the former, or in the century in which the Jews returned from Babylon. Not satisfied with the conclusions of either or both of these philosophers, in the year 65 A. D. Emperor Ming-ti sent an embassy to India in search of something better, and thus Buddhism made its advent into China. The real religion of the Chinese is to be found in the worship of ancestors, in the rites performed before the tablet at the family shrine, and addressed to the "two living divinities." Every April returns the annual general celebration of these rites. The members of the family assemble from near and from far; at the graves libations are poured out and paper is burned, and then follows a social feast attended with certain petitions and prostrations. There is no religious caste, and no ruling priesthood. The average Chinese mind is filled to overflowing with the grossest of superstitions relating to luck, the dragon and the tiger, the two principles Yang and Yin, the Fung-shui, or wind-and-water. Gongs are in great use to frighten away the multitude of ghosts.

With three religions already on hand, when Mohammedanism arose, and its adherents entered the empire to make proselytes, so hospitably were they received, and so excellent did their message sound that a strong and lasting foothold was gained, and 30,000,000 are said to be found to-day among the inhabitants of the western provinces. Four separate attempts have been made to introduce the Gospel. First came the Nestorians early in the sixth century, entering from the west and pushing resolutely across the vast spaces of desert and lofty mountain ranges. Little is known in detail of their achievements, but they appear to have made a multitude of disciples, and then to have lost their influence. No visible trace of their presence remains except the famous tablet at Si-ngan in Shansi, bearing the date 781 A. D., and in Chinese and Syriac characters telling something of the triumphs of the Cross which thereabouts had been wrought. Roman Catholic missionaries first made their appearance in the Flowery Land in the thirteenth century, entering also from the west and by the overland route. Quite an impression was made, and then set in a decline. The burning zeal of Xavier had been turned towards this populous region as a fit field for his labors, but death defeated his plans for evangelization. In 1580 Valignani, the Superior of Jesuit missions in the far East, selected Matteo Ricci and others, and sent them from Macao to push their way into the interior, to make to the perishing the proclamation of the way of life. They were clad in the garb of Buddhist priests, though later this was exchanged for the dress of the literati. Baffled again and again, but never despairing, after twenty-one years he was able to gain a lodgment in Peking, and soon success began to crown his efforts. For a hundred and fifty years great activity was displayed and converts were made by the hundred thousand. But the brethren, some of whom were Benedictines and Franciscans as well as Jesuits, fell to quarreling among themselves, and appealed too often to the Pope; moreover, on all occasions carried themselves too haughtily, and were persistent meddlers in matters political. And so after a hundred and fifty years an edict of expulsion was issued and a long period of severe persecution ensued. This occurred in 1736, and ever since Catholics have been feared and hated.

The fact should always be borne in mind that the exclusiveness of the Chinese, their determined policy of absolute non-intercourse with all other peoples, and especially with Occidentals, does not originate wholly in total depravity, or even in insane conceit, coupled with folly equally insane, and was adopted by the rulers only in times comparatively modern. The land is isolated by nature, is fenced in on every side by barriers, the ocean, the mountains, the deserts, which a few generations ago were practically impassable. But when after the doubling of the Cape of Good Hope intercourse was first opened with Europeans, the ports were open, no great prejudice was displayed, and trade was carried on with little difficulty. The case was somewhat changed after the conquest of the empire by the Manchus in 1644. But the outrageous behavior of the traders, who had no sort of regard for the rights of others, who scrupled not to deal with this highly civilized people as they would with savage African negroes, or American aborigines, must be regarded as the chief cause of the barriers which were afterwards reared. The Chinese who resorted to the Philippines to trade were treated by the Spaniards with peculiar severity. And moreover it was known what had befallen other nations in Southern Asia who had allowed

Europeans to land and open factories. It was largely through mortal fear of invasion and conquest that it was decided at length to close and bar every gate. The Portuguese had taken forcible possession of the peninsula on which Macao stands, but a wall was built across the narrow neck that joined it to the mainland, and a guard was kept to prevent egress or entrance. All trade with foreigners was to be confined strictly to Canton, and to a tract of fifteen acres outside the walls. Certain "hong-" merchants were constituted the sole intermediaries between the empire and the whole world. Only through these thirteen could any sort of communication be had with the emperor, or with any official of the government. It was a capital offence to teach the language to any "outside barbarian," alias, "foreign devil." Of course, the attempt was absurd, preposterous, and from the beginning was doomed to failure. It was the desperate expedient of conscious weakness, combined with amazing assumption of superiority. All British commercial transactions were then in the hands of the East India Company.

Such was the situation when this century opened; missionary zeal was rapidly rising and spreading, and the gaze of many earnest-hearted ones was fixed on the distant lands of darkness, with longings to bear thither the blessed light of life. The London Society was the first one to move China-ward, and selected Robert Morrison to be its pioneer, knowing full well the magnitude of the undertaking. The instructions given him at his departure help us to perceive how purely it was an act of faith. The directors say: "We trust that no objection will be made to your continuing in Canton till you have accomplished your great object of acquiring the language;

when this is done you may probably soon afterwards begin to turn this attainment into a direction which may be of extensive use to the world; perhaps you may have the honor of forming a Chinese dictionary, more comprehensive and correct than any preceding one, or the still greater honor of translating the sacred Scriptures into a language spoken by a third of the human race." Applying to the East India Company for a passage in one of its ships, he was refused, as Carey had been a few years before, and it became necessary to voyage via New York. And there it was, that after all the business arrangements had been completed, and he was about to leave the shipping office, the agent wheeled in his chair and with a look and tone of superior wisdom remarked: "So then, Mr. Morrison, you really expect to make an *i*mpression on the idolatry of the great Chinese Empire?" And quickly replied with emphasis this first missionary to the Middle Kingdom, with its hundreds of millions, and utterly closed against all foreigners: "No, sir, but I expect that God will." Nine months later he arrived at his destination and sat down before the huge fortress apparently so impregnable. Macao was his first halting place, and as soon as possible he secured a Chinaman to teach him the language, and gave himself to the arduous task with all his might. Such was his eagerness to make progress that he is said to have begun almost at once to offer up his secret prayers in broken Chinese. This city was so intensely and intolerantly Catholic that prudence seemed to require that the object of his coming should be concealed, and that so far as possible his presence should not be known. Disguised in Chinese clothing he also kept carefully within doors, only when his health suffered seriously from such confinement did he venture forth, and then only at night to the fields outside the city with Chinese attendants. Later Canton became his headquarters, and he soon found several good friends among the foreign residents, and a few from among the Company's servants. So excellent were his linguistic abilities, so intense was his application, and so rare were men possessed of a knowledge of the language sufficiently accurate and ample, that at the end of two years his services were sought by the Company as translator at a salary of $2,500, and later increased to $6,000. And thus it curiously came to pass, as in Carey's case, that the corporation whose spirit was so utterly sordid and antichristian, which had refused its consent to his coming, from this time forward to the end of his life enabled him to remain upon Chinese soil, and supplied in abundance the means to carry on his work.

Only a portion of his time being required for the performance of his official duties, Morrison was able to undertake the translation of the Scriptures. Ere long the Acts were ready for printing, Luke was next completed, and by 1813 the entire New Testament was issued from the press, the British and Foreign Bible Society donating large sums in aid of the momentous undertaking. Five years later the Bible was published complete in Chinese. During the same period the same busy pen was actively engaged in the preparation of both a grammar and a dictionary. The latter was a great work in six volumes, and was so highly esteemed that the entire expense of printing, some $60,000, was met by the Company. But nevertheless, the calling of the author was not that of a man of letters. From first to last, in heart and soul, it was the missionary who thus expended his energies, and all was done for the kingdom's sake, that the Gospel might be introduced into China. Therefore, though public services were impossible even in Macao, regularly for more than a quarter of a century, with the greatest circumspection, in the privacy of his own room, and behind bolted doors, a few, only two or three usually, were met for prayer and instruction. Six years passed without a companion or helper in burden-bearing, and then the London Society sent out Mr. Milne as associate. Landing at Macao, in a few days the governor issued a peremptory order for him to leave the city. Repairing to Canton, it soon became apparent that there was no room for him in China, and for reasons soon to be mentioned, he took his departure for other countries, carrying with him for circulation two thousand New Testaments, five thousand copies of a catechism which Morrison had prepared, and ten thousand copies of a tract, all in Chinese. Meantime an imperial edict had been issued strictly forbidding the printing of religious books, and to the pagan manifesto was added a "Christian" one, from the chief ecclesiastic at Macao, hurling anathemas against whoso should hold intercourse with the heretic Morrison, or receive his pestiferous literature, or supply him with Chinese works. He was also sharply reproved and warned by the Company that he was committing a grave offence by publishing the New Testament and religious tracts, and to the serious jeopardizing of British trade in the empire. But as an offset, as a grain of comfort in the midst of sore tribulation, in 1814 he was permitted to baptize his first convert, Tsai A-ko, who lived four years to honor his profession. Many days of wearisome waiting, however, were yet in store.

"O, Rock, Rock, when wilt thou open!" had been the exclamation of Valignani almost two hundred and fifty years before, and the wall of exclusion was even more impassable than then. Those who would enter must still remain outside, and wait, and pray. Determined not to despair or give over, and reduced to such extremities, while pushing to the utmost the important preparatory work of translating and printing, it seemed possible to bestow evangelizing labor upon certain natives to be found outside the bounds of the empire, and thus through them, in spite of edicts, introduce Christian teachers and books among the teeming millions. For it had been observed that a great tide of emigration was setting towards the south, and thousands of Chinamen were already thickly scattered throughout the Malay Peninsula and the Dutch East Indies. And so, curiously it came to pass that for some thirty years almost all efforts to redeem the Celestial Empire were put forth hundreds of miles away. It was to further this design that Mr. Milne turned his back upon Canton, and left Morrison once more alone. After a long tour of exploration, he finally fixed himself in Malacca, and with others who joined him began to preach and teach the things of the kingdom. Among the rest, a school was opened which developed into the famous Anglo-Chinese College, designed to impart to missionaries and others a knowledge of Chinese, and to the natives a knowledge of English. Penang and Singapore were occupied by several societies, Java also and Siam, the London Society, the American Board and the Presbyterians, being especially active. The task was an uphill one; it was entered upon merely as a make-shift, and nothing very substantial or enduring ever came of it. These results may be named. Between

1815 and 1842, when this phase of the work came almost wholly to an end, it is estimated by Mr. Medhurst, an active participant, that ten thousand children passed through the various schools, about one hundred were baptized, and several native preachers were trained, among them Liang A-fah, baptized by Milne in 1816, who till his death in 1855 was exceedingly useful.

A second temporary and provisional line of endeavor was resorted to during these discouraging times of trying to reach China while standing on the outside and off at arm's length. A noble and gifted company of men like Morrison, Milne, Medhurst, Gutzlaff and others were busy with pen and press furnishing a supply of religious literature, as well as other useful reading matter. And in the thirties the peculiar project was formed of defying to a certain extent the laws which forbade any intercourse with the people or touching of the sacred soil, and of making expeditions up and down the coast, so indented with bays, harbors and wide-mouthed streams, carrying a liberal supply of books, tracts, etc., landing wherever possible, and giving to all who would receive. The scheme evidently belongs to the order of the forlorn hope, and the last resort in the day of extremity, but was more rational in this case because it was understood to be a national trait to hold all printed paper in highest esteem. Gutzlaff made three entensive voyages in successive years, and Medhurst, with a companion, one covering several months. In the main the inhabitants were found to be good-natured and approachable, instead of misanthropic and hostile as had been anticipated, though the mandarins usually ordered them off sternly, though without violence, or much insult even. So hopeful for a season was the outlook in this direction, that Olyphant and Co., American merchants of Canton, devout Christians and friends of missions in addition, purchased a vessel to be used in these colportage expeditions. Besides, Liang A-fah, who had returned from the Straits' Settlements, and in 1824 had been ordained by Morrison, the first Chinaman to enter the Christian ministry, invaded Canton with religious books which he distributed in great numbers, especially to students who came to the city to take their examinations. But the authorities were soon in pursuit of him and his assistants on suspicion that they were in treasonable intercourse and league with the outside barbarians plotting the destruction of the empire; two were seized and severely beaten, and he was compelled to flee precipitately for his life. In all some fifty thousand volumes were placed in Celestial hands along the coast, and about twice as many in and around Canton and Macao. The only traceable results are found in the fact that a multitude were helped to a better feeling towards foreigners, having discovered that the "foreign devil" was not nearly so black as he had been painted, and over against this, the other fact that it appeared to be certain that, if missionaries could only enter the country, they would be fairly well received. And further, the publishing of Gutzlaff's Voyages excited wide-spread interest and enthusiasm.

Recourse was had to yet another indirect mode of operations, which almost at once showed itself to be an auxiliary to the Gospel most potent and of the greatest value, has continued to the present, and constitutes one of the marked features of evangelizing work in China. Gutzlaff was possessed of some knowledge of the healing art, and had ministered to many sick while playing the part of colporteur. But years before, in 1820, Morrison with Dr. Livingstone, one of the Company's servants, had begun to dispense medicines at Macao, and in 1827 Dr. Colledge had opened a dispensary at his own expense, though later the foreign population had contributed $6,500 to sustain it. However, the real father of medical missions is Dr. Peter Parker, who in 1836 opened a hospital in Canton for the gratuitous treatment of the suffering, with opthalmic and surgical cases as specialties. A great sensation was soon produced by his successful operations and remarkable cures. Howqua, the leading hong-merchant, hearing of the wonder, gave the free use of his building for years, though characteristically, suspecting that back of the seeming benevolence some selfish plot was concealed, he sent one of his clerks to keep an open eye on the proceedings. A medical society was formed to agitate for hospitals in other cities, and a few years later, in England and America, Dr. Parker made many and effectual appeals for the training and sending out of missionaries able to minister to the bodies of men whom they would rescue from the plague of sin. As might have been expected, and especially in China where so much needed, this instrumentality has been found scarcely second to any, for disarming bitter prejudice, and exciting confidence and esteem. No man can tell what the Gospel owes to the distinguished services performed in behalf of the wife of Li Hung Chang by Drs. Mackenzie and Howard. In addition to numerous hospitals, dispensaries, and medical schools, gifted physicians like Hobson and Kerr have written some fifty medical volumes for the instruction of the common people in matters of health, and whose circulation has been very great. At no other point can foreigners so easily and effectually demonstrate their superiority to the very wisest of the high-minded sons of Confucius. The eminent statesman just named is said to have expressed himself to this effect: "We Chinese think we can take care of our souls well enough; but evidently you can take care of our bodies better than we, so send us medical missionaries in abundance." And wealthy officials and merchants gladly contributed large sums every year to sustain this Good Samaritan feature of Christian effort.

Korea is said to have been opened to Europeans by the point of the lancet, but as for China, to accomplish this herculean task it was necessary to employ the terrible edge of the sword. The barriers would yield to nothing less violent than the savage and brutal assault of cannon. Morrison had toiled on and on, year after year, with none at hand to sympathize or help. Well may Dr. Milne say that "the patience that refuses to be conquered, the diligence that never tires, the caution that hides, and the studious habit that spontaneously seeks retirement, were best adapted for the first Protestant missionary to China." It was not until 1839 that Bridgman, of the American Board, came to his assistance, to be joined four years later by Wells Williams. And in 1834 he died, worn out with toil and hope deferred. In all the twenty-seven years of maintaining the siege of the stronghold of Satan, he had never been able to hold a public service, and had seen but three or four touched by the renewing power of the Spirit. But he died in full faith nevertheless. These words are found in the last letter he ever wrote: "I wait patiently the events to be developed in the course of divine providence. The Lord reigneth. If the command of God our Saviour prosper in China, all will be well. Other matters are comparatively of small importance." Eight years more were destined to elapse, and then the great wall of exclusion was to begin to crumble and fall. And the famous "Opium War" with Great Britain was to supply the shock required. Though the common idea is very different, the truth appears clearly to be, that the determination to continue the opium trade was in no proper sense the cause, was at the most but the occasion, of the bloody strife, was only the accidental spark that fired the magazine. For the cause we must go further back, and take a broader view of the situation, and it is to be found in the outrageous restrictions put upon commerce by the Chinese authorities, prompted in part by fear, and also in no small degree by a limitless conceit and arrogance, and these leading to intolerable methods of dealing with foreigners. There is but little to be said in commendation of the designs and disposition of either party. To aggravate the trouble, it was Occidental face to face with Oriental, with no language by which to communicate, so that endless misunderstandings could not but occur. Here, therefore, was one of the offences which must needs come, when the stronger and the weaker fall into conflict, though wo be to him through whom the offence cometh. The childish policy of communicating with the outside world only by means of petitions offered through the hong-merchants, utterly shut out from access to the central authorities, and compelled to take the attitude of a suppliant inferior, was bad enough from the beginning, but might possibly answer for a commercial corporation. But when in 1834 the East India Company was set aside, and the British Government took the direction of trade into its own hands, of course such servility and cringing were out of the question. Lord Napier was despatched as commissioner, and proceeded straight to Canton, and sent his credentials to the viceroy direct. They were returned unopened, with a rebuke to his presumption, and an order to return to Macao "immediately with speed." Various other outrages succeeded, culminating in 1839 in the command to deliver up all the opium in the hands of English dealers, and the imprisonment of the entire European population for days, with great indignities attending. Naturally war ensued, ending in 1842 in the treaty of Nanking, which opened five ports of the empire to residence and trade, and gave to Great Britain, besides, the island of Hongkong for a possession. Opium was admitted free, but only as all commerce was free. Here ends the first stage of missionary history in China.

Unfortunate and lamentable though it be, and scandalous in some of its phases, this transaction is to be classed among the great events in the spread of the kingdom of heaven among the nations. The wrath of man, and his folly, and his weakness also, played a leading part, but the Lord made them effectually to praise Him. And to China, though she knew it not, and neither yet is the fact discerned, accrued the lion's share of the priceless benefits resulting from the destructive clash of arms. The deepest humiliation and chagrin, with the addition of $21,000,000 in cash, were not too great a price to pay. Up to this time about sixty missionaries had been sent out by the various churches of Christendom for the evangelization of China, though only three or four had found it profitable to work and wait upon the immediate borders of the land. The remainder, at a distance, had been making ready for the fulness of times to dawn. Only the London Society and the American Board were represented in the field at the very gates of the fortress. But no sooner had the treaty been signed and the six cities, Canton, Hongkong, Amoy, Foochow, Ningpo and Shanghai, been thrown open, than a sudden and extensive enlargement was made. Almost at once the American Episcopalians, Baptists, and Presbyterians, came flocking in from Singapore and the region around about, where they had been sojourning, and many other societies hastened forward their quota of laborers to occupy the long coveted region, six of them in a single year, so that by 1848 instead of two organizations represented in the Flowery Kingdom, there were fifteen, with yet more soon to follow. The statistics for 1853 showed the presence of 118 missionaries, of whom 69 were ordained and 40 were women, with 29 native helpers. But at the same date, though forty-six years had elapsed since Morrison arrived, the churches numbered only 5 with 351 members, and the schools 32 with 812 pupils. Upon no other country had so much toil been expended for so long a period, with such slight return in converts gathered. Entering now the treaty ports, access was had to some two or three millions, but with minds and hearts fast closed by the increased prejudice and ill-will begotten by the recent war. To remove these barriers, hospitals and dispensaries were opened, schools were established, and in every possible way by the performance of kind deeds, the persistent effort was made to prove that these messengers of the Gospel came unselfishly, and as the truest friends.

But even yet we find ourselves in the midst of days primeval. Only six tiny points can be touched, while the vast empire is still closed against all foreigners.

The government is as determined as ever to stand aloof from the nations, in complacent and haughty self-satisfaction. England, America, and all the rest, continue to be but "foreign devils," and "barbarians," whom to abuse, and insult, and hold in contempt, is a virtue. And in particular, this capital point the rulers steadfastly refused to yield. Foreign ambassadors should not be allowed a residence in Peking and have direct and immediate access to the emperor, Son of Heaven that he was. Another war was required, which was but the concluding chapter to the first, before overweening pride would give way. And so, as in no other region the truth has sought to enter, in a sense it was necessary for the evangelist to wait until the soldier had done his preparatory work. Only by carnal weapons could the valleys be exalted and the mountains be made low, and in the desert a highway for our God be made straight. The conflict ensued in 1857-60, which ended forever the preposterous assumptions of the Manchu dynasty, and whose final act occurred in the capture of Peking by the combined forces of Great Britain and France, with other nations as interested spectators, and the looting and the burning of the magnificent Summer Palace of the emperor, as one of the most impressive incidents. The treaty of Tien-tsin settled it that ten more cities should be opened to trade, that the whole empire should be open for missionaries to pursue their beneficent calling, while their converts should be free from persecution, and that foreign ministers might take up their abode in the neighborhood of the imperial palace. However, it was yet thirteen years, and not till 1873, that under the persistent efforts of the representatives of Russia, the United States,

Great Britain, France and the Netherlands, an audience was allowed with the entire omission of the *kotow*, or prostration in the presence of His Majesty; the last remnant on his part of a claim to essential superiority, and on their part of the admission that they were but vassals. These were indeed days of severe chastening for China. For during the same period (1850-64) was raging the terrible Tai-ping rebellion, which covered a large portion of the Eighteen Provinces with conflagration and wholesale slaughter. It is estimated that not less than twenty millions of human beings fell victims to this political upheaval. In the later stages of the struggle with anarchy the European powers lent their aid, with "Chinese" Gordon and his "ever victorious army," as a most important factor. Then it was that this most thorough-going English Christian soldier fought side by side with Li Hung Chang, the future foremost of Chinese statesmen, and a warm friendship sprung up between them.

The radical revolution which had been wrought in the empire is well set forth in the statement of Wells Williams that, when in 1833 with two other Americans he arrived at Canton, they were reported to the leading hong-merchant as foreign devils who had come to live under his tutelage; and in 1874 as secretary to the American embassy at Peking, he accompanied the minister when in person he presented his letters of credence to the Emperor Tungchi, and was received on a footing of perfect equality! But this marvel did not occur until sixty-seven years after Morrison reached China, and forty years after he had gone to his reward. So far as treaties and diplomacy could avail, the way was now open for the messengers of peace to go up and down, here and there, wheresoever they would, proclaiming the glad tidings to the myriads of the needy. But other barriers remained, far less visible and tangible, but far more perplexing and difficult to remove. Such as the snares set by their false forms of faith, certain national peculiarities, lying, gambling, the extensive use of opium, as well as the bad feeling excited by the military operations. Nor was the fault altogether on their side. Mr. Medhurst tells of a tract written against him, which will help us to see how Occidentals appear in the eyes of the Celestials. The foreigners had introduced a poisonous drug, for their own benefit and the injury of others, and so were deficient in benevolence; "sending their armies and fleets to rob other nations, they could make no pretentions to rectitude; allowing men and women to mix in society and walk arm in arm through the streets, they showed that they had not the least sense of propriety; and in rejecting the doctrines of the ancient kings they were far from displaying wisdom; indeed truth was the only quality to which they could lay the least claim. Deficient therefore in four out of the five cardinal virtues, how could they expect to renovate others? Then, while foreigners lavished money circulating books, they made no scruple of trampling printed paper under foot, by which they showed their disrespect for the inventors of letters. Further, these would-be exhorters of the world were themselves deficient in filial piety, forgetting their parents as soon as dead, putting them off in deal coffins only an inch thick, and never so much as once sacrificing to their *manes*, or burning the smallest trifle of gilt paper for their support in the future world. Lastly, they allowed the rich and noble to enter office without passing through any literary examinations, and did not throw open the road to advancement to the poorest and meanest in the land. From all these it appeared that foreigners were inferior to Chinese, and not fit to instruct them."

We have now reached the third stage of missionary history in China, and enter the modern period, which covers only about thirty years, and brings us down to the present. The churches of Christendom began at once to improve the enlarged opportunity by increasing the force in the field, so that presently all the larger denominations were represented in the empire, and within a decade the number of societies engaged had risen to nearly thirty. The bulk of the missions, however, were in the coast region, while the vast interior was left wellnigh desolate. It was therefore a great event in the evangelization of China, when in 1853 the Rev. J. Hudson Taylor appeared upon the scene, and when, about ten years after, organized by his tireless energy and flaming zeal, the China Inland Society sent forward its first missionary. As the name declares, its object was to push in towards the central and western portions of the empire where the spiritual destitution was most appalling, and there is to be no rest day or night, until in every part of every province the sound of the Gospel is heard. The income reaches nearly $175,000, the work is undenominational, the number of workers was 592 at the close of 1893, of whom 361 came from England, 42 from North America, 34 from Australia, and the rest from Scandinavian countries. The number of baptisms is 5,627 from the beginning, and the communicants are now 4,206. In 1863 the English Presbyterians entered Formosa, an island some eighty miles off the coast from Foochow, the Presbyterians of Canada following nine years later, with the heroic genius Mackay as pioneer, and since then 60 churches have been gathered with a membership of 3,500. In 1867 the Irish Presbyterians began a gospel campaign in Manchuria, pushing inland from Newchwang to Moukden, and the Scottish United Presbyterians coming after as allies in 1873, the two have toiled together in harmony and with such vigor that upwards of 2,000 have embraced Christianity. John Ross is eminent among laborers in this field. In 1870 the London Society sent James Gilmour to begin his wonderful campaign of endurance and achievement in Mongolia, which lasted till his death a year or two since. No doubt, Shanghai is the center of evangelizing force. Nine societies maintain missions here, but far more important than all these combined in the vast range of its gracious influences, is the Presbyterian publishing establishment, with its list of over seven hundred works in the native language. From its presses have been issued of school and text books, 130 volumes; of medical books, 23; dictionaries and grammars, 40; Scripture commentaries, 25; hymn books, 21; religious books and tracts, 160; miscellaneous, 400. And every variety of edition of the Bible is included. The Methodists have similar publication houses at Foochow and Kiukiang. Tien-tsin is another center of power, and within the walls of Peking several strong missions are maintained.

But space is lacking to tell a tithe of the story of the marvels that have been wrought, and practically within a period of twenty years. It was only two decades ago that the time of blossoms and fruitage began to appear. Hitherto the statistics from the hard field had been discouraging, but in 1877 the 625 stations and out-stations could report 13,515 church members, and 73 ordained native pastors, with 519 other preachers. And from that date the gains have been steady in every department of the work, and at a rate constantly increasing. We have already seen how indispensable a part in the opening of China was played by the destructive operations of foreign navies and armies. But another infliction even more terrible and destructive to life, by the God of missions was overruled to the effectual opening of closed and stony hearts, and so the great furtherance of the Gospel. The reference is to the famine of 1877-8, said to be the worst of any recorded in history, and whose victims are estimated at from ten to thirteen millions. The Great Plain, so densely populated, was the theater of this appalling calamity, with the three provinces, Shansi, Shensi, and Shantung, as the chief sufferers, and the cause was found in the almost entire absence of rain during four successive years. With the missionaries in the forefront as leaders and actors, upwards of $400,000 were raised and distributed to the starving by foreigners, of whom some seventy contributed their time and strength, and four fell a sacrifice to exposure and overwork. The Government was astonished and deeply impressed by this unheard of example of pure benevolence, and expressed its appreciation in various effective ways. And as for the people, at first suspicious of sinister designs on the part of the distributors, they refused the offered charity, and were ready to mob and maltreat their would-be benefactors, and the utmost of wisdom, and caution, and tact were required to overcome the inveterate dislike and fear. Finally, however, confidence and even gratitude were won, though in Kaifung, the capital of Honan, to the very last the " foreign devils " were forbidden to remain with their food and other supplies, or even to carry on their relief work in the environs! From this time forward throughout most of the large region so sorely afflicted there was found a marked increase of readiness to receive visits from Americans and Europeans, and to hear the Gospel from their lips, while converts also began rapidly to multiply, the scores becoming hundreds, and the hundreds swelling to tens of thousands. Among the curious results of Chinese evangelization this statement may well stand. Since the Baptist mission was started at Swatow 1,670 persons have been received to membership, of whom nearly half were baptized after they were fifty years of age, 361 after they were sixty, 98 after they were seventy, 4 after passing their eightieth birthday.

A few additional statements are in order concerning medical missions, to which China owes so much. No less than 61 hospitals and 44 dispensaries have been established and are maintained by Christian hands. Several of these are built on an extensive scale, and are supplied with all modern appliances, as well as with the best of medical and surgical skill. Swatow is said to have the largest of mission hospitals. In Tien-tsin, the wife of Li Hung Chang having been brought back to health from the borders of death, through treatment by Christian physicians from the West, this eminent statesman and his government contributed large sums to secure and carry on a hospital, dispensary and medical school. In fact in all the cities of the empire where such undertakings are found, a large part of the running expenses are met by the gifts of Chinese officials and merchants, and of foreign residents. In the various fields of the world are found 350 medical missionaries, China alone has 126, of whom 26 are women. Down to the close of 1889 the total number of physicians who, for the kingdom's sake, had gone to the Middle Kingdom was 200.

In judging of the general statistics which help to an estimate of the labor performed, and the results achieved, in this immense and most difficult field, it must not be forgotten that forty-eight years were required to gather 500 souls into church membership, and that it is only thirty-three years since the empire was thrown open, or just a single generation. In 1877 the communicants numbered 13,035, and in three years more had increased to 20,000. At this last date there were 73 ordained and 511 unordained natives employed in Christian work. When the great missionary conference met in Shanghai in 1890 the statistical showing was full of good cheer, since it clearly demonstrated that the day of small things was about over, that the harvest season had already begun. Forty societies were represented by 1,296 workers, of whom 589 were men, and 316 were unmarried women. Besides, 211 ordained and 1,266 unordained Chinese were rendering efficient service. The entire missionary force reported was 2,953, or 1,296 Europeans, and 1,657 natives. Of the 522 organized churches 94 were fully self-supporting. The membership was 37,287, and the contributions of the native Christians for the year preceding amounted to $36,885. Besides this, the Roman Catholics are active and successful in the empire, with their 25 bishoprics, and claim a round 1,000,000, not including Thibet, Mongolia and Manchuria. Were the figures brought down to the present year, it cannot be doubted that they would prove even more encouraging. The latest reports indicate that the number of European missionaries is nearly 1,650, of whom about

650 are men, that the churches have a membership approaching near to 50,000, while something like 100,000 more have turned from idolatry, and have put themselves within reach of the transforming influences of the Gospel. So, well may the Church thank God and take courage, and press forward with zeal and full assurance of faith. The huge mass moves but slowly thus far, but is now fairly under way, and the momentum will presently become irresistible. The Word and the Spirit are mighty, and the divine promise cannot fail.

Korea.

For Korea, called by its inhabitants Cho-sen, the land of Morning Calm, a few paragraphs must suffice. For, as yet, it can scarcely be called open to foreigners, missionaries have but recently entered, and only the slightest beginnings have been made. Besides, many statements made concerning China and Japan will apply here almost equally well. The kingdom consists of a peninsula, lying between the Yellow Sea upon the west, and Japan Sea upon the east. The side which joins it to the continent borders upon China and the Russian possessions. Formerly a neutral strip some sixty miles by three hundred separated Korea from the Celestial Empire. The area is something over 80,000 square miles, and the population is perhaps 12,000,000, though the figures are but estimates. The statement is not much amiss that the Koreans are a sort of cross between the Chinese and the Japanese, since at various important points they strikingly resemble the former nation, and at others are closely akin to the latter. Nevertheless in many respects they differ radically from both. For one thing, the language is quite distinct. But written

Korean is employed only by the common people, while for all official and literary purposes, and by the upper classes, the Chinese is used exclusively. The Chinese Classics supply the substance of education. Politically, this peninsula may be termed independent, and at divers times invaders have been driven out. And yet from time immemorial China has asserted, and Korea has accepted, a suzerainty. As late as 1882 the claims of the over-lord were restated and reconceded. Every new ruler, and every heir-apparent, seeks investiture from the emperor, while year by year embassies are despatched to Peking to pay tribute and homage. Buddhism was formerly the ruling religion, but in comparatively recent times has been well-nigh displaced by the teachings of Confucius. The worship of ancestors is universal, and finds no rival among the people, except in the general and ever-present dread of evil spirits, and in the frequent performance of ceremonies, wherewith to circumvent their malevolent designs, and neutralize their power to do harm.

Some centuries since, Korea imitated her sister nations on either side in closing her ports against all comers, and isolating herself to the utmost; fully determined to travel her own way, and neither to take, nor receive, in the least degree, the knowledge or wealth to be derived from commerce, or from other forms of intercourse with mankind. Fear of encroachment increased almost to frenzy when, about 1860, Japan had been overawed by the visits of several fleets from the West, the allies had captured Peking, and had sacked and burned the Summer Palace, and Russia had seized the opportunity to lay hands upon vast territories in the region of the Amoor. From this time forward the Korean Gates to the northwest were watched most carefully both day and night, while strong guards patrolled every exposed point along the coast. Whoever approached was ordered off, and no communication was held with the feared and hated strangers from over the sea. The French had a serious grievance, and came with a fleet to obtain redress, but failed utterly. Twice over, the United States sent ships of war on a similar errand, and though some hard and successful fighting was done, no impression was made. Then Japan endeavored to secure a treaty which should be of advantage to both nations, and at length succeeded. And finally, in 1882, through the good offices of Li Hung Chang, a treaty was made with the United States, three ports were thrown open to commerce, and a minister-resident was received by the king, and permitted to reside at Seoul, the capital. About two years later occurred the genesis of Protestant missions.

But, more than a hundred years ago Christianity entered Korea. Through intercourse with Roman Catholic priests, while on embassies to Peking, some well-to-do Koreans had become acquainted with the teachings of the Gospel, received the truth as it was apprehended, and returning home, began zealously to teach and practice the same. The new religion seemed to meet a felt want, and spread rapidly. A few foreigners stole in at the imminent risk of their lives to impart instruction concerning doctrine and the forms of worship. But presently the number of the converts became so large as to attract the attention of the jealous government, and stern measures of repression were instituted. During the first half of the century seasons of persecution alternated with seasons of quiet and growth. But in the thirties the Korean mission came into the hands of

French ecclesiastics, who began to push measures of propagandism. More than a dozen priests, in disguise, had stolen across the boundaries, and were creeping here and there about the country, diffusing the leaven of faith and devotion. In 1864 a change of rulers occurred, and the new king speedily made a savage onslaught on all the Christians he could find. Bishop Berneux, and eight other Frenchmen, were seized and put to death, with insult, torture, and multilation, and whole communities died by the sword. It cannot but be counted most singular, that in each of the three hermit nations the evangelizing attempts of the Papacy ran so similar a course, and reached a conclusion so almost exactly the same.

It came to pass that in 1873 Rev. John Ross, sent out by the Scottish United Presbyterians, began work in Manchuria, and later paid a visit to the Korean Gates, where every year a great fair was held, and to which the people came in great numbers to trade with the Chinese. He found them exceedingly shy, suspicious, uncommunicative, and unapproachable. But returning a year later, the situation was so changed that he was able to hire a Korean to return with him to Moukden, and to teach him the language. As soon as possible he set about translating the Bible, and when the Gospel of Luke was in readiness, proceeded to put it in print, with the assistance of a second native from the peninsula. Later still, several were found willing to serve as colporteurs in the valleys among their countrymen, Mr. Ross supplying portions of the New Testament in Korean, and Bibles in Chinese. Such was the readiness to receive these books, and with such earnest, ingenuous purpose were they put to use, that messages began to come beseeching teachers and baptism. Several times he tried to pass the barriers upon the boundaries, but was stopped and turned back by the guards. However, eighty-five received baptism at his hands, and afterwards when missionaries were tolerated in the country, whole neighborhoods were found professing faith in Jesus Christ, and waiting to learn the way more perfectly. The American Presbyterians were the first to move in the matter of sending the Gospel message to Korea direct. In 1884 Dr. H. N. Allen was transferred from China to Seoul, while Mr. Underwood came a little after. And it was in the very nick of time. For in the autumn of that year a serious riot occurred in the capital, in which several men of high rank were slain, or covered with wounds. Among them was Prince Min Yong Ik, a nephew to the king, dreadfully cut, and at the point of death from loss of blood. Dr. Allen was called in and such was his surgical skill and success, that the court, and the whole city was filled with amazement. He was looked upon as an angel from heaven, and there was no limit to his popularity. He became court physician, and a royal hospital was built at great cost, with him in sole charge. When an embassy was sent to Washington, this Christian physician accompanied it as foreign secretary, his place in the hospital being filled by another missionary, while a third, Miss Ellers, M. D., was appointed physician to the queen. Naturally, ever since, the medical side of missionary effort has been put prominently forward in Korea.

In 1885 the American Methodists appeared upon the scene in Seoul, in the persons of Mr. Appenzeller and Dr. Scranton. The first opened a school which later became known as Yi Wha, which being interpreted, signifies "For the Training of Useful Men," and the latter opened a hospital, afterwards honored by receiving from the king a signboard reading thus: "Wide Spread Relief Hospital." And such a conception has been gained of the value of Western education, Christianity included, that three young men from the ranks of the distinguished nobility have been sent to the Methodist college in Shanghai. In 1887 this same denomination opened a printing establishment, which issues works in three languages, Korean, Chinese, and English. In 1888 missionaries entered this field representing two organizations in Canada. The year after, the Presbyterians of Australia joined their forces with those already at work, the Propagation Society (S. P. G.) came the same year, while in 1892 the Presbyterian Church, South, completed the list of societies thus far engaged in Korea. The three Presbyterian bodies have formed a council, for united effort, and looking to the existence of but one mission church of that order in the country. The last to enter was assigned to two provinces in the southwest, Chulla and Chung Chong. Eight organizations are now engaged in seeking the redemption of Korea with a total of upwards of seventy missionaries. The first baptism did not occur until 1886, a native church was formed soon after, while the number of converts to date is less than two hundred. The Catholics, however, have some twenty priests and fifteen thousand adherents. As recently as 1888 edicts were issued forbidding the public preaching or teaching of Christianity, and outside of the treaty limits the presence of foreigners is tolerated only through the non-action of the authorities. Though the people seem quite willing to listen and learn, the greatest prudence and caution are constantly required. Tours of observation can be made without serious opposition, with occasional opportunities for conversation, and Christian literature can be distributed, while every day the schools, hospitals, and dispensaries, lend most efficient aid.

Since the foregoing paragraphs were written the astonishing events of the Chino-Japanese war have occurred, with Korea as the prime occasion ; and rumors are just now changing into official statements that a treaty has been signed, which among other things secures independence to Korea, though no doubt, with the influence of Japan supreme. To each one of the three nations concerned changes of greatest moment cannot but ensue, and especially to China and Korea, including boundless confusion, strife and overturning. But whatever else may happen, ideas and forces inseparably conjoined with Christianity and the civilization of the West are certain to enter and bear sway. Nor can it scarcely be otherwise than that the call for evangelists and teachers will soon sound out with such a divine imperative that the churches of Christendom will not dare to disregard, while the kingdom of heaven will begin to go forward in Eastern Asia with most surprising velocity and momentum.

CHAPTER XVIII.

JAPAN.

AMONG other names are Dai Nippon, The Sunrise Kingdom, and The Land of Great Peace. This prodigy among modern empires is composed of islands numbering some three or four thousand, though only four are of any considerable size. The Kurile Islands are included at the north, and the Loo Choo Islands at the south. The entire area is estimated at about 160,000 square miles. The main portion of the mikado's domain stretches along the eastern coast of Asia in the shape of a bent bow, at one extremity lying at no great distance from Korea, and at the other approaching to within five miles of the Russian possessions. The principal island has a length of about eight hundred miles, and contains nearly half of the superficies of the empire. The surface is largely broken and mountainous, with scarcely more than twelve per cent. susceptible of cultivation. Twenty live, and numerous extinct, volcanoes proclaim the geological origin of the country, while earthquakes are frequent and destructive. Fuji-san, the loftiest of summits, which rises to an elevation of 12,365 feet, is a volcanic cone, and constitutes the crowning glory of the islands, as well as the pride of every Japanese. As to climate, general statements are likely to mislead, since the northern and southern limits are separated by something like thirty degrees of latitude, or two thousand miles, and approach, the one to arctic, and the other to tropical conditions. And further, down the western shores, through the Japan and Yellow Seas, sweeps continually an ocean current from the frozen regions, while up the eastern coast sets, summer and winter, the *Kuro Siwo*, Black Current, the Asiatic counterpart of our Gulf Stream, performing the double office of heat-bearer, and moisture-carrier. At certain seasons floods, typhoons, and tidal waves, are liable to work wide-spread disaster. According to Mr. Griffis, " Nature's glory outshines her temporary gloom, and in the presence of her cheering smiles the past terrors are soon forgotten. The pomp of vegetation, the splendor of the landscape, and the heavenly gentleness of air and climate come to soothe and make vivacious the spirits of man. The seasons come and go with well-nigh perfect regularity; the climate at times reaches the perfection of that in a temperate zone—not too sultry in summer, nor too raw in winter. The majority of the inhabitants rarely see ice over an inch thick, or snow more than twenty-four hours old." Rice is the principal food product, though the ocean and the streams are most bountifully stocked with fish of excellent quality.

The population of Japan somewhat exceeds 40,000,000, making an average of nearly two hundred and sixty to the square mile, though in many sections the density is very much greater. The inhabitants are thought to have entered the islands originally both from the north and the south, and as well, to some extent, from China and Korea. The Ainos at the north are reckoned as aborigines, whose numbers are but small. Two races are easily discernible, distinguished by marked differences of feature and mental quality, the one constituting the upper, and the other the lower classes. The people in general, the average of the nation, possess not a few attractive and lovable traits. They are quick-witted, inquisitive, ready to learn, but also mercurial to the borders of fickleness and beyond; are enthusiastic, and polite in the extreme, and hence have been dubbed "the French of the Orient." Respect for parents is universal, the family is the great thing, the individual is almost nothing by comparison. The last named conviction, or instinct, will explain the meaning back of the astounding reply to a question, "I have lived in this locality, or I have wrought at this trade, for four hundred years!" Reverence for superiors is also bred in the Japanese bone, especially for the heaven-descended emperor, while patriotism is often a passion, a frenzy. Death is despised on comparatively slight occasion. Of course, we should not be surprised to find that much brass, iron and even clay are found mingled with the gold of mental and moral constitution. Among national sins may be set down lying and licentiousness. Where Christianity has not brought reform, truth for truth's sake is a phrase without force or meaning, while concubinage was provided for in the legal and social *regime*, prostitution was legalized, and without any shock to the moral sense, girls were sold by their parents to lives of shame and accepted the dreadful fate meekly, and as a matter of course. Life too was held in light esteem, and assassination and suicide frequently rose to the rank of virtues. Further, with all its delicacy and refinement of make, the Japanese mind is affirmed to have no capacity for musical performance and appreciation, at least, according to occidental standards.

Japan, like China her neighbor, is possessed of, not one religion, but several. The oldest is the Shinto, which is thought to be scarcely worthy to be called a religion, consisting in ancient times of not much more than a form of nature worship and reverence for ancestors, and now being mainly an affair of the state, and employed to regulate the relations between the emperor and his subjects. Then the ideas of Confucius are widely afloat, through the prevalence of Chinese as the language of literature, and the use of the Chinese Classics in the schools of the empire. Buddhism was introduced from China in 552 A. D., was some six centuries in fighting its way to universal acceptance, and then passed through a period of development, receiving extensive and radical modifications. How prominent is the place held by these pagan faiths in the daily life of the people, is seen by the fact that the Shinto shrines number 196,242, and of Buddhist temples there are 108,-109, with nearly 70,000 priests, so that there is a temple or shrine to about every 130 inhabitants.

The Japanese claim at least twenty-six centuries of existence for their empire, and the career of this nation can be traced quite well, far back towards the Christian era. For many generations the islands were divided between various tribes or clans, independent, and often at war, but finally all were brought under the sway of a single ruler. Then little by little grew up a military class, which also gradually became subject to a hereditary commander-in-chief (shogun, the tycoon of later times), while the other generals became princes (daimios) in possession of castles and extensive landed estates, each also keeping about him a body of armed retainers (samurai), who owed him fealty and loyal service in the field, and for whose support he provided. In other words, a complete feudal system was established, which lasted for seven hundred years and until its overthrow in

1868. And finally this head of the army became the *de facto* ruler of the state, holding his court in Yedo (the Tokyo of the present day), while the mikado, the ruler *de jure*, dwelling in far off Kyoto, held only the ignoble semblance of dominion.

The Land of the Rising Sun was first heard of by the western world when, late in the eleventh century Marco Polo, returning from a long residence at the court of Kublai Khan, told incredible stories about a certain Zipangu. It was in search of this same land of wonders that, two hundred years later, Columbus set out, and for which at his first landing he inquired of the natives. The Portuguese, following in the track of Vasco da Gama, were the first of Europeans to reach the islands by sea. Mendez Pinto was the pioneer, and others of his countrymen came after to trade. Christianity was introduced in 1549. Xavier, in southern India, had met a Japanese, who on account of crime had fled his country, but later had repented and embraced the Gospel, and asked him if the people would be likely to receive the Gospel. The reply was notable and wondrously significant: "His people would not immediately assent to what might be said to them, but they would investigate what I might affirm respecting religion by a multitude of questions, and above all by observing whether my conduct agreed with my words. This done, the king, the nobility and the adult population would flock to Christ, being a nation which always follows reason as a guide." Such a nation must not be passed by, and in due season the Apostle of the Indies landed in Japan, with two other Jesuits and two natives. Xavier did not undertake to master the language, but spoke through interpreters, and had a varied experience. All available expedients were resorted to, and when the aspect of poverty, austerity, and asceticism, failed to attract and excited only contempt, he turned to the other extreme of ecclesiastical pomp and display, and made costly presents to the emperor and princes. After some successes, and various failures, he took his departure, leaving the work in other hands, and sending in additional laborers. By the end of five years considerable progress had been made, and before the first generation had passed the churches numbered two hundred, and the converts a hundred and fifty thousand. In 1583 four nobles were sent on a visit to the Pope, kissed his feet, had an audience with Philip II., and returning brought with them seventeen more Jesuits. Spanish missionaries also flocked in from the Philippines, friars of the Dominican and Augustan orders, full of faith and zeal. Oratory was fervid concerning the Cross of redemption, and was reinforced by generous measures of images, pictures, gorgeous altars, and all such paraphernalia as Rome knows so well how to employ, whereby the imaginative and impressible multitudes were stirred to the depths, were led away captive to the charmer. Moreover, divers miracles were conveniently wrought just then, while all along, the transition from Buddhism to Catholicism—systems which have so much in common—was made extremely easy. As the result, several princes, large numbers of the high officials and nobility, officers in the army and navy, gave in their allegiance to the Church. These were the palmy days of the Inquisition, and in Japan carnal weapons were wielded in the service of the Lord. Certain daimios ordered their retainers to be baptized, with banishment from the realm as the hard alternative. And the neophytes were incited to acts of violence against the Buddhists. The character of the bonzes was attacked, and shrines were desecrated and destroyed. One perfervid noble razed many temples, and burned three thousand monasteries. It is estimated that the number of converts at one time reached a million, and it seemed certain that Japan would become wholly Christian.

But, alas, such prosperity was the ruin of the mission, and the empire received a shock from which it did not recover for centuries. First the Jesuits and the friars fell out, and fell to anathematizing and excommunicating each other. It was Portuguese against Spaniard, and Spaniard against Portuguese. Then, to make confusion worse confounded, the Protestant Dutch and English began to resort to the islands for trade, and proceeded to malign the whole race of Catholics as rogues and scheming villains, who were plotting mischief for the Japanese. Suspicion was aroused, and fear, and dislike. The Jesuits and friars were ordered to take their departure, and public services ceased to be held. Later a plot was discovered to betray the country to Europeans and persecution ensued against the Christians, and finally was much intensified in severity when under severe sufferings they rose in rebellion. Thousands were put to death with the accompaniment of savage tortures, borne as steadfastly and heroically as any inflicted since the days of the apostles, and thousands more fled to other countries. All Europeans were banished, and with them from henceforth there should be no intercourse whatsoever. Only a handful of Dutch might remain to trade; cooped in a tiny island, Deshima, might send out one ship-load a year, but must not bring in any Bibles or Christian books, and must not buy, or take any books on Japanese history. No natives must leave the country on any consideration, and to make the attempt was death. All ships of any considerable size were to be destroyed and no more were to be built. It was also death, and deepest disgrace besides, to teach or to practise Christianity. Edicts against this "evil sect" were posted everywhere throughout the empire, in every city and village, on every highway, by the ferries and in the mountains, and reading in this vigorous fashion: "So long as the sun shall warm the earth, let no Christian be so bold as to come to Japan; and let all know that the king of Spain himself, or the Christian's God [thought to mean the Pope] or the great God of all, if he violate this command, shall pay for it with his head!" And for more than two centuries the attempt was kept up to stamp out utterly the least traces of the Gospel. The name of Jesus was held in the utmost loathing and abhorrence. And Japan, like her sister nations, China and Korea, closed and barred her gates.

The isolation, however, was not perfect. All along, some intercourse was maintained with her near neighbors to the west. And in numerous ways also the Dutch, though so carefully cabined, cribbed, confined, and most jealously watched in the neighborhood of Nagasaki in the extreme south, yet in various most efficacious ways served as a connecting link, a medium of communication between the would-be hermit empire and "outside barbarians." Numerous news items crept in through this channel, and much valuable information was picked up in Deshima and diffused far and wide. We now approach the period when under very different and far better auspices, Christian missions were destined to have a re-beginning upon Japanese soil. For in the meantime

Protestant powers had come to the front in commerce, colonization and conquest. In 1842, China had been compelled by British cannon to open certain of her ports to trade, and in considerable numbers the heralds of the cross were flocking thither. A most remarkable providential preparation for the opening of Japan was also in progress. And it was meet that from first to last America should play a leading part in the sublime transaction, and further, that the achievement should not be made through a bloody conflict with fleets and armies, but should stand in history among the glorious victories of peace. Only a few years before, in our amazing national movement westward, the Pacific coast had been reached, and by the discovery of gold, through the consequent vast influx of population had suddenly risen to importance. Thus the United States was brought face to face with Japan, and stood as her nearest neighbor to the east, with only the ocean as a convenient highway between. In those same days, helped by a liberal treaty with Russia, the northern Pacific was thronged with whalers, whose crews, every now and then shipwrecked upon the rock-bound coast of the Sunrise Kingdom, had suffered shameful maltreatment. Moreover, it happened not seldom that unfortunates from the islands, caught upon the open sea in a storm, had been driven along the Black Current to the opposite shores, or had been picked up midway, and the effort had been made, though frequently repulsed with rudeness, to return the waifs in safety to their friends.

As a result of these and other similar facts, early in the fifties the idea began to dawn upon the minds of various persons that the opening of Japan was a consummation devoutly to be wished, and that the government should make a bloodless but resolute attempt to secure sailors' rights in this quarter of the globe, as well as to secure an enlargement to American commerce. And in due season, the powers that be reached the same conclusion, and preparations began to be made for an expedition which should lack nothing of appliances, or methods of procedure calculated to ensure success. Fortunately the command was given to Commodore M. C. Perry, a brother of the hero of Lake Erie, who devoted months to careful working out of details for a scheme which should not only inspire respect, and kindle a healthy fear to the borders to terror, but in equal measure should convince the Japanese that the dominant feeling was friendly, and that they had much to gain from intercourse with the western world. July 8th, 1853, is a notable date, for it was then that Perry and his fleet anchored in Yedo Bay. He had four ships of war, two of them steam frigates, whose like in those waters had never been seen, and when propelled by some invisible force they moved about with flame and clouds of smoke, the paralyzed natives could only explain the phenomenon by supposing the barbarians had caught, and tamed, and harnessed, a volcano for the task. A request for an interview was sent on shore, and in reply came an order to hoist anchor at once and be off. Not so, but he must communicate, for he bore a message to the Emperor from the august President of the United States. Then he must transfer himself to Nagasaki, and speak through the Dutch, for the laws forbade all direct intercourse. He would not budge, and so much the worse for the laws. He would wait three days for a reply, and they must look well to the consequences of refusal. A veritable panic ensued in the breasts of both people and rulers. After much solemn conference in Yedo, it was finally concluded to meet the terrible Unknown (for as yet no Japanese eyes had been allowed to look upon Perry), but on his vessel. No, he must be allowed to land, and confer upon their own soil. At length every essential point was yielded, and with great ceremony, and show of dignity, a meeting was accorded with a high official representing the crown, the gold box containing the letter from the President, and the articles of the treaty desired, was given and received, notice was served that an answer would be called for at some time during the next year, and a few days later the fleet steamed away and disappeared. After about six months had passed once more the " black ships " hove in sight from the headlands, but this time there were nine instead of four, and anchor was cast much further up the bay than on the former occasion, indeed almost in sight of the capital city. After divers delays, and subterfuges, and protests of *non-possumus*, on their part; and on his, sturdy persistence relating to certain particulars, it was agreed that American sailors should be well treated, that at two ports a consul might reside, and supplies of coal, water, provisions, etc., might be procured, and though just now trade could not be allowed, perhaps in a few years the privilege would be granted. Then followed an exchange of presents on a grand scale. Among Perry's were a telegraph complete, a locomotive with rails and cars, both of which were put in order and set to work, with many other products of modern invention and skill. The transaction ended with feasting on ship and on shore, **the freest of social intercourse, and abundance of good feeling all around.**

It may seem that the outcome was but slight for so much endeavor, but it is to be remembered that all the rest to be related resulted easily and naturally from the achievement then made. Other nations followed and secured similar concessions, and before 1860 the urgency of our ambassador had gained the consent of the government to the opening of six ports, in which, and for twenty-five miles about them, foreigners might trade and travel. In 1861 an embassy was sent on a visit to the United States, and the year following another to Europe. True, the Japanese were still suspicious, and fearful that the irresistible barbarians had political designs which would work mortal mischief. A little later a tide of reactionary feeling set in, some foreigners were assassinated, and even vessels of war were fired upon from the shore, though with such a taste of vengeance inflicted in return that never since has occidental wrath been thus provoked. And what were the churches of Christendom doing meanwhile for the evangelization of the Land of the Rising Sun, which had now become in some measure accessible? Many an eye had long been watching for the hour to strike. Especially had the missionaries in China been scanning the political signs of the times. As early as 1855 an attempt was made to reach Japan from Shanghai, but passage could not be secured. In 1859 however Messrs. Liggins and Williams, representing the American Episcopalians, landed in Nagasaki, and began work for the kingdom of heaven. And before the end of the year to the same city, bent on the same heavenly errand, came three more, Messrs. Verbeck, Brown and Simmons, sent by the American (Dutch) Reformed Church, while a few weeks before Messrs. Hepburn and Nevius, American Presbyterians, in the Lord's name had entered Kanagawa on the Bay of Jedo, the scene of Perry's exploit, to remove afterwards across to Yokohama. The American Baptists followed in 1860, and for almost a decade no more societies joined in the work. Among the names mentioned are some of the intellectual and spiritual giants of this part of the mission field. But their sphere of toil was exceedingly narrow, and limited on every side. With no especial ill-treatment, though sometimes their lives were in danger from fanatical assassins, no public services could be held, the people were afraid of them, and spies were continually on their track. They could only quietly prepare, busy themselves laying foundations, and in patience possess their souls. They could study the difficult language, circulate Christian literature in Chinese which all the upper classes could read, let themselves be seen as much as possible in public, and by numberless kind deeds and acts of mercy finally compel the confidence and esteem of the sensible and candid. And presently they were in demand as teachers of English and other secular studies, even the government resorting to them for assistance in many things. They were able at length satisfactorily to demonstrate that they were actually what they seemed to be, not emissaries in disguise of any foreign power, with political designs back of religious performances, after the fashion of the Jesuits with whom Japan had had such sorry experience.

It is evident that as yet Japan is not open to the world, except in a very partial and superficial way. Foreign nations had done their part, but vastly more that was just as essential remained to be performed within the nation itself. And verily changes and overturnings, most sweeping and astounding, were at the door. Here was a case where things "sacred" must needs wait on things "secular." The longings of patriots, and the schemes of statesmen, must precede and prepare the way for the heavenly offices of the herald of the cross. And various mighty influences were at work within the Japanese body politic, which were destined marvellously to give free course to the Gospel. An intellectual ferment had been in progress for years. Through the Dutch traders, through European sailors shipwrecked upon the coast, and through Japanese sailors who, in spite of themselves, had been driven to foreign climes, many an exciting account of lands beyond sea had entered the islands, and been eagerly passed from lip to lip, whereby the curiosity of not a few, and hunger for knowledge had been quickened. Scores of young fellows like Neesima, bright, ambitious, and plucky, had been running away of late to see the wide world. And intercourse with foreigners in the treaty ports had added fuel to the flame. But most of all, the spirit of patriotism was finding a new voice, and was nerving many an arm to strike. As we have seen, the military head of the nation had long since usurped supreme authority, while the power of the emperor was but shadow and sham. Dissatisfaction has long been growing, and only a fitting occasion was wanting to produce an outbreak to humble the shogun, and to exalt the mikado to his proper place as the sacred head of the people. And the results of the coming of Perry's fleet supplied the required stimulus. The American commodore, in his excusable ignorance, supposed he was dealing directly with the emperor; whereas it was only his chief general, and also he that signed the treaty, as well as all similar engagements soon after entered into with other western nations. This last act of aggression was worst of all, and was, in short, intolerable. Against the law, he had presumed to communicate with the abhorred barbarians, had entered into league with them, had given them liberty to land, and dwell, and travel, and trade! After years of growing excitement the crisis befell in 1868. A variety of cross purposes, schemes and counter-schemes, were curiously combined in the bitter and bloody strife which ensued, and raged for ten or fifteen years. The noisiest cry was reactionary in its aims and demanded, "Restore the emperor," and, "Expel the barbarians." With the first half in mind, the shogun was soon persuaded to abdicate, and turn over all his power and glory to the mikado, though a number of the daimios, whose political fortunes were involved with his, resorted to arms.

Fortunately for Japan, there was a body of influential statesmen of a make much more liberal and more modern. And, though for years their startling project was concealed, it meant nothing less than the overthrow of feudalism in all its forms and phases, a cordial welcome to foreigners, and the adoption of all good ideas, customs, and institutions, to be found in the western world. Where in all history can such sublime daring and venturesomeness be found? And such was their skill and energy, and such the wave of generous enthusiasm which now swept over the whole land, that the bulk of the daimios, great and small, voluntarily resigned all claim to their castles and landed estates, and to the fealty of their retainers, and from being rulers of the people, consented to take the place of mere citizens! Where else can there be found a case of such self-sacrifice, and self-abnegation on so vast a scale? Among the rest, some two millions of samurai, soldiers and literati, who had always lived upon the bounty of their over-lords, were suddenly left without occupation, or means of support. And finally, to cap the climax of innovation and departure from the sacred precedents of centuries, the mikado conveniently dying just them, his youthful successor came out from the closest seclusion in which his lofty kind had always hid themselves from the gaze of the vulgar, appeared in public like common clay, and from hallowed Kyoto, where in dread majesty the emperors had dwelt from the beginning, changed his residence to Yedo, the former seat of the shogun now defunct, but with the name changed to Tokyo. At length came the crowning wonder, and when one day The Honorable Gate, as his imperial title signifies, "came in person to the meeting of the Council of State and took an oath as an actual ruler promising that a deliberative assembly should be formed; all measures should be decided by public opinion; the uncivilized customs of former times should be broken through; and the impartiality and justice displayed in the works of nature be adopted as a basis of action; and that intellect, and learning, should be sought for throughout the world, in order to establish the foundations of the empire."

Suiting the action to the word, an embassy, composed largely of high officials of the government, was despatched to the United States, and afterwards made a progress through Europe, not for show, but for earnest business; appearing in Washington in February of 1872. And it was this event " that marked the formal entrance of Japan upon the theater of universal history." A very furore for change set in. " Everything domestic came to be looked upon as inferior; everything from abroad was accepted as superior, and adopted with little inquiry as to its merits." European costume for men and women, modes of cooking, beer and wine, dancing and cards, among other "improvements," became exceedingly popular. But together with abundance of folly, choice was also made of much that was among the best and most characteristic in the western world. Like the Code Napoleon, navy, army, coinage, post-office, steamships railroads, telegraphs, lighthouses on every prominent point of the coast, cotton and paper mills, a school system extending from the kindergarten to the university, with educational works by the hundred and thousand, as well as modern medicine and surgery. Yes, and commencing with January of 1874, the Gregorian calendar came into use, and the Christian Sabbath became a rest day for all teachers and government employees. Provision was made for a constitution, to go into effect in 1890, which gave the country a legislature of two houses, and in part elected by the people. Some hundreds of thousands of *eta* and *hinin*, outcasts held in contempt, and with no protection from the laws, were made citizens. Some hundreds of choice young men were sent to the United States to be trained in our best institutions of learning, and as many more to those of Europe. To meet the present emergency, until natives could be educated in sufficient numbers, scores ot foreign scholars, engineers, military men, jurists, physicians, etc., etc., were called in to construct and set in motion the new machinery. Resort was also had in liberal measure to Christian missionaries who were already upon the ground, for, not unwillingly, their manifold gifts and graces were received and utilized as an integral and important part of the admired civilization of the west. Christian scholars like Verbeck, and others, were in higher favor from the fact that, while the great embassy was in Germany, where much was seen and heard that made a profound impression, the Emperor William and Bismarck hesitated not to speak plainly and emphatically to the Japanese princes of the value and the imperative need of Christianity among the people, if a nation is to prosper. And what an unmatched spectacle it was, taken in all its parts! A renascence vastly more wonderful than Italy beheld in the famous days of the Medici. Only to be equaled, for sublimity and significance, by the first months of the French Revolution. A nation was born in a day. At one leap the gulf was spanned which separated the Dark Ages from the Nineteenth Century!

Just about twenty years after Perry's cannon aroused the hermit nation from the sleep of ages, Japan was found open and accessible. At least the Gospel could enter with a fair chance to make its way forward. The edicts were removed in 1873, which for two hundred years had threatened death to every soul that dared to love Jesus, or to speak for Him. To this day, however, church property can be held only upon the concessions granted in the treaty ports, while elsewhere ownership must be in native hands. Neither are foreigners allowed to reside in the empire beyond the twenty-five mile limit, unless in the employ of the government, or of some native company, or individual. In order to travel in the interior, passports are required, and these are granted only upon grounds relating to "health" and "science." Though these two terms are commonly construed by the officials with almost limitless liberality, consciences not a few hesitate about preaching Christ under such a subterfuge, and with at least the semblance of law-breaking.

But in spite of these and other obstacles, and with the rising tide of enthusiasm for things foreign to largely counterbalance, when for substance the tremendous political revolution had been achieved, a great and effectual door for evangelizing labor was found standing open, and inviting entrance. All along, ever since their advent nearly fifteen years before, the half-score of pioneers had been making the most of their limited opportunities, though as yet with next to nothing to show of visible results. The first baptism had occurred in 1866, but the first church, with a membership of nine natives, was not organized until 1872. The missionary force was now greatly enlarged by the entrance of other organizations. The American Board and the English Church Society had sent their representatives in 1869, or soon after the abdication of the usurping shogun, and within five years five more followed, and in this order, making ten in all: The Union Woman's Society, the Methodist Episcopal, the Canada Methodist, the Propagation Society, and the United Presbyterian of Scotland. By the end of that decade fifteen organizations were in the field, and by 1890 the number has risen to twenty-six. During the period of armed strife, and while the stunning political changes were in progress, so intensely occupied were men's minds in other realms that little time was left to attend to religious affairs, nor to any extent had the disposition to listen to what the missionaries might say begun to be as yet. Prejudice had penetrated to the heart's core. The ogre of Jesuitism still terrorized the multitude, and *kirishitan* (Japanese for Christian) was a synonym for the devil and all his damnable works. The ice of ignorance and dislike was first broken by the passionate desire to become acquainted with the marvels of the western world, the languages, sciences, forms of government, and all the rest. And who so accessible as the clusters of missionaries to be found in the treaty ports. To gain what was desired, all sorts of schemes and subterfuges were resorted to, and large doses of doctrine and moral precept were swallowed. Classes were formed, and schools were opened. And it came to pass, such was the power of the truth, and such the docility and ingenuousness of the Japanese mind and heart, (*vide* the statement concerning the people made to Xavier by the convert from the islands), that it was not long before, in many cases, baser motives began to be exchanged for far worthier ones, and earnest seekers after salvation began to multiply.

And this phenomenon presently came into view. A fact became evident, which, though in steadily diminishing degree, has ever since characterized Christianity in the Land of the Rising Sun. It came to pass, as nowhere else in the annals of missions either ancient or modern, that the bulk of the inquirers and converts were not from the poor, the ignorant, the pariahs of society; but from among the middle-upper class, samurai, the knights of the feudal days, the literati, young men of social standing and culture, of intellectual force and political influence; the future leaders of the people, statesmen, officials of the government. These were now crowded into the large cities, were the first to come into contact with foreigners, and to feel the impact of the new ideas. Even yet, the masses, the inhabitants dwelling in the interior, have scarcely been touched by the glad tidings. A distinct and memorable advance was made in Yokohama in 1872, when Christians of every name united to observe the Week of Prayer. So delightful were the meetings, and so manifest the unusual presence of the Spirit, that they were continued through the month, and to the end of February, with spiritual power steadily growing. Much earnest supplication was mingled with the instruction, and the Book of the Acts was read in course, and studied, and prayed over. It was a season of remarkable religious quickening and exaltation of thought and feeling. "For the first time the Japanese were in a prayer-meeting, and upon their knees pouring out their souls for a blessing on their country." It was verily Pentecost come again. As a direct result, early in March nine young men were baptized, and with two older ones were united in Christian fellowship, forming thus the first church in Japan. From this prophetic beginning the blessed work spread to other portions of the field, though for ten years nothing else so noticeable occurred. As reinforcements poured in, new stations in quite large numbers were opened. The native Christians were fervid and had a mind to work, and before long began with great effect to play the part of evangelists to their neighbors and friends. In 1877 the first native was ordained, and set over a church in Osaka. Two years before this Joseph Neesima, after an experience full of elements touching and romantic, and a thorough course of training, had returned from America to his native land overflowing with zeal, and longing to see his people turned to the Gospel, in due season to lay the foundations and rear the walls of his Doshisha (One-Purpose Company), a Christian university, and his monument for all time. As far back as 1871, Captain Janes, a soldier, had been engaged by an ex-daimio to open a school for young men in Kumamoto. For three years not much was said about Christianity, though he had gained the admiration and affection of his pupils, but then one day he said : " I shall teach the Bible on Sunday ; any one who wishes may come to my house." A few accepted the invitation, but with no serious purpose, and only out of regard for their instructor. After another year several who had begun to be impressed followed Captain Janes' counsel and spent a New Year's vacation reading the Gospel of John, and in prayer for themselves and their schoolmates. A revival followed in the school lasting for several weeks, during which about forty confessed Christ, and as many more took up the study of the Scriptures. Finally, one Sunday, a company of the Christian students " made a solemn covenant together that, as they had thus been blessed by God in advance of all their countrymen, they would labor to enlighten the darkness of the empire by preaching the Gospel, even at the sacrifice of their lives. They prayed kneeling, and wrote an oath-paper, on which they signed and sealed their names." Sharp persecution from their relatives followed to a portion of the number, under the effect of which a few turned back, but the most—the oldest was under twenty—were immovable. Presently they appear at the Doshisha, to form its first theological class, and to-day, with a few exceptions, are found in the ministry, or in other related callings, and the members of the "Kumamoto Band" will always rank high among the mighty molding forces which operated early in New Japan.

The period of 1870–80 was one of quiet and not extensive growth. The seed was sown beside all waters, but the abundant harvest was not yet. In 1879 the number of converts was only 2,701 and of these 1,084 had been received during the year. Then followed a series of years during which the kingdom of heaven in Japan advanced by strides and leaps. The converts increased marvelously, at the rate of fifty per cent. annually, and during one year at the rate of sixty-seven per cent. And the Christian world looked on with amazement, scarcely able to believe the reports of ingathering sent home by the rejoicing missionaries. It looked as though the complete evangelization, and even Christianization, of the empire was in sight. But then, under the influence of a variety of co-operating causes, the flood of zeal began to subside, and the work goes forward much more slowly and heavily. In 1889 the additions to the churches amounted to 5,677, but in the next year they fell off to 1,199, with a number still smaller in 1891. The craze for foreign products was now over, had run its roaring and turbid course, and a violent reaction had set in. An almost frenzy began to rage for nationalizing and Japanizing everything, and in religion as well as elsewhere. Besides, a rationalizing spirit entered the churches, derived from Unitarian and German sources. But now the indications are abundant that once more the pendulum has begun to swing towards the center. As one token from a number, in 1892 the accessions to the mission churches rose to 2,144, or double those of the year preceding. These figures will tell something of the progress made to date in laying the foundations of the Gospel in Japan. The number of organizations engaged is 32, which are represented by 226 men and 625 women, of whom 210 are unmarried; and 258 ordained natives, and 536 unordained preachers and helpers. The fruits of toil appear in 365 churches gathered, and 39,240 communicants. Besides, the Roman Catholics report 44,812 adherents gathered in 244 congregations, and the

Greek Church (Russian) 20,325 in 219 congregations. Upwards of 10,000 Japanese were baptized in 1892.

But what are these few thousands among so many millions? The bulk of the population has not yet even heard the sound of the Gospel message. The missions are mainly in, or near, the few treaty ports, while the masses in the interior are left to their idols, and without hope. For generations to come, the Macedonian cry will come to Christendom from these islands, and their deep spiritual needs will demand in large measure the gifts, the prayers, the toils, of all those who would see the kingdom spread over all the earth.

Before passing from this mission field so interesting and at many points so unique it may be well to notice two or three of its most striking peculiarities. And first, from the beginning, there has been a lack of appreciation almost utter for the theological and ecclesiastical differences which separate the numerous sects engaged in evangelizing work in the empire, coupled with a persistent disposition to ignore them. The Japanese idea is this: Why should the numerous quarrels and schisms of Protestant Christendom be introduced and perpetuated among us? Why may we not build directly upon the Word of God, the teachings of Christ and his apostles, instead of upon the creeds and customs which divide western churches into warring camps? Like the disciples of early times, why cannot we be all one, united in a single national church? This desire, so strong as to amount to a settled determination, often springs in great measure from an inborn indifference, and inability, as touching all subtleties of logic and metaphysical hair-splittings, and an overwhelming proclivity to lay the chief emphasis upon the practical in religious affairs. It was significant that when the first church was organized in 1872, though Presbyterian in paternity, the only name taken was "Church of Christ." And so general and imperative has been the demand for union, at least for federation, that the thirty-two societies are found combined in twelve ecclesiastical bodies, and five of these cover all but 1,644 of the native Christians. Seven Presbyterian and Reformed societies are joined in "The Church of Christ in Japan," four Episcopal churches unite to constitute Nippon Sei Kokwai, while a remarkable degree of harmony and fraternal co-operation exists between the residue. As a notable example of this, in 1872 the various missions met and chose a representative committee to prepare a translation of the Scriptures which should suffice for all. A number of native scholars were also chosen to add their knowledge and judgment. The New Testament was issued eight years after, the Old Testament was not completed until 1888.

Again, and quite kindred to the fact just mentioned, the Japanese display a remarkable readiness to be independent, to cut all leading-strings, to stand alone. Ordinarily in mission fields, the great difficulty has been to persuade converts in any measure to think and act for themselves. They had no ambition in that direction, or the capacity was wanting. But not so in Japan. Intellectual force is abundant, with national pride (not to say conceit) to reinforce it. In explanation we are to recall the fact already stated, that the majority of the conversions have hitherto been from among the samurai, young men of the cultured upper-middle class, and not from the pariahs of society. And further, since the recent reaction set in, jealousy of all foreign interference or influence has received an astonishing impulse, even to the point of regarding the missionaries as intruders, and would-be rulers. And so the churches, with refreshing confidence in their ability thus to do, proceed to fashion creeds and covenants to suit themselves, to do this and that with slight regard for occidental precedent. And with this is coupled a phenomenon still more strange. In a multitude of cases these unique saints insist with all their might upon exercising the privilege of doing the work of evangelizing their fellow countrymen, and of paying their own bills. In 1878 a native home missionary society was formed, which has done much to spread the Gospel in neglected and benighted regions; the contributions for self-support have always been liberal beyond precedent; of the sixty-five churches formed in connection with the work of the American Board, forty-one now receive no outside help, while several have never been thus aided.

CHAPTER XIX.

SPANISH AMERICA.

UNDER the phrase Spanish America is included the entire region lying between the southern boundary of the United States and Cape Horn. The area under view equals in size the vast Russian possessions in both Europe and Asia, or Europe twice over with three German empires in addition, and contains a population of 47,500,000. For many reasons there is a fitness in grouping together these twenty states which politically are altogether separate and distinct. The general physical features are quite similar. The peerless Andes, with their northern counterpart the Mexican Cordilleras, extend from end to end, with here and there volcanic peaks the loftiest in the world. The land of the Montezumas is "probably the richest known argentiferous region in the whole world," the output being estimated at the prodigious figure of twelve thousand millions of dollars, while in Peru, Potosi alone, a name which ranks with Ophir and Golconda, has added a thousand millions to the world's stock of silver. Then except in the extreme south the climate is either tropical or semi-tropical. Besides, the composition and character of the population differ but little. The ruling class is everywhere Spanish, Brazil only excepted, and there the Portuguese are in power. Some ten or twelve million Indians hold their original seats between the Gulf of California and Cape Horn, a large portion still in paganism and savagery. A larger element of the population is composed of a mixture, in every conceivable degree, of European and aboriginal blood. To these are joined other millions of Negroes, once slaves but now free, while in later times has occurred a large emigration of Germans, Italians, Jews, etc., and also of Chinese and Hindu coolies. For the masses illiteracy is the rule.

Still further the history of each one of the score of states is in outline at least almost indentical with that of all the rest. Spanish America was the first section of the New World to be discovered and overrun by the greedy gold hunters from the Iberian Peninsula. In the story which sets forth their doings the truth is far stranger than fiction. In an incredibly short space of time, by an unparalled series of tours of exploration and feats of arms, the whole coast region, both on the east and west, was visited by a mere handful of daring spirits and fell a prey to "civilization." Colonies were founded in Brazil as early as 1504. The conquest of Mexico was achieved by Cortes with five hundred and fifty men in 1510-21, while Pizarro in 1531-2 with one hundred and eighty men marched against the Inca, and reduced his empire to vassalage. In Buenos Ayres the foundations of dominion were laid in 1535, in Paraguay in 1536, and in Chili in 1541. For the better part of three centuries the original conquerors retained possession, and then suddenly and almost simultaneously (1809-21), by a common and irresistible impulse imparted from the Napoleonic wars, the inhabitants of every province, from Texas to Tierra del Fuego, rose in rebellion, cast off the foreign yoke, proclaimed independence, and one after another adopted a republican form of government. It is, however, a sad commentary upon the intellectual and moral condition of the people, that such a multitude of would-be despots have made their appearance from that day to this, and that revolutions with immense expenditure of blood and treasure have been so absurdly frequent. Evidently fitness for self-rule has not yet been attained.

Finally, from the beginning, the entire region under view has been under the same ecclesiastical domination, and the same religious training has been bestowed. In the palmy days of the Great Discovery the privileged Pope had the whole world at his disposal, and graciously bestowed the New World upon his most loyal servitors, Spain and Portugal, to wit, and a horde of priests and friars sped across the Atlantic to rescue the souls of the pagans. And ever since in realms spiritual the papal church has all things to its liking, has not failed to rule with a high hand, and the fruits of ten generations of the Roman *regime* appear in forms most characteristic, if also lamentable and heart-sickening. The outcome is even worse than that to be found in southern Europe. The civilization is of a low grade, while the masses are left to grovel in dense ignorance and gross superstition. Too often the priesthood is scarcely above the people for intelligence and is grossly immoral, while the religious teaching and practice are a curious compound of Christianity and heathenism, and the elements of the latter preponderating. With fine and costly architecture, and stunning spectacular display, the church routine is an empty form, while all that represents the pure and blessed Gospel of the Kingdom is dragged down to the low level of the current political and social life, and with shockingly easy accommodation to the semi-pagan and semi-barbarous environment. Of course the tropical climate, with excessive heat and moisture combined, adds to the demoralization and degradation. Let Paraguay stand for Rome's most illustrious achievement in the New World. For nearly a hundred years here was the veritable paradise of Jesuitism. The Franciscans were the first upon the ground, but later the wily disciples of Loyola entered, and soon ordered off all rival missionary toilers, and from 1690 to 1768 held exclusive possession. There was no lack of propagandizing zeal, and from among the simple-minded natives converts were made by the ten thousand. These were gathered into villages for more thorough discipline. A theocracy was set up, a "philanthropic despotism." Private ownership of property was abolished, and in its place community of goods prevailed. In a spirit truly paternal, the holy fathers managed all the secular (as well as sacred) affairs of the people, directed their labor, taught them various useful handicrafts, and in almost every way fairly outdid Louis XIV. himself in his precious dealings during the same period with his *habitans* on the St. Lawrence. Minds, and hearts, and consciences, were as clay in the hands of these matchless potters, obedience was perfect, while of individual volition there was nothing left. Humanity was even transmogrified into a machine. Only let the Jesuit touch the spring, and action would follow strictly according to law. Since the political revolutions occurred, several of the states have made no inconsiderable advances towards enlightenment of every kind, in most popular education and religious liberty are provided for by law, and yet quite a number have made next to no progress at all. Almost anywhere between New Mexico and southern Patagonia to introduce the Bible, or any form of teaching other than that of the

Catholic type, is to face fierce denunciation and mob violence, if not also death. The roll of Protestant martyrs in Spanish America contains already names not a few and is a lengthening one. For, practically everywhere a bigoted priesthood is supreme in the hopes and fears of the sorely benighted millions. And it was mainly on account of this universal and abject bondage to Rome, with the consequent intolerance to the extent of horror and loathing for the ideas and practices flowing from the Reformation, that missions in these parts are of such recent origin, have as yet scarcely emerged from the estate of feeble infancy, and so South America with strict propriety can be termed " the Neglected Continent."

Let us begin our more minute survey with the southern half of the New World, reserving Mexico and Central America for the latter portion of the chapter. Between the Isthmus of Darien and Cape Horn lies a vast mass of land 4500 by 3200 miles in its greatest length and breadth, and covering some 7,500,000 square miles. The most remarkable physical features are found in its mountains, its mighty rivers, and its vast grassy plains (pampas). The Amazon has no equal on earth, it drains an area of 2,600,000 square miles, or twice the size of the Mississippi Valley, while sending into the sea a flood six times greater than that of the Father of Waters. The bulk of this huge continent is situated within the tropics, the equator stretching westward from the point where the Amazon enters the Atlantic, but an ever narrowing extension reaches far towards the southern pole. The continent is parcelled out among thirteen nationalities, and these figures will give the area and population of each one.

	SQUARE MILES.	POPULATION.
Brazil,	3,209,000	14,000,000
Argentine Republic	1,125,000	4,086,000
Venezuela,	600,000	2,323,000
Bolivia,	570,000	1,200,000
Colombia,	505,000	3,880,000
Peru,	465,000	2,622,000
Chili,	295,000	2,820,000
Ecuador,	120,000	1,270,000
Uraguay,	75,000	700,000
Paraguay,	100,000	330,000
The three Guianas,	200,000	500,000
Total,	7,264,000	33,830,000

Passing by for the moment the original enterprise looking towards carrying a pure Gospel into South America, the first successful attempt at evangelization was made in 1735, by the Moravian Church, and in Dutch Guiana (Surinam). This was more than one hundred and fifty years ago, only thirteen years after that body of Christians had begun to be, and while all the rest of Protestant Christendom was sunk in a deep sleep as touching obedience to the Lord's last command. And what an anomaly it is, that more should have been accomplished to date for the redemption of this southern continent by this feeblest and humblest of the denominations, than by all the others combined, and that more than half of all the Protestant Christians of South America should be found in the less than least of all the states, whether for size or population! In accordance with the policy settled at Herrnhut of preferring fields spiritually most barren and forbidding, after selecting the enslaved Africans of the West Indies, and then the Eskimos of Greenland, the northeast coast lying between the mouths of the Amazon and the Orinoco was chosen as the seat of the third mission. And verily here the Brethren found sin and sorrow, suffering and shame, to their hearts' content, and for themselves in sowing and watering for the Master long waiting and discouragements numberless. "The low-lying coast land was deadly for Europeans, and the dense forests, through which the Surinam and other rivers wend their earlier course, are still more deadly. It was there that for a time *every soul won cost a missionary's life.*" Men and women died by the dozen and the score, but there was no lack of others to fill their places. For various reasons progress was slow for almost the entire first hundred years. Three classes in particular were sought after. First the Arawack Indians, and if possible worse off than these, the bush negroes, who had once been in bondage, but had fled from their masters and taken refuge in the back country, and for the most part led the life of outlaws and desperadoes. After the toil of forty-eight years only fifty converts had been made. The third class was composed of the slaves upon the plantations. The Dutch masters eyed the missionaries through the spectacles of *odium theologicum*, their ideas and ways were so different from those of the Reformed, and in addition were much afraid that piety of the Moravian type working in the black breast might seriously interfere with his value as a field hand. Some generations passed before much access could be gained to these wretched creatures. Wars came in to further interfere, and also famines and pestilences. But nothing could daunt the courage of these ambassadors for Christ, or at all chill the fervor of their zeal for souls, and finally they conquered by sheer patient continuance in well-doing, coupled with unbounded good nature, kindness, sympathy, and true affection, even for the very vilest. In the early decades of this century the skies began to brighten. The emancipation of the slaves in the sixties led to much confusion, and compelled the facing of new and grave problems, but a few statistics will help us in some measure to appreciate the magnitude of the revolution social, intellectual, and moral, which by the matchless power of the Spirit and the Word has been wrought. The missionary force numbers 80, of whom 37 are ordained, with 7 native ministers and 437 other native helpers. The churches contain 8,572 communicants, while 30,000 adherents are identified with the mission. Paramaribo, the chief city, is a stronghold for the Gospel. More than half of the colony is connected with the Moravian congregations, and since, besides these, there are some 10,000 Lutherans, Reformed, Episcopalians, etc. Dutch Guiana may now fairly be called Christian.

It was considerably more than a century later before the second assault was made upon this great kingdom of darkness. The extreme southern point, Magellan's Land of Fire, was selected as the most desirable location for a mission. The immediate results were tragic to the terrible, so that abundant opportunity was afforded to the indifferent and worldly-wise to cry out, " failure," and " waste." And yet, not to know the story of Allen Gardiner, is to have missed one of the most pathetic and thrilling and inspiring narratives ever put upon paper, and also, judged by the New Testament, the Divine test, one of the most glorious achievements which have attended the spread of the kingdom. The childhood of this notable saint and martyr was prophetic of mature years, for he used often to sleep upon the ground " because he intended to travel, and would inure himself to hardship." Entering the British navy, he voyaged the whole world over, taking careful note of the condition and needs of the various peoples, and while witnessing the heathen worship in a Chinese temple received the impulse which controlled the residue of his life. His wife dying in 1834, he soon, and with all his might, determined "to become the pioneer of a mission to the most abandoned pagans." South Africa was his first field, but the Zulu war soon breaking out he was compelled to flee, barely escaping with his life. A way of entrance was sought to New Guinea, but sought in vain; and then South America was fixed upon. Three of the principal English missionary societies were importuned to send him thither, but all declined. He assayed to herald the glad tidings upon the western coast, and again in the northern portion, but only to be baffled. Returning to England for assistance, at length the Patagonian Missionary Society was formed, and thrice over Gardiner led a forlorn hope to Tierra del Fuego to gain a foothold in that dreary and dreadful waste. Finally in 1850, when everybody but himself was utterly disheartened, with unconquerable faith he tugged away until £1,000 were secured to fit out yet another expedition. And since to undertake to dwell upon land among such incorrigible thieves was to run daily risk of losing all things, while sudden massacre by the brutal savages would be unceasingly imminent, four boats were fitted up to hold the needful supplies, and to furnish a place of residence. With six companions this intrepid soldier of the cross was transported to the island, and left with provisions for six months. By a most calamitous blunder, the powder and shot were overlooked and forgotten, and carried away by the vessel which brought them, so that the little company was doomed to subsist without meat, nor could they defend themselves against attacks. "The climate is always dreadful with frequent rainy squalls in summer, with snow and sleet in winter. The sky is seldom clear and the winds are ferocious." Great suffering presently ensued. In a tempest the smaller boats were lost, and the anchor to one of the larger ones. Sometimes protection was sought from the intolerable cold in caves so damp as to produce rheumatism. To fill to the full the measure of disaster, communication from home bringing relief was delayed beyond all expectation, and food began to fail, with slow starvation as the result. They wandered up and down the coast, dying one after another, Gardiner the last to succumb. September 6th was the fatal day for him, as his diary stated, and the ship bringing supplies did not arrive until the last of October. Marks upon the rocks, and papers fastened here and there, revealed the place where the bodies lay moldering. And what sublimer token can be found than faith triumphant in the darkest hour? Hard by the spot where this hero had breathed his last his feeble hand had traced Psalm 62; 5-8: "My soul wait thou only upon God, for my expectation is from him," etc. A solemn charge was also left to his friends not to neglect the object for which he had gladly sacrificed his life. As the result of all, the South American Missionary Society soon came into being, the ship *Allen Gardiner* was purchased, and other bands of missionaries were despatched. The "failures" were not yet over and one entire party of nine was murdered while engaged in worship without the least suspicion of danger. This catastrophe befell in 1859. Already the policy was adopted which ever since, and with the greatest care, has been pursued, of making Kepple

Island, one of the Falklands, a few hundred miles to the east, the chief seat of the mission, and carrying thither from time to time certain of the better class of the Patagonian men and women, when tamed, civilized, Christianized, and educated somewhat, to be returned to their homes as a nucleus for work among their friends. After a while genuine conversions began to occur, and such has been the general transformation that this field now differs little from any other located in the midst of a degraded people. Even so calm and sagacious an observer as Darwin (not to say prejudiced and sceptical), who had seen much of the Fuegians when in their original brutishness and ferocity, and as he judged, the lowest specimens of humanity—even he was filled with wonder at the matchless power of Christianity there displayed, and to the end of his life was a regular contributor to the funds of the society.

We pass next to Brazil, almost equal to all the other South American states combined, for it covers nearly half the area of the continent, and holds about half the population, while so central is its location and so extensive are its boundaries, that it touches every other state, Chili only excepted. As is most fitting, therefore, much the largest number of organizations are here represented, by a far larger force of missionaries. And it was also upon the soil of this imperial domain that the first Protestant attempt was made to proclaim among the heathen the Gospel of salvation. This was in 1555, two hundred years before Carey was born. Calvin and Coligny, with the French Huguenots, were concerned in it, but since the scheme meant colonization much more than Christianization, and soon came to an end in disaster, we may dismiss it without further notice. Two

Methodists are found at work in Rio Janeiro as far back as 1836, but before the language had been learned, or anything had been undertaken in behalf of the natives, one died and the other, on account of crushing financial troubles at home, abandoned the field. Two years later Dr. Kalley, a Scotch physician, undertook the task of evangelizing the same city, and afterwards extended his labors to Pernambuco, gathering churches and establishing out-stations. In 1859 the Presbyterians entered the capital, and have ever since held on, lengthening the cords and strengthening the stakes. Earnest men and women have gone up and down the coast, and far towards the interior, selecting, one after another, important centers, like Sao Paulo, Bahia, Brotas, Soracaba, Campanha, and Rio Grande da Sul, and around each opening clusters of preaching-places. The Southern Presbyterians followed in 1869, occupying such strategic points as Pernambuco, Campinas, Bagagem, etc., and pushing out into Ceara, Maranhao, Alagoas, and other provinces. In 1888, in response to a general desire both on the part of the missionaries and the native ministers, the work of these two denominations was federated, the three presbyteries were readjusted and joined in the Synod of Brazil. This body now reports 87 missionaries of whom 59 are ministers, 65 churches with 4,780 members, 383 joining last year. The contributions for twelve months amounted to $37,874. The Methodists re-entered this field in 1876, and the Southern Baptists came in 1881. Bishop Taylor has a self-supporting mission at Para; the Episcopalians are doing somewhat; both the American Bible Society, and the British and Foreign Bible Society supply the Scriptures in the vernacular, and the South American Missionary Society maintains a number of chaplains for the benefit of English-speaking persons. At Sao Paulo is located a Protestant college, where also is the seat of the chief law school of Brazil, and a Presbyterian training school for native ministers and teachers. Such in briefest outline is the evangelizing work undertaken by Protestant Christendom for the 14,000,000, who for the most part sit in darkness and the shadow of death. Almost all the missions are planted upon the coast, or near it, while the vast interior is altogether untouched.

The Argentine Republic is the second state in South America for size and population. In this glance both Uraguay and Paraguay will be included, since for our purpose they present no distinctive features. In all three the Catholic Church is established by law, though all other churches are tolerated. In the country first named, the government is liberal, and education and public improvements are fostered. We find ourselves again in the region made sacred by the prayers and toils and sufferings of Gardiner, and as we saw, the South American Society was formed to carry on his work. Besides Keppel, in the Falkland Islands, it has two stations near Cape Horn, Ooshooia, and Wollaston recently removed to Tekeenika, with the schooner *Allen Gardiner* plying often between, and is represented elsewhere by chaplains who render service in behalf of British colonists. The Methodists entered Argentina in 1836, beginning work in the city of Buenos Ayres, and since have extended the theater of their beneficent work into Paraguay and Uraguay, as well as far back towards the interior. This denomination is represented by 7 missionaries with their wives, 15 ordained and 43 unordained native preachers, by 1,200 church members, by probationers and others enough to make a total of 10,000 adherents, and 2,000 pupils in the schools. The American Bible Society supplies efficient co-operation.

Let Chili, across the Andes, come next into view. Its shape is most peculiar. Situated between the mountains and the ocean, it stretches from Peru to southern Patagonia, with a length of 2,600 miles, while the breadth varies from 240 miles down to but forty. Catholicism is enthroned as the state religion, but the law grants toleration to Protestants. Education is free, and schools are provided of various grades up to a university, with departments of law, medicine, and the fine arts. The press is also untrammeled. The Presbyterians sent missionaries in 1873, and work out from four centers, Santiago, Valparaiso, Concepcion, and Copiapo. The force now consists of 7 ministers, 6 of them with wives, 3 ordained and 12 other native helpers. In the 5 churches are 295 members, and 400 children in the schools. Bishop Taylor has missions (Methodist), with flourishing church and school work, in Santiago, Concepcion, Coquimbo, and Iquique. In 1878–89 he sent to the west coast of the continent for his self-supporting work 26 preachers, with 9 male and 46 female teachers. The American Bible Society is present to supply the printed Word, and the chaplains of the South American Society preach in their mother tongue.

Bolivia has in its population 1,500,000 Mestizoes, a mixture of Spanish and Indian, and 1,000,000 Indians. The Catholic Church is established by law, and no other may hold public service of any kind. With this important limitation, religion is free. The intellectual condition appears in the fact that, with inhabitants numbering 2,500,000, only about 25,000 children are found in the schools. The American Bible Society is the only exponent of a pure Christianity.

Peru contains 350,000 uncivilized Indians, and 50,000 Chinese coolies, and of the population remaining, twenty-three per cent. is composed of a mixture of white races and red. The constitution prohibits the public exercise of any but the Catholic religion, and yet this clause is so far disregarded that Jews and Anglicans maintain services in Callao and Lima, and the Methodists are at work in the same cities, with Rev. T. B. Wood as presiding elder. A colporteur of the American Bible Society also pushes his work, quietly and " without observation." It was however this same man, F. Penzotti, who a few years since was arrested for circulating the Word of God in the vernacular, and expiated his " crime " by lying for months in prison.

In Venezuela, with the Roman Church in the place of civil power, other faiths are " tolerated " except that " they are not permitted any external manifestation." The only form of missionary toil is found in the circulation of the Bible in Spanish by the American Bible Society.

Colombia is in a religious case slightly better, for here the Catholics suffer Protestants and others to preach and propagate their opinions freely, so long as they do not go " contrary to Christian morals nor the law." Under the gracious protection of this shield the Presbyterians entered Bogota in 1856. Fierce opposition was aroused at once on the part of the jealous priesthood, but fortunately the civil authorities stood by the missionaries, and they have continued to this day. Political revolutions have hindered much, and for various reasons progress has been slow. With 5 ministers, 7 women, and 16 native helpers, 4 stations are occupied, 3 churches, with 144 members, have been formed, and 250 children are in the schools. The Bible Society is a stanch helper.

Ecuador stands last in more senses than one. The Catholic Church is supreme everywhere, is all in all. "The constitution excludes all other creeds." As the name implies this country lies under the equator, and so is extremely hot—for all heretics. Not China, Japan, or Korea, was ever more effectually closed against the entrance of a living Gospel.

In summing up for South America, before proceeding northward, we must not fail to take especial notice of the exceedingly prominent part played by the two great Bible societies, of Great Britain and the United States. The one has 11 colporteurs constantly at work while the other maintains 37 agencies and about 30 colporteurs, and in cash donations expends upwards of $60,000 a year. In all, between the Isthmus and the Cape, are found 117 male, and 134 female missionaries, and 44 native ministers, a total force of 885. But this is only at the rate of one Protestant minister to every 225,000 of the population. Into the mission churches are gathered 14,809 communicants, and a little over 6,000 into the schools. A liberal estimate would make the adherents number not more than 60,000. Only so many, out of a population 34,000,000, or but one out of 566 in any degree associated with a pure and intelligent faith.

Central America.

Central America can be dismissed with few words. As to physical characteristics, climate, and population, it differs but little from its neighbors to the south and north, while of missionary work bestowed there is next to none.

The five little republics, which are grouped together under this term, are sometimes confederated, sometimes independent, and frequently at war with each other, or distracted and desolated by internal strife. Great Britain has a crown colony in this same region. The following table will show the area and population of the several states.

	SQUARE MILES.	INHABITANTS.
Guatemala,	46,800	1,460,000
Nicaragua,	49,500	313,000
Honduras,	46,400	432,000
Costa Rica,	37,000	243,000
Salvador,	7,225	777,900
British Honduras,	7,562	31,500
Total,	194,487	3,257,400

Everywhere the people are Roman Catholics, in Costa Rica the papacy is established by law, but in all the states Protestantism is tolerated. Only two denominations are represented among these millions of Spaniards, Indians, Negroes, and a multitude composed of a promiscuous mixture of the three. Since 1847 the Moravians have sustained a mission upon the Mosquito Coast of Nicaragua, where ever since the days of the buccaneers, every conceivable influence which makes for evil has been working wickedness and shame. Bluefields was taken as a center, and for almost a half century the Brethren have been patiently founding and building all manner of good institutions among the Indians, delivering them from bondage to their gross vices and superstitions. Traveling from station to station is largely by water, and a vessel is kept for the purpose. Many precious lives have been sacrificed to the tropical and malarial climate, and to overexhausting labors, but 697 communicants, 5,171 baptized adherents, and 634 children in the schools, stand for gains much more than commensurate with the cost. Of late the government has given permission to enter the interior.

The other mission in Central America was founded in 1883 by the Presbyterians, and is located in Guatemala City, the capital of the state of the same name, about sixty miles from the seaport, San Jose. The first missionary, Rev. John C. Hill, was sent out at the request of President Barrios, who also paid the traveling expenses of his family, the freight charges upon furniture, as well as purchased the equipment necessary for the establishment of church and school work. But the pathway since has not been always strewn with roses. Let the last report present the situation. "Guatemala as a mission field is encompassed with difficulties. Of the inhabitants 300,000 are Ladinos, people of mixed blood, and of the remainder a large majority are of the indigenous races, many of them descendants of the ancient Toltecs, and constitute the coolies and beasts of burden of the country. The condition of the people, socially, morally, and religiously, is deplorable. The first house of worship was dedicated a year ago and during the past year two churches have been organized, one of Spanish-speaking, and the other of English-speaking, persons. "Two ministers with their wives and a native teacher carry on the work."

Mexico.

Mexico forms the third general division of Spanish America, and constitutes the New Spain of former days. Once this was a viceroyalty of imperial proportions, extending along the Pacific from the Isthmus to Puget Sound. But two-thirds of this vast territory was lost by the separation of Central America, the secession of Texas, and the war with the United States in 1845-7. The present area is about 770,000 square miles. The extreme length is 1,900 miles upon the western side, while the width varies from 1,000 miles at the north, to but 130 at the Isthmus of Tehuantepec. A coast-line of 6,000 miles affords but three or four good harbors. The Tropic of Cancer divides the land into nearly equal parts. But the climate is determined less by distance from the equator, than by certain features of the relief. The surface consists mainly of a plateau, to which the ascent is quite abrupt from the low-lying plains along the coast, and whose general elevation varies from 4,000 to 8,000 feet. Then, from this table-land rise various mountain ranges to 12,000 feet and upwards, at least ten extinct volcanoes exceed 16,000, while some, like Orizaba and Popocatapetl, approach 18,000. Not a river is to be found of any considerable value for navigation. Silver has always been Mexico's prime production. A metaliferous belt of extraordinary richness stretches southeastward from Sonora to Oajaca, a distance of 1,200 miles. The population numbers about 11,500,000, and is composed of Spaniards, 2,200,000; Indians, 4,425,000; and a little less than 5,000,000, a mixture of the two. In large part as a result of three centuries of rigid discipline under Castilians and the Catholic Church, the Indians are peaceable, docile, and fairly industrious. For generations they were esteemed only for their silver-producing capacity, for the benefit of the Spanish crown, by a ruthless system they were parcelled out among the plantations, and the mines, and whether held to service above ground, or below, their condition was tantamount to slavery.

The earliest European settlements in Mexico were made almost a century before the first upon the northern Atlantic coast. And Spanish domination lasted exactly three hundred years, or from the death of Guatemozin in 1521, to the departure of the last viceroy in 1821. The beginnings of the struggle for independence came in 1808, and when that revolution had reached a successful termination, a long and dreary period followed of anarchy and strife, but on the whole, with steady and substantial gains for liberty and national prosperity. In 1857 a liberal constitution was adopted, which after radical revision in 1873-4, is now the organic law. When the republic was established, it also came to pass that the Castilian element of the population began to lose the place of power which it has always held, while the plebeian Indians began to rise to controlling influence in the state. Moreover, by that event the days were numbered of the tyrannical, and demoralizing, sway of the Catholic Church. Until 1857 no other faith had been tolerated. The Jesuits had been supreme, and the Inquisition was an institution honored and revered. One-third of all the real estate of the country was in the hands of the priesthood, and *one-half* of the city of Mexico is said to have consisted of churches, convents, and other ecclesiastical structures ! When by law religious liberty was granted, in fact nothing of the kind existed, and it was not until after Maximilian was dethroned and executed, in 1867, that the great victory was fully achieved. Then all ecclesiastical orders were suppressed, convents were emptied of their occupants, and all superfluous church establishments were appropriated by the state. These wholesale confiscations amounted to upwards of $300,000,000. And now " the liberal party has strangled the church and stripped it of every possession. No priest dares to wear a cassock in public, and in politics the clergy are powerless, while parish schools are prohibited." As far back as 1886, there were in existence 11,000 primary schools, with 600,000 pupils, and it was estimated that not far from 2,500,000 persons were able to read and write.

"The Bible was borne into Mexico by General Scott's army," and there can be little doubt that, by the direct and indirect results of the war with the United States, the day of spiritual redemption for that benighted and priest-ridden country was hastened. Within ten years of the close of that lamentable and iniquitous struggle, a constitution was adopted which made it possible for Protestantism to live and propagate itself within the boundaries of the republic. And the first missionary was a woman, Miss Melinda Rankin, who early in the fifties established a school in Brownsville, on the American side of the Rio Grande, later crossed to Matamoras, and in 1866 began work in Monterey. With money raised by herself, she trained and sent out colporteurs to distribute the Scriptures. For twenty years her efforts continued, and bore abundant fruit. In the meantime the American Bible Society had entered the field with its agents, sending the first one in 1860, and ever since has stood among the chief of evangelizing forces in all that region. Last year 48 colporteurs were actively engaged, the cash contributions, for the Mexican work amounted to almost $20,000, and 23,614 Bibles, or portions, were distributed, and 125,050 during the last ten years. But the full measure of Miss Rankin's influence has not yet been set forth. For it was through her that the attention of Rev. H. A. Riley was directed towards the land of the Aztecs. He had been over a Spanish congregation in New York City, and was sent by the American and Foreign Christian Union to the Mexican capital in 1869. Arriving he found that a most remarkable preparation had already been made. Several priests had months before openly renounced the errors and corruptions of Rome, had made converts to their new convictions, and were ready to adopt the creed and ritual of Episcopacy. Soon these and others were united in the " Church of Jesus." For a trifling consideration a confiscated church was turned over for their uses. But this shocking religious innovation was not wrought without furious opposition from the papal church. The excitement culminated in disturbances so violent that upwards of forty Protestants lost their lives.

The time had now arrived for the American churches, as such, to begin to go up and possess the land for Christ. And two decades almost cover the entire period of organized missionary effort. The Friends crossed the Rio Grande in 1871, to enter upon the crusade against ignorance, superstition, and priestcraft. In 1872 the Presbyterians and the American Board sent forth their pioneers. In pursuance to the action of the General Assembly, a party of seven proceeded to the capital, and found a large body of believers awaiting their arrival. Nor was it long before solid foundations had been laid. The next year Zacatecas was occupied, and from these two centers enlargement has gone steadily on, until missions have been opened in twelve out of the twenty-seven states, of which Mexico is composed. Outbreaks, and mobs, and murders, have by no means been wanting, but in spite of all, the churches, and schools, and the mission press, have continued to diffuse the best that

Christianity and civilization can produce. The Presbyterians are now represented by 7 men and 9 women; 25 native ministers, 20 licentiates and 54 other native helpers; by 93 churches, 4,462 members, of whom 374 were received last year; and by 1,769 pupils in the schools. The American Board entered from the west, sending two men from California to break ground in Guadalajara. At first the attempt seemed to meet with quite general favor, though the priests were bitterly hostile. The next year an out-station was opened ninety miles away, at Ahualulco, where presently the leading ecclesiastic stirred up a mob to set upon Mr. Stevens. His doors were broken open, and all the goods were stolen or destroyed, he himself was brutally assassinated, with mutilation, and one of the converts was also killed. A succession of mishaps followed until 1882, when after reorganization a period of growth set in. During the year just named Chihuahua was occupied, and with a beautiful and commodious house of worship just completed, has already become quite a stronghold for the Gospel in northern Mexico.

In 1873 the Methodists, both North and South, began to lay foundations, the former beginning in the metropolis, and later branching out into such cities as Guanajuato, Puebla, Tlascala, Oaxaca, etc., in eight states; while the latter have invaded no less than seventeen states, including several important centers of population. These two denominations report respectively 2,853, and 5,154 members, probationers included. The Baptist Home Missionary Society was already engaged in the same region and in 1884 both the Southern Baptist Convention and the Associate Reformed Presbyterians took up their share of the burdens. And finally, in 1888, the Cumberland Presbyterians sent in a force of missionaries. Including the American Bible Society, twelve organizations are now united in shedding light in the midst of the great darkness. In the City of Mexico alone, with its 350,000 inhabitants, are found 8 missions, 18 congregations, 16 native ministers, 13 day-schools, and 3 boarding schools for girls. The Methodists are in possession of a building which was once put to the accursed uses of a dungeon and torture-room for the Inquisition. In 1893 there were engaged in behalf of the 11,500,000 Mexicans, 187 foreign and 546 native workers, distributed among 87 centers, and 469 congregations. In the churches are now nearly 17,000 communicants, and with them are associated enough to make at least 50,000 adherents. There are 7 theological schools with 88 students, 23 boarding, and 164 common schools, with over 7,000 pupils. Eleven Christian papers are published, and the total of missionary property approaches to $850,000 in value. These results, representing the toil of only twenty years, cannot but be regarded as remarkably large, and full of encouragement, as well as abundantly worth all it has cost to gain them, even though nearly sixty lives have been destroyed by bigotry and fanaticism. The entire republic lies open, inviting the entrance of the messengers of peace, and if the churches were only half in earnest, and would undertake with vigor to complete the occupation of every state in the north, south, east, and west, the full redemption of Mexico would soon come.

CHAPTER XX.

THE AMERICAN INDIANS.

The term as here employed, relates not to the entire 12,000,000 of aborigines dwelling between the Arctic Ocean and Cape Horn, but only that portion to be found within the limits of the United States and the Dominion of Canada, and numbering in all, probably, not much more than 400,000. Of these Alaska contains about 35,000, the various states and territories of the Union 250,000, and the British Possessions 125,000. A former chapter told in outline what was undertaken in their behalf by Eliot, the Mayhews, Brainerd, the Moravians, etc., during the seventeenth and eighteenth centuries, in the Eastern and Middle States, and noted the lamentable fact that after the Revolution, from the co-operation of various causes, work for the evangelization of the red men almost entirely ceased. After the evil passions excited by the frequent Indian wars (1750-1815) had died out, and as Christian zeal and solicitude for the spiritually needy and perishing had been marvelously quickened by the revivals which marked the early decades of this century, once more attention began to be turned towards the heathen at home, located upon the various reservations, or hovering upon the vast frontier.

The Moravians, with Zeisberger as most eminent from first to last, had held faithfully on, in spite of almost unparalleled discouragements and disasters, in Ohio, in Michigan, in Canada, back in Ohio, again to Canada, and finally once more to the Muskingum, though only to fail, and in 1824 to relinquish their lands. The American Board early planned a mission to the Indians in Canada, but the war of 1812-15 brought the project to naught. But by the same society, in 1815-38, Cyrus Kingsbury, S. A. Worcester, and many others were sent to preach the Gospel among the Cherokees of Georgia, the Chickasaws, the Choctaws, and the Osages of the southwest. For years the work prospered. Large congregations were gathered, many turned to the Lord, and large advances were made towards civilization. Mission Ridge became famous in those days, taking its name from the abundant works of mercy and grace performed upon its summit. But, as has so often happened before and since, these aborigines were in the way of white settlers, their lands were coveted, and in utter disregard of their rights and their welfare, after various exasperating encroachments they were finally compelled to emigrate to the far west. Out of 16,000 who made the enforced exodus in one body, more than 4,000 perished from exposure and hunger while on the journey. In the long and bitter struggle which preceded, the missionaries had taken sides with their converts, protesting against their wrongs, and two of them, for righteousness' sake, lay for fifteen months in a Georgia penitentiary. During the same period other tribes were visited with the message of salvation at Mackinaw, Green Bay, etc., and in 1834 a mission was commenced among the Dakotas (Sioux) on the upper Mississippi, not far from where Minneapolis now stands. Later the central stations were located upon the upper Minnesota, with Messrs. Riggs and Williamson as devoted leaders in labor and endurance. After thirty years had passed, and when churches and schools were prosperous, and many substantial results for Christianity and civilization had been gained, of a sudden, and instigated wholly by the pagan Indians, the dreadful "Outbreak," occurred of 1862, attended by wide-spread conflagration and massacre, and ending in the removal of the Dakotas from the state. It is pleasant to recall that not a Christian Indian was implicated in the deeds of violence and blood, while not a few of them gave timely warning to their white friends, and the missionary families were piloted across the vast prairies to places of safety.

But already had the messengers of glad tidings crossed the Continental Divide, and made their proclamation upon the remote Pacific coast. The origin of missions beyond the Rocky Mountains is connected with one of the most pathetic incidents on record in the history of the Kingdom, and well illustrates how, at least sometimes, the heathen mind in its darkness is stirred with deep, though vague longings and feelings after God, if haply it may find Him. When, just as the century was opening, Lewis and Clark, first of civilized men, crossed from the head waters of the Missouri to the mouth of the Columbia, among the rest, they and some members of their party, in telling the natives about the wonders of the East, told them also of the religion of the whites, and in particular, of God's Book of books. Before the expedition returned a request was made that missionaries might be sent, though to this no sort of attention seems to have been paid. It is said that fur traders, who soon after entered this region, gave similar information to the Indians, but that certain among them, taking advantage of the desires excited, sold cards to the simple-minded savages, alleging that these were leaves from the Bible.

Some of the Cayuses were so wrought upon that they began to meet upon the Sabbath to worship the unknown God. Year after year passed, but they waited and longed in vain for the appearance of teachers. And finally the Nez Perces despatched a delegation of four, two aged chiefs, and two braves in their prime, to make the journey of over 3,000 miles to St. Louis, to bear their petition for some one to be sent to point out to them the way of life. Mr. Clark was now Indian commissioner, and the message was communicated to him, but, for reasons not known, received no notice whatever. Weeks went by in perplexity and disappointment, half the number died, and a third one on the return journey, but not a word of encouragement came from any quarter. A little later, however, something of this strange story reached the ears of the Christian public, and the Methodist Church sent Jason Lee and a missionary party to Oregon in 1833, and three years afterwards the American Board commissioned Dr. Whitman and Mr. Spaulding for the same field. These were among the very earliest to make their way through the South Pass, and pushed on to the valley of the Willamette. Dr. W. soon became one of the most important factors in securing to the United States that whole vast region, whose ownership was then in dispute, and bent on this patriotic errand, ventured a trip in mid-winter, on horseback, across the mountains with incredible suffering and the imminent risk of his life, and proceeded to Washington to conjure the authorities not to heedlessly fling away such a priceless national treasure. Quite a body of missionaries were soon engaged among the Cayuses, and Nez Perces. Mills were built, schools were opened, and the story of divine love was told so effectually that thousands of converts were gathered. And then, all without warning, came overwhelming disaster in the massacre of 1847, in which Dr. Whitman, his wife, his assistant, and six others fell victims, while nearly fifty were taken captive. Even yet the cause of this terrible outburst of Indian fury is unknown, but is widely believed in some way to have been connected with the then recent occupation of the country by the United States, and the consequent removal of the agents of the Hudson's Bay Company, who had long been in possession. The mission was broken up for years, and when at length resumed, was presently turned over to other hands, and with excellent results has ever since been maintained. As settlers crowded in, other stations were opened by various organizations, at points here and there, from the British line to Mexico.

The beginning of Methodist missions among the Indians was mentioned in a former chapter, and was made by a Negro in behalf of the savage Wyandots on the upper Sandusky. Through converts there gathered the Gospel was carried in 1820 to the Ojibways of Canada. In after years ten stations were maintained, which were eventually transferred to the Canadian Conference. Not far from the same date, Methodist missionaries made their appearance among the Creeks, Choctaws, and Cherokees, and at the end of about twenty years had gained some 2,000 members, but then followed the troubles and excitements which ended in the expulsion of these tribes, and most serious damage to the work of the Gospel. Though followed to their new homes in the Indian Territory by their religious teachers and pastors, such suspicion and hate had been engendered that for a long time scarcely anything could be done. At the present day this denomination has an Indian Conference with 3,356 members. When the Methodist Church was divided, in 1845, the Southern branch became heir to the work in the southwest, and now reports 89 missionaries in the Indian Territory, 181 native preachers, and 12,759 members. At quite an early date the Baptists undertook the evangelization of the aborigines in New York, and afterwards in Indiana, and Illinois, as well as some of the tribes in the Indian Territory, and report in all 21 white, and 72 native missionaries, and about 6,000 members. The Southern Baptists also occupy the field last named. So far towards being Christian has the Territory become, that out of a population of 69,000, not less than 28,521, or 41 per cent., of the population are communicants in the churches; there are 785 church organizations, while services are sustained in 422 houses of worship and 308 halls.

The Episcopal Church first carried the Gospel to the Oneidas in 1815, ten years later extended the work to Wisconsin, but it was not until 1860 that much was undertaken in a vigorous effectual way. The Dakotas of the upper Minnesota were now visited with the Word of life, and presently Bishop Whipple appears upon the scene, to enter on his long career of most loving and unwearied service. No voice has been lifted oftener or to better purpose than his in pleading the cause of the Indians, and in crying out against the iniquities which have been practised upon them. The agencies at Leech Lake, Red Lake, and White Earth have been in part the theater of his toils. And in later years Bishop Hare, among the Indians of Dakota, has proved himself a most worthy coadjutor. The Presbyterians, separating from the American Board in 1870, took the Oregon missions, and proceeded to open others in the southwest among the tribes of the Indian Territory, New Mexico, Arizona, and California, and also in Dakota. And the American Missionary Association has several stations among the Sioux. These three organizations together have gathered out of this single tribe, the wildest and fiercest of all, upwards of 4,000 communicants, and a number of native pastors have been trained and set over the people.

Our British brethren have not been behind, in labors of love in behalf of the red men inhabiting the northern portion of the continent. And to their efforts this important advantage has providentially been accorded. With a settled Indian policy, and with treatment on the whole rational and righteous, Indian wars have been rare indeed, and so the work of evangelization has seldom suffered serious interruption. The Canadian Presbyterians have gathered about 400 into their churches. The Methodists sustain missionaries in the eastern, central, and western provinces of the Dominion, and to the number of over 100; the annual expenditure is more than $50,000, while the nearly 4,500 church members are organized into eight conferences.

But the greater part of the Indian work, at least if judged by the extent of territory covered, is in the hands of the English Church Society. The region occupied is mainly hyperborean, and largely arctic. The beginning was made in 1826 upon the Red River of the North, not far from Lake Winnepeg, a point then almost at the ends of the earth. Since then steady enlargement has been made, until now six grand divisions are found, extending through eight dioceses. The mere names are enough to make one shiver and shudder. Moosonee lies upon the east, south, and west, of Hudson's Bay. Rupert's Land and Qu'Appelle is in and about Manitoba. Saskatchewan to the north of the last, and Calgary to the west, lie on the flanks of the Rockies. Athabasca lies to the north of Calgary, with Mackenzie River to the north of that and extending to the Polar Sea, while in the extreme northwest, across the Rocky Mountains, is found Selkirk, bordering upon Alaska, and including the upper waters of the Yukon. Mackenzie River is the "largest, most desolate, most sterile, and most frigid of them all." Travel is on foot, by canoe, by sledge, or on snowshoes. Ten months may pass without letters or other communication from the civilized world, while for companions only Eskimos are to be had, or other savages as filthy and groveling. And this statement relating to Moosonee will tell something of what it costs to carry the Gospel to those regions: "In March, Mr. Lofthouse visited York Factory, walking the whole distance, nearly one hundred and seventy miles, in five days. There he spent Easter, about sixty Indians coming for services, several of them traveling eighty or a hundred miles. No one in England can conceive what walking forty-three or forty-four miles for four consecutive days on snowshoes means, and at night sleeping under a tree, with the skies for a covering. My feet were so blistered that for nearly a week I could only hobble around." Surely if anybody, men like Bishop Bompas, and Bishop Horden who from 1854 until his death a few months since, gladly endured exile for Christ's sake on the bleak shores of Hudson's Bay, are entitled to the meed of sainthood. The Church Society reports 56 stations in this boundless field, held by 33 European and 17 native clergymen, and a total missionary force of 177. The communicants number 2,448, and the adherents 14,076. If we add those gathered by the Methodists, and Presbyterians, the Indian communicants in Canada, number 7,348.

But the most unique, and in many respects the most remarkable attempt to evangelize the aborigines of the Dominion belongs to the Northwest Coast, at first in British Columbia, and since removed to Alaska. This also originated with the Church Society, which in 1857 commissioned William Duncan, a layman, and sent him forth via Cape Horn. Stopping at Vancouver he heard nothing but words to discourage and terrify, but kept on, and in due time was set down at Fort Simpson. Several tribes of savages of the Tsimshean family dwelt in the vicinity, and he soon had a taste of their fiendishness in certain orgies performed just outside the walls, lasting several days, attended by all manner of drunken excesses, including several murders, and a cannibal feast upon raw flesh. For months he did not dare to risk his life among those he had come to turn to righteousness, but busied himself learning their language. At length a visit was ventured, and the story of the Gospel was told. Later it was found possible to open a school for children and adults, and later still the warriors united to build a schoolhouse. Such was the genius of the man, so full was his heart of love, so manifold and so unwearied were his efforts to do them good, and that upon the material as well as spiritual side, that within a year he had won admirers, and had made not a few fast friends. And yet on several occasions he narrowly escaped death from the hate of confirmed evil-doers, and especially from the medicine men (shamans), by whom he was regarded as a dangerous rival. After long pondering, Mr. Duncan was convinced that it was necessary to separate from their heathen surroundings all such as were disposed to follow his teaching and counsel, and so undertook to found a colony with strict rules and regulations. Several hundred were found ready to remove some twenty miles down the coast, when, in 1862, all the preparations had been completed to lay the foundations of Metlakahtla, and the number steadily increased, until the village contained upwards of a thousand inhabitants. He himself filled the office of civil magistrate, with power to enforce the law, a council was chosen by popular vote, and a force of constables was maintained. A tax was levied of a blanket for each adult male, and a shirt for each youth. Roads and wharves were constructed, slides for canoes, drains, and houses for the entertainment of strange Indians. Among the institutions were a fire brigade, a brass band, a rifle company, and a two-gun battery. The rude settlers were taught improved methods of fishing and hunting, and in order to aid in exporting what was produced, a schooner was purchased, exchanged later for a steamer, which plied up and down the coast. A soap factory was opened, and a store on the joint-stock plan, with a savings bank attached. Weaving was taught, as well as carpentry, shoe-making, brick-making, blacksmithing, etc. To crown all, a saw-mill was built to run by water-power. When this project was first broached, an aged ex-cannibal exclaimed: "If it is true that the missionary can make water saw wood, I will see it and then die." Then the huts were exchanged for two-story dwellings, clap-boarded, and shingled, and supplied with chimneys, cooking stoves, bedsteads, window-curtains, clocks, and some even with pictures upon the walls. Two schoolhouses were constructed of size sufficient to accommodate seven hundred, and a town hall large enough to hold the entire population. But the church was easily the *chef d'oeuvre* of toil and skill. The material was yellow cedar, a graceful spire, with belfry and bell, were in place. The seating capacity was twelve hundred. Groined arches were overhead, there were stained windows, a carved pulpit, organ and choir, and Brussels carpet in the aisles—in short all the appointments of a well-furnished Christian sanctuary. And as the crowning wonder, from foundation to capstone everything was wrought by native hands! The cost of all these improvements was not far from $100,000, a part of which came from generous friends in England, but the bulk was derived from various business transactions in which Mr. Duncan was leader and helper.

All along the school was maintained, and so the young were trained to intelligence, industry, and good morals. Nor was the religious side of character and life in the least neglected, in the multitude of schemes for the material betterment of the natives. Some Chilcats, who had paid a visit to the village, took home incredible accounts of how they had found there a body of " Indians who had become white, could talk on paper, and hear paper talk, wore white folks' clothes, and lived in houses with windows; had forsaken their medicine men and no longer ate dog's flesh, or killed each other." When the schooner made her trips down the coast, it was nothing unusual for two hundred letters to go, written by Indian hands. And, as the supreme proof of the presence of divine power, when only a year after Metlakahtla was founded, the Bishop of British Columbia visited the mission, after several days spent in examining candidates, fifty-six witnessed such a good confession that they were baptized. The next year fifty-five more were admitted to the church, eighty-four others in 1871, while by 1879 no less than 579 adults, and 410 children, had been baptized, and also 137 couples had been joined in Christian marriage. Other helpers came, and other stations were opened upon the same general basis. After twenty-five years of such exhausting toils, crowned with such striking successes, it is sad to be obliged to record that serious differences of judgment and conviction arose between this devoted schoolmaster-missionary and the great society which had sent him out. For years excitement, and not a little ill-feeling, pervaded the settlement, and at times the entire work seemed to be in the greatest jeopardy. And when at length no place for compromise appeared, by Mr. Duncan and the entire body of Metlakahtlans it was decided to forsake their entire possessions, houses, public buildings, and their contents, and remove across the line into Alaska, which fortunately was not far away. Upon application at Washington, Annette Island was assigned to these exiles, and in the autumn of 1887 the painful exodus was made, and the foundations of New Metlakahtla were laid. The location is described as delightful, and admirably well chosen; the population is nearly as large as it was in the palmiest days; signs of progress appear on every side, and the future is full of hope. Such, in briefest outline, is the story, which in its details reads like a romance, from the first chapter to the last, and proves once more that sober truth may be stranger than baldest fiction. Metlakahtla is a name every way worthy to stand in the same category with Serampore, Tranquebar, Kuruman, or any other illustrious scene of apostolic labors in heathen lands, while the most remarkable results of evangelistic toil there achieved enable us to gain a glimpse of the signs and wonders possible to the Gospel, in the midst of difficulties most appalling, when Divine grace co-operates with human qualities of a high order, when to boundless devotion and heroism are also joined boundless good sense, breadth of view, and genius for invention and leadership. Well might Lord Dufferin, then Governor General of Canada, exclaim that he "could find no words to express his astonishment" at what he saw. And Charles Hallock wrote: "Metlakahtla is truly the full realization of the missionaries' dream of aboriginal restoration." And N. H. R. Dawson, Commissioner of Education: "The story is one of the wonders of the age." And Sheldon Jackson: "There are few chapters in missionary history more full of romance or more wonderful."

As for Alaska and its 35,000 Indians there is not much to say. Only a few years have elapsed since the first Gospel messenger was despatched to make proclamation of Christ to the few tribes dwelling upon the coast, and along the streams. With a large part of this region communication is infrequent and difficult. The Presbyterians began at Fort Wrangel in 1877, and from the tiny seed then planted have grown 7 churches with 580 native communicants, and about 750 children in the schools. The Moravians located a mission upon the Kuskokwim in 1885, and the Episcopalians another upon the Yukon the year following. About the same time entered also the Methodists, the Baptists, the Friends, and also some missionaries sent by the Swedish Mission Union. But in 1889 came a call for beginnings much further to the north, and among the Eskimos dwelling to the north and east of Bering Straits. In response, the American Missionary Association chose Cape Prince of Wales, the Episcopalians Point Hope, 220 miles beyond, and the Presbyterians Point Barrow, 310 miles further still, and the most northern point on the mainland of the continent. The heroes who hold this outpost are 4,000 miles to the north of San Francisco, far beyond the Arctic Circle, and so near the pole that sometimes the summer passes without the ice thawing sufficiently to allow a vessel to penetrate so far. How dreary are the winters, and the natives how filthy, and stupid, and vile. But even here the Gospel is a power unto salvation.

CHAPTER XXI.

THE LAND WHICH REMAINS TO BE POSSESSED.

TAKEN altogether, the pages which precede set forth the stage of advancement now reached by the work undertaken for the world's evangelization, and at the end of the first hundred years from the date of the glorious re-beginning of Christian missions, under the lead of William Carey. And indeed the fact has been abundantly demonstrated, that a marvelous development of the kingdom of heaven has taken place. The ingathering of souls in pagan lands has been great. Millions have turned from the worship of idols to the service of the living God, probably as large a number as were reached by the Gospel during the first three centuries after the advent of the Redeemer of men. And the territorial expansion, the portion of the earth's surface visited for the first time with the message of salvation, witnessed since 1793, vastly exceeds all that occurred from that date back to Pentecost. Besides, far more barriers have been removed, more doors of entrance have been opened. Every continent and island around the whole globe has been discovered, and visited, and explored, and made accessible; and by the railroad, the steamship, the telegraph, and excellent postal facilities has been brought near. In addition, the ruling powers of to-day, those possessed of fleets, and armies, and commercial enterprise, are almost wholly Christian, and by them in many ways the intolerant heathen and Mohammedan governments are restrained from evil, and impelled to rational and righteous doing. More than a third of the followers of the prophet of Arabia are subject to Great Britain alone. In well-nigh every region the lives and property of missionaries are secure. Societies by the hundred have sent forth by the thousand consecrated men and women, while by the million the money to sustain them is regularly bestowed. And finally evangelizing methods have been perfected under the tuition of large experience, potent instrumentalities have been fashioned in great variety, and all needed appliances have been set to work. Christendom, if not yet fully awake to the magnitude and importance of the task, is at least steadily arousing to solicitude and zeal. The passing century of wonders has beheld no phenomenon more astounding than that connected with the diffusion of the truth as it is in Jesus since the notable day when the poverty-stricken cobbler-preacher-school-master, with consuming fervor exhorted his fellow-Baptists to "Expect great things from God," and, to "Attempt great things for God." How changed in every particular, how enlarged and strengthened beyond conception, are Christian missions, both as to their condition and the outlook for the future. When Carey set forth for India, the heart of Christendom was dead as touching conviction and desire. And only this was Protestantism doing for the redemption of a perishing world; in and about Tranquebar was a decaying Danish mission, and the Moravians were maintaining a few stations among the most benighted of the human family.

So regarded, viewed with only such facts in mind, the last century constitutes an illustrious period in Christian history. But this is by no means a complete statement of the essential facts in the case. There is another aspect of a different sort, one far less flattering, and far more serious. It is that which relates to what has *not* been accomplished, the things that remain to be done. The case for this generation is much like the one to which Joshua called the attention of the chosen people when near the close of his life. By the divine hand they had been brought safely through the desert of wandering, the Jordan had been opened that they might pass over dry-shod, great victories had been won at Jericho, and Ai, and Beth-horon, and when loyal and obedient to Jehovah, no force however great had been able to stand before them. But after all, the Canaanites were not expelled. Many choice tracts were still in alien hands. And the situation was summed up in these solemn words, with specifications following: And there remaineth yet very much land to be possessed. And this is the supreme fact for the consideration of the disciples of Christ at the present time, and for long years to come. With profoundest and abiding gratitude for past achievements, thanking God and taking courage, we are to address ourselves with might and main to the completion of the tremendous task yet on hand. At no point, and in no particular, is the undertaking finished. At the best, only a fair beginning has been made. The momentous campaign has simply opened. A world-wide reconnoissance has been made to gain a needful knowledge of the field, a few scattering skirmishes have been fought to feel the strength of the enemy, and to find where he is drawn up in force, and some comparatively trifling successes have been won. The main battle, which shall mark the turning point, the beginning of the end, belongs in the unseen future. With this thought in mind, or with this conception of missions, let us give a closing glance at the entire field.

With India a beginning can most fittingly be made, India the chiefest bulwark of the kingdom of Satan. Amazing revolutions have been wrought since Carey landed, an "interloper," in Calcutta. In every realm is felt the beneficent influence of British dominion. Law and order exist everywhere, and for all. Railways, highways, and other public works have been constructed, sanitary measures, and popular education, are carefully provided for. Religious worship and teaching are free, the missionary can go, and abide, and ply his calling where he will, while all fanaticism is kept within the proper bounds. No other field has been occupied by so many societies, with so large a force, and in no other country have so many converts been made. The mass movements are significant, and prophetic of sweeping ingatherings in days to come. Every now and then entire villages, and groups of villages, are found ready to destroy their idols, to receive teachers, and asking for baptism. But over against all this; ah, the myriads to be evangelized! One-fifth of the earth's inhabitants are crowded into the triangular space lying between the Himalayas and Cape Comorin. Of these 175,000,000 are Hindus, more than 50,000,000 are Mohammedans, and about 50,000,000 are degraded devil-worshippers. And the entire number of "Christians" (non-heathen, non-idolatrous), Roman Catholics, etc., included, is but 2,275,000. Only about 250,000 found in Protestant churches. Only some 800,000 are reckoned as connected with Protestant missions. More than 250,000,000 are unable to either read or write. Everywhere are appalling ignorance and superstition. Upon all rests the curse of caste, that most cunning and effective of all devices for ensnaring souls, for making damaging divisions between man and man, ministering to pride and self-righteousness, as well as to indifference and contempt for one's fellow men. Partly on account of climatic conditions, there is an almost universal lack of ambition, and of love of independence, lack of nerve, and energy, and push, and a disposition to be content with things as they exist, no matter how full of evil. With this, and the religious and social systems long fixed and hoary with age, who can measure, or imagine, the mass of *vis inertiæ* concentrated in this vast peninsula. It is evident that redemption has not yet come to India, and that there remaineth yet very much land to be possessed.

Colossal China takes rank among the foremost of political, social, and religious organizations, hostile to Christianity, and able long to resist any onset likely to be made. Something like a quarter of the human family dwell within the boundaries of this oldest of nations. Deepest poverty, and ignorance most dense, are the common lot. The civilization is highly developed, and its existence is measured by millenniums. This people make boast of one of the wisest of ancient sages, and can imagine nothing loftier than his moral teachings. Three religions have long coexisted, and are strangely blended in the hearts and lives of multitudes. The national conceit of wisdom, and of all manner of superlative excellencies, is preposterous almost to the sublime, with prejudice and contempt for all foreigners to match. The Chinese mind is exceedingly cautious, conservative, slow-moving, and averse to change. In place of caste, as the supreme hindrance to the Gospel, ancestral worship is found, and coupled with it full faith in the ever-present and potent operations of geomancy (fung-shui). For two hundred years all foreigners were rigidly excluded. Until 1840 no footing was gained for the Gospel upon Celestial soil. Not until 1860 was it possible to penetrate to the interior, and not yet by any means has gravest peril to life from infuriated mobs passed away. After about a generation of comparative freedom for evangelizing effort, something substantial and enouraging in the shape of results can be named. A few limited sections have been fairly well supplied with opportunities for hearing the word of life. At least to some slight extent, most of the Eighteen Provinces, as well as Mongolia and Manchuria, have been visited by the heralds of salvation, though Thibet with its 700,000 square miles and 7,000,000 inhabitants, still keeps its gates shut and barred. But, beset as it is upon both the south and east, by several earnest and determined companies, who are praying and watching and waiting for admission, and meantime studying the language, and translating the Scriptures, so preparing weapons for the holy campaign, it is scarcely possible that more than a few years will pass before at least the outworks of this, almost the last of the strongholds of heathenism, will yield to the assault. In China proper just enough has been achieved to prove that great results are within reach, and are not far off, if only Christian efforts are put forth at all commensurate with the magnitude of the task. Mainly within twenty years, about 45,000 have been received into church membership, and many of these have shown themselves to be disciples of the steadfast and stalwart sort. Yes, but what are 45,000 among 350,-000,000? A drop in the bucket, a fragment infinitesimal. Of China also it must be written: There remaineth yet very much land to be possessed.

Until within a decade Korea continued to be a hermit nation, determined to hold no manner of communication with the great world, to think only her own thoughts, to live altogether for herself. Persuaded since to forsake this absurd and suicidal policy to some extent, on the political and commercial side, so that foreigners are tolerated in the treaty ports, the work of missionaries is still contrary to law, is limited and hindered at almost every point, and on the nation as a whole scarcely any impression has been made. The people appear to be well-disposed, and medical missions are full of bright promise. But, Korea has been entered, and that is all. Only a few initiatory steps have been taken towards imparting to her 10,000,000, or 12,000,000 the way of life through a crucified Saviour.

As for Japan, it is the marvel of missionary history. Nowhere else in the annals of the race have changes political, social, intellectual, and religious ever occurred so numerous and sweeping, upon a scale so vast, in so brief a space of time. And all these have wrought together to break down barriers, to throw up a highway for the entrance of the Gospel. Much of what is best and most characteristic of Christian America and Europe, has been transplanted to Japanese soil. Changes, which commonly have cost the toil and suffering of centuries, have been effected within a single generation. Already since 1873, within twenty brief years, 40,000 have been gathered into the Protestant churches, mainly, too, from the brainy, forceful, middle classes, and enough more into the Catholic and the Greek churches to raise the number nearly to 100,000.

And they differ from almost all other converts made in mission fields in being eager for independence, determined to think, conclude, and act for themselves, ready to sustain the institutions of the Gospel where these are already planted, and also ready to carry the Gospel into the "regions beyond." Just now, however, a serious reaction is in progress. Much of the old spirit is returning, including jealousy of foreigners, and dislike of western ideas, and ways. There is danger that liberty will lapse into license. The government is still a despotism. The old pagan faiths are by no means dead, and their priests are rallying in their defence. But the prime fact is this: What are 40,000 by the side of 40,000,000 of the unevangelized? We may call one in a thousand Christian indeed. Perhaps five in a thousand have barely heard of what occurred in Bethlehem and on Calvary. And hence in the Sunrise Kingdom, too, there remaineth yet very much land to be possessed.

In our rapid review, crossing this hugest of continents, we glance next at the realms of Islam. According to the best estimates the prophet of Arabia has not less than 200,000,000 followers. Of these upwards of 50,000,000 are found in India, as many more in northern and central Africa, 30,000,000 in China, 15,000,000 in the Malay Peninsula and the Malay Archipelago, 28,000,000 in the Turkish Empire Arabia included, and 9,000,000 in Persia. This one-seventh of the earth's population represents one of the most arduous and disheartening tasks connected with the universal diffusion of the Gospel. And towards its accomplishment hitherto no progress whatever has been made. At least with these two exceptions. A few scores, or hundreds, of converts have been gained from this obdurate class in northern India, and a few thousands in the Dutch East Indies, while the Bible has been translated and quite widely circulated in Arabic, the sacred language of the entire Moslem world, and because in it the Koran was written. In European Turkey, and Asia Minor, and eastward to the Euphrates, for sixty years a noble company of consecrated men and women have been toiling along evangelistic, educational, and literary lines, and have wrought a most surprising revolution. In Syria, to the north and south of Beirut, and upon the flanks of Lebanon, a similar work has been done, and with results equally excellent. In Palestine a number of societies of various sorts have long been occupied. Considerable progress has been made in the northwestern portion of Persia, while in the central portions the foundations have been laid. On the outskirts of Arabia, to the east, and the south, and the west, Christendom is actually represented by seven Europeans and Americans, and four natives. Only so many to care for 1,000,000 square miles, and 10,000,000 souls. But though at work in Mohammedan realms, alas none of these, or next to none, are devoting themselves to the redemption of Mohammedans. The nearly 40,000,000 are passed by. The calls of mercy are not addressed to their ears. Everywhere is found Moslem hate and contempt for all other religions, with perfect satisfaction concerning their own spiritual case. In Arabia the people are said to be fairly approachable, and the Shah of Persia is counted a liberal-minded ruler, allowing some measures of freedom, even in religion. The death penalty for apostasy is abolished in Turkey, but notwithstanding, whoso forsakes Mohammed for Christ takes his life in his hand, and is far more likely to die than to live. In Afghanistan Christian missions are not allowed. So that practically, there are no missions to Mohammedans, and from Thibet, in Central Asia, to the Mediterranean and the Balkans, the beginnings of the Gospel among the dominant races are still to be made. What believing and ardent soul does not cry, O Lord, how long? And who can deny that, as touching this more than one-eight of the family of man, there remaineth yet very much land to be possessed.

Continuing our survey, and entering Africa, we light upon a dark continent indeed. There is no occasion to forget the marvels of exploration and occupation, which have come to pass since Livingstone died in 1873. These are sufficiently suggested by the notable achievements of Stanley, the creation of the Congo Free State, the opening of missions by the score in the Congo Basin, and about the great African lakes, and the setting up of "protectorates," and "spheres of influence" by the leading governments of Europe. And even the terrible slave trade is about to die the death. But nevertheless, what has Christendom done towards banishing the grossest heathenism and savagery from those 5,000 miles by 5,000, or those more than 160,000,000 souls? The first missionaries in modern times to enter this boundless realm of degradation and sin landed at the Cape more than one hundred and fifty years ago, and the London Society sent Vanderkemp thither in 1799. And to-day the American United Presbyterians hold a line of flourishing stations in the Nile Valley, extending from Alexandria far south to the Cataracts, but almost wholly for the benefit of the Copts (Christian in name already). The North Africa Society sustains a body of men and women in the four other states bordering upon the Mediterranean. Dotting the West Coast, from Sierra Leone to the mouth of the Niger, and on the banks of that river, several scores of heroic toilers are wearing out their lives for the love of the Lord Jesus and of perishing souls. Within only fifteen years another long line of stations has been established on the lower and upper waters of the Congo. Yet further down the coast the American Board has occupied three centers back from Benguela, and on the table-lands, while back of these Mr. Arnot holds other strategic points along the road to Garenganze. South Africa is a field fairly well tilled. So extensive and mature is the work of the Gospel, and so large is the immigration of Europeans, that the region may not improperly be termed evangelized, if not also Christianized. The Wesleyans alone have upwards of 32,000 converted natives organized into a conference. Upon the east coast, lying between Zululand and the mouth of the Zambesi, other companies of preachers and teachers are witnessing for the Master, and ministering to the needy in His name. The Paris Society through its representatives has penetrated to the Barotse, inhabiting the region of the upper Zambesi. In like manner groups of missionaries are to be found building for the kingdom to the north and south of Zanzibar, and about the shores of Nyassa, Tanganyika, and Victoria Nyanza. Uganda is already famous among missions. But everywhere in East Central Africa the work is still in the period of feeble infancy. Advancing towards our starting point, and passing through Abyssinia, and along the Red Sea, not a herald of glad tidings can we discover. The great Soudan remains, so vast and so densely peopled, stretching nearly across the continent, and containing about one-third of its population, largely Mohammedanized but without an evangelist or a follower of Jesus. Two or three Soudan missions have recently been organized, two or three companies are pushing in that direction, from the West Coast and northward from the upper Congo, and that is all. As for Africa as a whole this is the situation. The northern and central portions, including much more than half of the area, and approaching to half of the inhabitants Moslem, and the remainder in a pagan estate most woful, and horrible in the extreme. Scarcely one in a thousand has tasted of saving grace, scarcely one in a hundred has ever heard the saving Name pronounced. Then there can be no doubt, that between Cape Blanco and the Cape of Good Hope very much land remaineth to be possessed.

Nor shall we find the Islands of the Sea in a much better case. In this portion of the world-field some of the most remarkable of the conquests of the cross have been made. Entire peoples have been lifted up from the lowest depths of barbarism and beastliness to decency and an orderly life, to a fair degree of intelligence, to character and life truly Christian, so that by the ten thousand they have honored their profession of godliness. Let these names stand for the incredible story. The Society and Hawaiian Islands. Fiji inhabited by devils incarnate, creatures given to cannibalism, and all nameless vices. New Zealand as bad, and the New Hebrides as terrible as any. But now so marvellously transformed as to send of their own number to tell to other brutal islanders of the divine love which brought salvation to their own souls. Glory to God for what the Gospel has wrought. But yet, the bulk of these are only children in spiritual estate, and perhaps for generations to come must needs be nurtured and instructed. Ceylon is well advanced on the road to evangelization. The Dutch East Indies have received the truth from various Netherlands' and German societies, to such a degree that a large district of Celebes is no longer heathen or Moslem; in various other regions are found missions which enjoy such measures of prosperity that the converts are counted by tens and scores of thousands. The head-taking Dyaks of Borneo have learned to esteem human life sacred. But for all this, it is true that in the entire Archipelago (Malaysia) there are only 300,000 nominal Christians, and in Java which holds 24,000,000 of the 31,000,000, not much of anything has been accomplished. Madagascar ranks next to Japan, perhaps, among missions for the wonderful workings of the Spirit of God. Scarcely another organization has been able to record successes to match those vouchsafed to the London Society among the Malagasy. Upon no other body of new converts ever befell so relentless and protracted a persecution as tried the souls of these. And when the dreadful stress was over, seldom if ever was seen such a wholesale turning to the Lord. In the churches of the three missions 70,000 members are found, while the adherents number 350,000 with 35,000 Catholics in addition. For the other side, we are bound to take note that the Christians are confined almost wholly to a single tribe, the Hovas, and that of the entire population nearly five-sixths remain in their original darkness. Therefore, not only in Asia, and Africa, but in the Islands of the Sea as well, there remaineth yet very much land to be possessed.

Turning next to countries nominally Christian, but

under the rule of the Papacy, what do we find? And first in the Spanish American states, which extend from southern California to the Straits of Magellan. The population approximates to 50,000,000, and is composed of Spanish, Portuguese, and Indians, and the blood of these joined in every degree of mixture. Many of the aborigines are still in rank paganism, and over all the residue the Roman Church has borne absolute sway for centuries. The common grade of morals and religion is low indeed, even for Catholic countries. In most of the states religious freedom is accorded by law, with Catholicism established as the ruling faith. In two or three of the republics Protestants are forbidden to teach or worship publicly, while in Equador, with intolerance worse than that of China, Korea, or Turkey, and equalled only by Thibet, to be a Protestant and to make it known, is to be a malefactor worthy of fines and imprisonment, or of expulsion. From Mexico to Patagonia, some 50,000 Protestant church members are found, with twice or thrice as many adherents, or in proportion to the population, one in 500 of the latter, and one in 1,500 of the former. In Spanish America, too, there remaineth yet very much land to be possessed.

A closing word concerning Papal Europe, including France, Spain, Portugal, Italy, Austria, Belgium, a large part of Germany, etc. No apology is required for zealous attempts to evangelize and educate the masses so ignorant and priest-ridden. For these 150,000,000 not much has been even undertaken, though Italy since 1870 has received considerable attention. The churches are not toiling, but only playing at missions in behalf of Catholics. Or, grouping with the Papacy the Greek Church, which at so many points bears to it so great a resemblance, is in despotic control from St. Petersburg and the Adriatic, across two continents, to Bering Sea, and is shaping the destinies of some 75,000,000, the situation is even worse. For the Czar far outdoes the Sultan in determination to allow no dissent from the orthodox faith. The bulk of Europe, and the whole of northern Asia, are yet to be leavened by a pure Gospel. Again the divine word to Joshua applies: There remaineth yet very much land to be possessed.

To state in a single paragraph the conclusion of the whole momentous matter: One hundred years after Carey made his sublime venture, Christendom is represented in Heathendom by about 11,450 Europeans and Americans of both sexes. Of these about 4,300 are ordained, something less than 1,000 are unordained, 3,650 are wives, and 2,575 are unmarried women. With them are associated 4,200 ordained and 43,000 unordained natives toiling as pastors, evangelists, teachers, etc. The entire missionary force numbers not far from 55,000. These messengers of the churches are sustained at an annual cost of more than $15,000,000. As a part of the ingathering, the mission churches contain not far from 1,000,000 members, and the mission schools as many pupils, while the adherents may reasonably be reckoned at a figure three or even four times as large. So many have turned their backs on idolatry, and have turned their faces towards the kingdom of God and its righteousness. And all things considered, a most wonderful achievement to be made in a single century. To God be all the glory, and to his faithful children a tenfold increase of courage, ardor, and holy zeal, of prayer, giving and consecrated toil. For over against those totals standing for what has been accomplished, must be set these overwhelming figures: 800,000,000 heathen, 200,000,000 Mohammedans, and 225,000,000 adherents of the Greek Church and the Church of Rome. To make the statement complete it would be necessary to add the many in Protestant churches who have but a name to live in Christ, and the multitude outside of the indifferent, the skeptical, the godless and the abandoned.

All that innumerable company of the unevangelized are included in the Great Commission, in the last command of the risen Lord. Nothing less than putting forth the utmost of effort to compass this stupendous achievement will fill the measure of obligation, of privilege. A task so solemn, so sublime in the wise and loving providence of God is laid upon the shoulders of Protestant Christendom. This is its mission, its heavenly calling. Who is sufficient for these things? It is the little David going out against the giant; a handful making assault upon a host. The force is ridiculously impotent if standing alone, but is abundantly able, wholly adequate with the Great Captain to devise and lead, to inspire and supplement. What more is needed to beget the full assurance of faith: Go ye into all the world; Lo I am with you all the days; Every knee shall bow, and every tongue shall confess that Jesus Christ is Lord; The kingdoms of this world are become the kingdoms of our Lord, and He shall reign forever and forever

THE END.

INDEX.

ABYSSINIA, Conversion of, 19; Krapf a missionary to, 227, 233.

AFRICA, Missions in, chapter on, 187–238; physical features of, 187; population, 190; races, 191; religions, 192; slavery in, 193, 213; rum, 193; discovery and exploration of, 194–9; partition of, 199; steamers, railroads, etc. in, 200; early Christianity in, 202; summary of results, 236.

AFRICA, East Central, 226; Church Missionary Society in, 227, 229; United Methodist Free Churches, 227; Universities' Mission, 228; Scottish Established Church and Free Church, 230; Berlin, London and Paris Societies, and Moravians, 231.

AFRICA, North, 232; first missions in, 233; United Presbyterian Church, 234; North Africa Society, 235.

AFRICA, South, 204; first mission to, 205; London Society, 207; English Wesleyans, 208; Paris Society, 209; German societies, 210; American Board, 210; Scottish missions, 211; summary of results, 213.

AFRICA, West, 213; mission to, proposed, 99; Moravians in, 214; Church Missionary Society, 214; Wesleyan, 216; American Baptist and Presbyterian, 217; Basle Society and American Methodist, 218; United Brethren, Episcopalian and United Presbyterian of Scotland, 219; North German, and American Lutheran (General Synod), 220; Southern Baptist Convention, 221.

AFRICA, West Central, 222; English and American Baptists in, 224-5; Swedish Societies, 225; Congo Balolo Mission and Arnot's, 225.

ALASKA, Missions in, 401.

AMERICA, Central, section on, 380–2.

AMERICA, Discovery of, effect of upon missions, 32, 34.

AMERICAN BOARD, Causes which led to the founding of, 100–107; sends missionaries to India, 110, to Ceylon and the Cherokees,

116, 390; Sandwich Islands and Palestine, 117; South Africa, 210; Sumatra, 272; Borneo, 273; the Armenians, 286, 289; Nestorians, 287, 299; European Turkey, 302; China, 320; Japan, 357; Mexico, 386.

ANGLO-SAXONS, Conversion of, 21; significance of, 34, 68; the missionary race, 130.

ANSGAR, Missionary to Scandinavia, 24.

ARABIC BIBLE, Value of, 297.

ARMENIA, Conversion of, 19.

ARGENTINE REPUBLIC, The, Missions in, 377.

Ars Magna, Raymond Lully's, 30.

BAPTIST, American, Missionary Union, founded, 101, 112, 120; change of name, 122; adopts Judson and Rice, 122; mission of, in Burmah, 170; among the Telugus, 176; in West Africa, 217; Congo Free State, 224.

BAPTIST MISSIONARY SOCIETY, English, organized, 76; enters India, 79, 163; West Africa, 214; Congo Basin, 224; West Indies, 279.

BAPTISTS, Free, organize for missionary work, 125, enter India, 179.

BAPTIST SOUTHERN CONVENTION, organizes for missionary work, 125; in Brazil, 376; Indians, 394.

BASLE MISSIONARY SOCIETY, organized, 96; enters India, 178; West Africa, 218.

BEIRUT becomes a mission station, 285, 295; importance of, as, 297.

BERLIN MISSIONARY SOCIETY, organized, 96; enters Burmah, 172; South Africa, 210; East Africa, 231.

BIBLE SOCIETY, American, organized, 104; number of copies of the Scriptures printed by, 137; value of work of in Spanish America, 378, 379, 380, 388.

BIBLE SOCIETY, British and Foreign, organized, 96; number of versions printed by, 137; of copies, 137.

BOERS, The Dutch, 205, 207.

BOGUE, Dr. David, part of in organizing the **London Missionary** Society, 83-5.

BOLIVIA, Missions in, 378.

BOMBAY, founded, 59, 151; first mission in, **114.**

BONIFACE, The apostle of Germany, 23.

BOYLE, Robert, gift of for missions, 61.
BRAINERD, David, 66, 67, 99, 137.
BRAZIL, Missions in, 54, 375.
BUCHANAN, Claudius, "Star in the East by," effect of, 103, 106, 158, 168.
BURMAH, Missions in, 112, 121, 123.

CALVIN, sends missionaries to Brazil, 54, 375.
CANADA, Jesuit missions in, 37; Protestant missions to the Indians of, 395–401.
CANNIBALISM, in Figi, 258; New Zealand, 263; the New Hebrides, 266.
CAREY, William, Early career of, 71; missionary treatise of, 74, 76, 81; sermon of, 75; sails for India, 78; impulse given to missions in the United States by, 100, 121; work in India, 163.
CAREY EPOCH, The, in missions, why properly so called, 70.
CASTE, in India, the evils of, 149.
CEYLON, Dutch missions in, 57–8; Newell arrives in, 115; reinforcements sent to, 116; English Church enters, 168; Dr. Coke sails for, 173.
CHILI, Missions in, 378.
CHINA, Chapter on missions in, 307–32; physical features of, 307; people, 307; languages, 308; religions, 309; Nestorian missions in, 26, 309, 310; Roman Catholic missions, 38, 310; why closed against foreigners, 311; Morrison the first missionary to, 312; Milne, 315; early methods of work, 316–20; opium war, 321; later wars, 324; enlargement of missions, 323–327; medical mission in, 318, 330; summary of results, 331.
CHINA INLAND MISSION, The work of, 328.
CHURCH MISSIONARY SOCIETY, Organization of, 95; enters India, 167; Ceylon, 168; West Africa, 214; East Africa, 227, 229; North Africa, 233; New Zealand, 263; West Indies, 278; Persia, 302; Canada, 395; British Columbia, 397.
CHURCH AND STATE, Union of, evil effects of, 20, 45, 54.
CLOUGH, Rev. J. E., Work of among the Telugus, 176.
CLOVIS, Conversion of, 22.
COKE, Dr., founds a mission in Antigua, 82, 278; sails for Ceylon and dies, 173.

COLIGNY, Admiral, founds a mission in Brazil, 54, 375.
COLOMBIA, Missions in, 379.
COLUMBA, founds a monastery in Iona, 22.
COLUMBAN, The apostle of Gaul, 23.
COOK, Captain, voyages of, effect of upon missions, 49, 72, 249, 260.
CORNWALL, Conn., Mission school in, 104, 117.
CROWTHER, Bishop Samuel, 215.
CRUSADES, Value of as a missionary agency, 28.
CYRIL AND METHODIUS, apostles of the Slavs, 24.

DANISH MISSIONS, 47, 58; at Tranquebar, 63, 156, 179; in Greenland, 64.
DARWIN, Charles, testimony of to missions, 259, 375.
DEMOCRACY, Value of to missions, 46.
DISCOVERY OF AMERICA, Effect of, upon missions, 32, 34.
Duff, The, sails for the South Seas, 88; captured by the French, 94.
DUFF, Alexander, 73.
DUFFERIN, The Countess of, organization of medical work by, 181.
DUNCAN, William, Work of at Metlakahtla, 138, 397–401.
DUTCH, Missions of, in the East Indies, 56–8, 274, 275; West Indies, 58.
DYAKS, Head-taking, of Borneo, 273.

EAST INDIA CO., Charter of given, 59; opposition of to missions, 112–115, 134, 158; dissolved, 161.
EAST INDIES, Missions in, 270–5.
ECUADOR, Missions in, 380.
EDINBURGH MISSIONARY SOCIETY organized, 86; sends two men to the Foulahs, 89.
EDUCATION AND MISSIONS, 138.
EDWARDS, Jonathan, pamphlet of on missions, 73; missionary work, and life of Brainerd, 99.
EGEDE, Hans, missionary to Greenland, 64.
EGYPT, Modern missions in, 234.
EIGHTEENTH CENTURY, The, missions of; Danish-Halle, 63; to American Indians, 63; Moravian, 65.

INDEX. 423

ELIOT, John, first missionary to the Indians, **61, 99.**
ENGLAND, Conversion of, 21.
ERASMUS, Missionary treatise of, 53.
EUROPE, Missionary beginnings in, 15; Western, 15, 21; Central, 23; Northern, 24; Eastern, 24.
EXPANSION, Missionary, the phenomenon of, chapter on, 126–41; described, 127–8; causes which co-operated to produce, 130.

FIJI, Evangelization of, 257.
FISK and Parsons, the first missionaries to Palestine, 118, 285.
FRANCKE, Connection of with missions in the Eighteenth century, 63.
FREE CHURCH, of Scotland, enters India, 173; South Africa, 211; East Africa, 230; Jewish mission in Turkey, 288.
FREDERICK IV. OF DENMARK, Mission founded by, in Tranquebar, 63; in Greenland, 64.
FRIENDLY ISLANDS, Evangelization of, 256.
FRUMENTIUS, Apostle of Abyssinia, 19.
FULLER, Andrew, visits Carey, 73; counsels American Baptists, 122.

GARDINER, Capt. Allen, career of, 372, *et seq.*
GEDDIE, Rev. John, missionary in the New Hebrides, 267.
GENESIS OF MISSIONS IN AMERICA, Chapter on, 97–125.
GLASGOW MISSIONARY SOCIETY, organized, 86; sends two men to the Foulahs, 89.
GOODELL, Rev. Wm., opens a mission in Constantinople, 286, 289.
GORDON, Rev. G. N., killed in the New Hebrides, 269.
GORDON, Rev. J. S., killed in the New Hebrides, 269.
GOSSNER'S MISSIONARY SOCIETY, Work of among the Kols, 169, 178.
GOTHS, The Conversion of, 19.
GUTZLAFF, Work of in China, 317, 318, 319.

HALDANE, Robert, Mission to Bengal planned by, 86.
HALL, Gordon, Evangelizing zeal of, 106; sails for India, 110; reaches Bombay, 114.
HAMLIN, Rev. Cyrus, enters the Turkish Mission, 289; founds Robert College, 294.

424 INDEX.

HASSELTINE, Ann (Mrs. Judson), Heroism of, 171.
HAWAIIAN ISLANDS, Evangelization of, 117, 260.
HAWEIS, Dr., Zeal of for missions, 84, 91, 102.
HERVEY ISLANDS, Evangelization of, 253.
HOPKINS, Rev. Samuel, proposes a mission to Africa, 99
HORNE, Melville, Letters on missions by, 103.

INDIA, Physical features of, 143; population, 144; religious practices, 147; caste, 149; history, 150; British rule, 152-4, 180, 185; public works, 154; native states, 154; beginnings of the Gospel, 19; advent of Carey, 157, 163; effect of the Mutiny, 160-1; missions of the Church Society, 167; American Board, 110, 169; American Baptists, 170, 176; Wesleyans, 173; Church of Scotland, 173; Presbyterians, 175; woman's work, 180; medical missions, 180; summary of results, 163, 182.
INDIANS, American, Chapter on, 389-402; early missions to, Eliot and the Mayhews, 61; Edwards and Brainerd, 67; Zeisberger, 67, 82; the American Board, 116.
INDUSTRIAL MISSIONS, Value of, 138.
INGLIS, Rev. John, missionary in the New Hebrides, 267.
IRELAND, Conversion of, 22.
ISLANDS OF THE SEA, Chapter on, 247-280.

JAPAN, Chapter on, 239-264; physical features of, 339; people, 340; religions, 341; history, 342; Roman Catholic missions in, 343; closed against foreigners, 346; Commodore Perry's expedition to, 347; first Protestant missionaries in, 350; political revolution, 351; open to the Gospel, 356; summary of results, 361.
JAVA, Mission work in, 271.
JESUIT MISSIONS, in Canada, 37; in India, 38; in Paraguay, 368.
JEWETT, Dr., missionary to the Telugus, 176.
JUDSON, Adoniram, at Andover, 106; sent to London, 108; sails for India, 110; is immersed, 112; enters Burmah, 123, 170.

KATHIAWAR, first of native states to be entered by missionaries, 160.
KIERNANDER, missionary in Calcutta, 82, 157, 158.

INDEX.   425

KING, Rev. Jonas, a missionary in Greece, 288.

KOREA, the country and people, 232–3; Roman Catholic missions in, 333; Protestant missions, 335.

KRAPF, John Ludwig, missionary in East Africa, 197, 198, 222, 227, 228.

LEIPSIC MISSIONARY SOCIETY, in India, 179.

LIVINGSTONE, David, 196, 208, 228, 230.

LONDON MISSIONARY SOCIETY, The organization of, 83–5; opens missions in the South Seas, 87; in South Africa, 92, 207; India, 167; East Africa, 231; Madagascar, 241.

LOVEDALE, 138, 211.

LUTHERAN MISSIONS, Early, in Tranquebar, 63; in Greenland, 64.

LUTHERAN CHURCH (General Synod), Missions of, in India, 125, 179; West Africa, 220.

LUTKENS, Chaplain to Frederick IV., connection of with Tranquebar Mission.

MADAGASCAR, Physical features of, 238; population, 239; beginning of missions in, 241; persecution, 243; great ingathering, 245.

MADRAS, Missions in, 168, 169, 170, 173, 186.

MALABAR COAST, St. Thomas Christians of, 19, 156.

MANCHURIA, Missions in, 328.

MARSDEN, Rev. Samuel, Work of for New Zealand, 263, 265.

MARTYN, Henry, 158, 168.

MASS CONVERSIONS, 140, 167, 177, 178.

MAYHEWS, The, missionaries to the Indians, 61, 99.

MEDICAL MISSIONS, The value of, 138, 180; in China, 330; Korea, 336.

METHODIST CHURCH, The missions of, origin of, 123; in Africa, 124; in India, 177; in Bulgaria, 302; South America, 376; Mexico, 387; American Indians, 124, 393.

METHODIST CHURCH, South, Missionary organization of, 125; work of among the Indians, 394; Mexico, 387.

METLAKAHTLA, Mission of Wm. Duncan at, 138, 397.

MEXICO, Section on, 382–8.

MICRONESIA, Evangelization of, began, 262.
MILLS, Samuel J., 104; befriends Obookiah, 117.
MILNE, Dr., arrives in China, 315; to Malacca, 316.
MISSIONS, Christian idea of, 5; Christ's teaching concerning, 10; Holy Ghost and, 14.
MISSIONS IN AMERICA, Genesis of, chapter on, 97–125.
MISSIONARY EXPANSION, The phenomenon of, chapter on, 126–141.
MISSIONS, Home, in the United States, magnitude of, 98.
MISSIONS, Medieval, Methods employed in, 23–5.
MISSIONS, Protestant, The beginning of, why so long delayed, 40; zeal was anti-Catholic, 43; Church and State were united, 45; the people had no power, 46; no contact with the heathen world, 47.
MISSIONS, Roman Catholic, Origin of, 36; features of, 37; Xavier, 37; Jesuits in Canada and India, 38, 163; China, 310; Korea, 334; Japan, 343; failure of, 38; in Japan, 343.
MOFFAT, Robert, 196, 207.
MOHAMMEDANISM, The rise of, 26; spread, 26, 27; crusades against, 28; Lully's mission to, 29; restrained by Christian powers, 135, 410, *et seq*.
MONGOLIA, Missions in, 328.
MORAVIAN MISSIONS, 65; in South Africa, 205; West Africa, 214; East Africa, 231; West Indies, 276; Dutch Guiana, 370; among the Indians, 389.
MORRISON, Rev. Robert, first missionary to China, 312; translates the Bible, 314; patient waiting of, 320.
MUTINY, The Indian, Effect of on missions, 160, 161.

NEESIMA, Joseph, 352, 359.
NEPEAN, Gov. Evan, orders Hall and Nott to depart from Bombay, 114; allows them to remain, 115.
NESTORIANS, Early missionary activity of, 25, 28, 310; mission to, 287, 299.
NETHERLANDS MISSIONARY SOCIETY, organized, 90; in the East Indies, 274.
NEWELL, Rev. Samuel, in Andover, 106; sails for India, 110; to Ceylon, 115; to Bombay, 115.

NEWELL, Mrs. Harriet, dies, 114; worth of brief career of, 115, 137.

NEW GUINEA, Introduction of the Gospel into, 270.

NEW HEBRIDES, Evangelization of, 266-70.

NEW ZEALAND, Work of the Gospel in, 263-6.

NOBILI, Robert de, Imposture of, 38.

NORTH AFRICA MISSIONARY SOCIETY, The work of, 235.

NORTH GERMAN MISSIONARY SOCIETY, Mission of in West Africa, 220.

NOTT, Rev. Samuel, in Andover, 106; sails for India, 110; early experiences in Bombay, 114.

OBOOKIAH, 117, 260.

OBLIGATION, Missionary, rests on all alike, 6, 9; as Moravians hold, 7; as Carey felt, 8; and the early church, 10, 12, 16.

PALESTINE, Mission of the American Board to, 117, 285, 287; of other societies, 298.

PARAGUAY, Jesuit missions in, 368.

PARIS MISSIONARY SOCIETY, organized, 96; enters South Africa, 209; the Zambezi valley, 231.

PARK, Mungo, Exploration of the Niger by, 195.

PARKER, Dr. Peter, the founder of medical missions in China, 319.

PARSONS AND FISK, the first missionaries to Palestine, 118, 285.

PATTESON, Bishop, killed in the Santa Cruz Islands, 269.

PATRICK, St., Missionary zeal of, 22.

PERKINS, Rev. Justin, carries the Gospel to the Nestorians, 300; translates the Bible into Syriac, 301.

PERSIA, Mission to, founded by the American Board, 300; English Church Missionary enters, 301.

PERU, Missions in, 379.

PLASSEY, Battle of, effect of upon missions, 48, 67, 153.

PLUTSCHO, missionary to Tranquebar, 63.

PRESBYTERIAN CHURCH, The, joins in the work of the American Board, 119; withdraws for separate work, 119; enters India, 175; West Africa, 217; Syria, 298; Persia, 301; Brazil, 376; Central America, 382; Mexico, 386; among the Indians, 394.

PRESBYTERIAN CHURCH, South, Missions of, in Brazil, 376; Mexico, 386.

PRESBYTERIAN CHURCH OF CANADA, Missions of, in the New Hebrides, 269; West Indies, 279.
PRESBYTERIAN CHURCH, Reformed, American, Mission of in Syria, 299.
PROTESTANT MISSIONS, Chapter on, 40-52.
PROPAGATION OF THE GOSPEL, Society for, charter of, 66; enters India, 168; Burmah, 172; South Africa, 212; Borneo, 274; West Indies, 278; Korea, 337.
PROTESTANT EPISCOPAL CHURCH, organized for missions, 125; in Greece, 125; China, 125; West Africa, 219; Indians, 394.

QUEBEC, Capture of, effect of on missions, 48, 67.

RANKIN, Miss Melinda, Work of in Mexico, 385.
REFORMATION, The, effect of upon missions, 32-4.
REFORMED (DUTCH) CHURCH, co-operates with the American Board, 120; mission in India, 179.
REFORMERS, The, why lacking in missionary zeal, 41-52.
REVIVALS, Stimulus from to missions, 49, 68, 141.
RHENISH MISSIONARY SOCIETY, Missions of, in South Africa, 210; East Indies, 271, 272, 275.
RICE, Rev. Luther, 109; sails for India, 110; is immersed, 112, 120; returns, 122.
ROMAN EMPIRE, Conversion of, 15; forces which aided in, 16.
RUSSIA, Conversion of, 24.

SAMOA, Evangelization of, 255.
SANDWICH ISLANDS, Evangelization of, 117, 260.
SAXONS, The, Conversion of, 23.
SCANDINAVIA, The conversion of, 24.
SCHWARTZ, Christian Frederick, 64, 82, 156, 158.
SCOTLAND, The conversion of, 22.
SCOTLAND, The Established Church of, missions of, in India, 173-4; East Africa, 230.
SCOTLAND, Free Church of, missions of, in India, 173; South Africa, 211; East Africa, 230; Jews in Turkey, 288.
SELWYN, Bishop, Work of in New Zealand, 264, 269.
SERAMPORE, Founding of, 59; Carey removes to, 165; the brotherhood of, 166.

SEVENTEENTH CENTURY, The Protestant missions of, 54.
SHAW, Barnabas, 208.
SIERRA LEONE, 67, 195; missions in, 215, *et seq.*
SIXTEENTH CENTURY, The Protestant missions of, 53, 62.
SLAVE TRADE, 187, 192, 213, 275.
SLAVS, The, Conversion of, 24.
SMITH, Rev. Eli, Translation of the Bible into Arabic by, 297.
SOCIETY ISLANDS, The evangelization of, 250; results flowing from, 253, 260.
SOUTH AMERICA, Physical features of, 369; area, 370; Protestant missions in, 370, *et seq.*
SPANISH AMERICA, Chapter on, 365-380; area and population of, 365; conquest of, 366; Roman Catholic missions in, 367; Protestant missions in, 370, *et seq.*
STILES, Rev. Ezra, proposes a mission to Africa, 99.
SUMATRA, Missions in, 272.
SYRIAN MISSION, Founding of, 285, 295; results of, 298.

TAHITI, Evangelization of, 87, 91, 250.
TAYLOR, Rev. J. Hudson, China Inland Mission founded by, 327.
TELUGU MISSION, Baptist, 121, 176.
THOMAS, Dr. John, meets Carey, 77; sails for India, 79; later career of, 157, 163, 165.
TRANQUEBAR, Founding of, 59; the mission in, 63, 156, 179.
TURKISH EMPIRE, The, Chapter on, 281-306.

ULPHILAS, apostle of the Goths, 19.
UNITED BRETHREN, Mission of in West Africa, 219.
UNITED PRESBYTERIAN CHURCH, American, Missions of, in India, 179; in Egypt, 234.
UNITED PRESBYTERIAN CHURCH, Scottish, Missions of, in India, 179; South Africa, 212; West Africa, 219; West Indies, 279.
UNIVERSITIES' MISSION TO CENTRAL AFRICA, 228.

VANDERKEMP, 90; sails for Africa, 92; missionary zeal of, 94, 207, 241.
VAN DYCK, Dr., Translation of the Bible into Arabic by, 297.
VENEZUELA, Missions in, 379.
VLADIMIR, King, The conversion of, 24.

WARNECK, Dr., Estimate of Zinzendorf by, 66; on mass conversions, 140.
WELZ, Von, Missionary zeal of, 62.
WESLEYAN REVIVAL, The, Effect of on missions, 49-50, 68.
WESLEYAN MISSIONARY SOCIETY, Organization of, 96; enters India, 172; Burmah, 172; South Africa, 208, 213; West Africa, 216; Friendly Islands, 256; Fiji, 257; New Zealand, 265; West Indies, 277.
WEST INDIES, Missions in, 275-80.
WHITMAN, Dr. Marcus, Career of as missionary in Oregon, 392.
WILLIAMS, John, Work of, in the Society Islands, 253; Hervey Group, 254; Samoa, 255; New Hebrides, 266.
WILLIAMS, S. Wells, missionary in China, 320, 325.
WILSON, Captain, sails in the *Duff*, 88; returns, 91.
WOMAN'S PART IN MISSIONS, Early ideas of, 111; importance of, 138; work in India, 180-2.

XAVIER, St. Francis, 37; in Japan, 343.

ZENANA WORK, 180.
ZEISBERGER, David, Work of, among the Indians, 67, 82, 389.
ZIEGENBALG, Founding of Tranquebar mission by, 63.

www.ingramcontent.com/pod-product-compliance
Lightning Source LLC
Chambersburg PA
CBHW051726300426
44115CB00007B/485